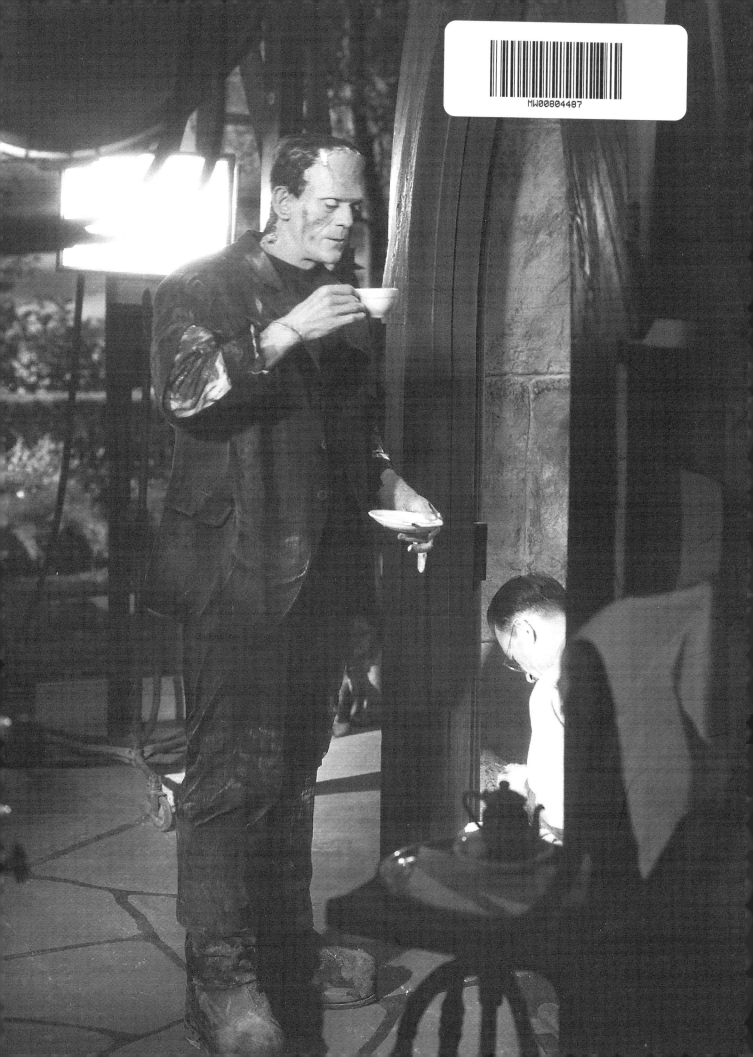

Midnight Marquee #80

Editor
Gary J. Svehla
Aurelia Susan Svehla

Graphic Design Interior
Gary J. Svehla

Front Cover
Seddok, Son of Satan
by David Robinson

Back Cover
Frankenstein (1932) montage
by David Robinson

Copy Editor
Janet Atkinson

Writers
Nicholas Anez
Barry Atkinson
Christopher Gullo
Troy Howarth
Ernie Magnotta
Gary J. Svehla

Artists
Allen Koszowski
David Robinson
Mark Robinson

Special Thanks!
Matt Berry at Kino Lorber; Beth Cox at McFarland; Warner Archive; Richard Klemensen; David Colton and the CHFB; Dave "Charlie" Ellis; George Stover; Susan Svehla; Bob Gehring

Publisher
Midnight Marquee Press, Inc.
Gary J. Svehla
Aurelia Susan Svehla

Midnight Marquee #80, April 2018, copyright © 2018 by Gary J. Svehla; Midnight Marquee is published irregularly at 9721 Britinay Lane; Parkville, MD 21234; email Gary at midmargary@aol.com; website:http://www.midmar.com; phone: 410-665-1198. Issues sell for $11.00, postpaid (Media Mail)

Playing at the Midnight Marquee

What a difference five years can make.

Since the end of 2013 when our 50th anniversary issue of *Midnight Marquee* #79 appeared, the world has seen tons of changes, including far too many horror celebrity deaths.

Just think, all these icons have passed away since the last issue appeared: Christopher Lee, Wes Craven, Tobe Hooper, Yvonne Monlaur, George Romero, John Zacherle, Bill Paxton, Martin Landau, Noel Neill, Carrie Fisher, Rod Taylor and many, many more. It is with a heavy heart that we both acknowledge their passing and remember the importance of their cinematic work. This magazine, for over 50 years, exists as their eulogy.

And on a more personal level, many of the *Midnight Marquee* family have faced pretty tough blows during the past five years. Not to get into the gruesome details, but artists Allen Koszowski and David Robinson have been facing personal health issues and writer Greg Mank (and his family) are weathering a recent personal tragedy. And Sue continues to face health issues, dealing with chronic pain in a world where opiate pain medications are no longer available to those people who need them the most. I guess longevity has drawbacks for all of us who survive long enough.

So our thoughts and prayers go out to everyone needing a little support.

But let's get down to the fun stuff!

When so-called Monster Kids were children, back in the *Famous Monsters of Filmland* days, the Universal classics were only 20 or 30 years old, and to our generation these were the creaky classics that inspired us. Now we are 80-plus years beyond the release of the Universal classics, most of them restored on Blu-ray, but these movies look far less creaky today than they did in 1957, when we first watched their revival on fuzzy TV broadcasts!

Our Baby-Boomer generation saw the birth of the 35-cent monster magazine, printed on inky newsprint and bound with a few staples down the middle of the folded page. Black and white interior was all that was expected and having a glossy color cover was an incredible thrill (I still remember how my jaw dropped the first time I saw the classic *Bride of Frankenstein* colorized cover on issue #21 of *Famous Monsters*). We collected monster bubble gum cards, plastic monster models, silent and sound 8mm and 16mm condensation home movies released by Castle Films and others. We filled our walls with theatrical movie posters and lobby cards, or at least had a few of the Jack Davis comic-style horror art displayed. And we happily walked a mile or two to go to the local newsstand to buy issues of *Castle of Frankenstein* or *Famous Monsters* (or perhaps *Fantastic Monsters, Horror Monsters, Mad Monsters, Shriek, Monster Mania, Modern Monsters,* etc.).

The post-Boomer horror movie generation is more closely bound to Euro-horror and the Continental tastes of 1960s, 1970s and 1980s, singing the praises of masters such as Mario Bava, Dario Argento, Lucio Fulci and Jess Franco. However, the 1970s generation produced new fan-favorite American masters as well: George Romero, Wes Craven, Joe Dante, John Landis and John Carpenter. The love of everything Universal belongs to the Boomers (and along with it comes the beloved schlock of PRC, Monogram, Allied Artists, American International and Columbia).

Only Hammer Film Productions appears to be cross-generational, reminding Boomers of their beloved classic Universals, here remade in color with a heavier dose of sex; and post-Boomers, who associate Hammer with the birth of Euro-horror and link the Hammer classics with the work done by Bava, Argento, Fulci and beyond.

Gone are the days of the horror film celebrity, stars such as Boris Karloff, Bela Lugosi, Lon Chaney (father and son), Christopher Lee and Peter Cushing, whose work defined the genre (even though they all made non-genre movies), or celebrated celebrity directors such as Tod Browning, James Whale, Terence Fisher, Tobe Hooper, Joe Dante, Wes Craven and John Landis, who are defined by their horror film work.

Very few names (if any) occur when recalling producers/directors who work almost exclusively in the horror film genre today. Perhaps James Wan and J.J. Abrams come to mind, but today's franchise horror series (*Saw*, *Insidious*, *The Conjuring*, *Paranormal Activity*, *Final Destination*, *Cloverfield*) are typically directed by varying individuals called to the franchise instead of being the creative personalities who guide it. Directors come and directors go, but the franchise series lives on, in most cases as studio controlled product.

Fortunately, for better or worse, the horror film genre not only survives but also prospers, still remaining date bait for teenagers and college students across the world. While Marvel Universe comic book movies make hundreds of millions during the first weeks of release, the typical low-budget horror movie programmer makes 10 to 20 million upon its total theatrical release (playing in theaters for a few weeks and then disappearing). However, such genre movies make a relative killing when released to home video (via DVD/Blu-ray or streaming services such as Amazon Prime, Netflix, Roku, Hulu and Streampix). Very few horror films will gain immortality, yet there are worthy horror movies that flood the streaming market and eventually rise above the rest. But just like today's music scene, too much product is released every week that even the gems tossed among the crap are often buried in debris and forgotten. Too much product exists where even the most dedicated horror movie buff might find it difficult to discover the best.

Isn't it curious that the film genre that defined the mythology of America, the Western, the genre that ruled the movie screens during the 1950s and 1960s and the television airwaves during this same period, is mostly forgotten today, or at least has become irrelevant, with a few Westerns released each year to lackluster reviews and box-office muscle.

So, why has the horror film genre maintained both its artistic and financial

relevance dating from the birth of cinema (*The Cabinet of Dr. Caligari*, *The Golem* and *Nosferatu*) to today (*It Follows*, *Get Out*)? Perhaps the answer, at its most simple, is that people love to be frightened, witness good conquering evil (or sometimes the other way around) and metaphorically see life win out over death. At its most complex, the horror genre represents the inventiveness and cutting-edge technology of visual style that is always pushing the envelope forward. Horror may just be more mythological (good vs. evil, life vs. death, the price paid for immortality, the mortal vs. the godly, etc.) than even the American Western and perhaps becomes the genre that best feeds our inner imagination and creative soul. Even the bad horror movies prosper and sometimes it appears that quality does not matter. Technology,

special effects, make-up effects and just a gonzo visual style are enough to satisfy the horror genre fan. Plot and characterization be damned, as just like our dreams, at times the horror film universe creates a trance-like visual zone free of logic and common sense, but a world that speaks to our sub-conscious and satisfies some unexplained urge inside.

The fact that we cannot actually put our finger on the reason why the horror film reigns supreme is the very reason why it always has been and will be so popular. We simply do not understand why we like what we like, but we definitely want more, both the good and bad.

Go figure!

—Gary J. Svehla
February/March 2018

ATOM AGE HORROR

BY BARRY ATKINSON

Following the unprecedented world-wide success of Hammer's garishly gruesome *The Curse of Frankenstein* in 1957, a new kind of sub-genre was created within the sphere of horror cinema—contemporary medical/surgical horror. And along with it came censorship hassles. Riccardo Freda's *I Vampiri*, shot in Italy, actually preceded Terence Fisher's groundbreaker by a year, a mad doctor tale having its origins in the Gothic cinema of the 1930s and 1940s but brought up-to-date, garnished with science fiction-related overtones to suit a newer kind of audience looking for fresh thrills to whet the appetite in cinema's atomic age. In Freda's ornate mix of science and Gothic motifs, which suffered minor cuts at the hands of the British Board of Film Censors, Antoine Balpetré drained the blood from young women to preserve the fading looks of Countess Gianna Maria Canale, a much-favored theme that was to flourish in European cinema over the next two decades. Falk Harnack's 1959 *Artz Ohne Gewissen (Physician Without Conscience)* maintained this increasingly popular trend, deranged scientist Ewald Balser preserving the hearts of dead prostitutes in his laboratory, donating the organs to those he thought worthy of a transplant, the director's bold (for the time) enterprise clashing head-on with the German film censor en route. Georges Franju's *Eyes Without a Face* (1959), reviled in some quarters when first released to a disgusted panel of English critics in June 1960 and trimmed by a few minutes for public consumption in Britain, endures as a classic of its type from the early years of Continental horror cinema, showing us just what the Europeans could accomplish by sourcing their material from elsewhere

MÁS ESPELUZNANTE QUE EL MISMO FRANKENSTEIN!

LION'S FILMS presenta SEDDOK (EL HEREDERO DEL DIABLO)

A Spanish poster for *Seddok, Son of Satan*

(notably the Americans) and turning it into something unique, a surgical masterpiece to beat them all. The film focused on yet another preferred concept which Continental filmmakers got hooked on, that of rebuilding the face destroyed by accident or malicious intent.

By the early to mid-1960s, Italian, Spanish and French horror movies were making steady inroads into territory previously dominated by the Americans and, to a lesser extent, the British. But this bizarre overseas product was an entirely different kettle of fish altogether to what the public was used to sitting through, bucking long-accepted ideals by serving up a whole set of quirky values deemed, at the time, unsuitable for a mainstream audience. This is why most of these pictures were relegated, in the United Kingdom, to the art-house circuit or those independent cinemas specializing in the offbeat. Many were Anglicized in an attempt to make them appear less foreign to a Western au-

dience, unfamiliar Latin names replaced with more familiar English names: Riccardo Freda became Robert Hampton; Luciano Martino was changed to Martin Hardy, and so on, and so forth. Taking as their templates the more extreme bloodletting and overt violence depicted in the Hammer productions of the period, these highly stylized programmers, verging on the subversive, contained stark black-and-white or flashy color cinematography, unorthodox soundtracks, hammy performances, awful dubbing, a different-from-norm monster/maniac, sensuous damsels in distress and a salacious accent on sadism, sleaze, sensation, cruelty, nudity, lesbianism and gratuitous gore, guaranteed to have the censor (in Britain at least) reaching for his scissors before passing each and every one of them with an "X" certificate. Continental Gothic/medical horror was born, exhibiting those selfsame exploitive traits promoted in the burgeoning European X-rated sex/porn

market; this wasn't run-of-the-mill fare by any stretch of the imagination, one of the main reasons why the majority of these movies with their distinct international flavor were misunderstood and ignored both by critics and public on initial release and remain misunderstood to this day. The fundamental belief behind people's way of thinking was this: Why pay good money to watch an incomprehensible non-American/non-English horror movie cursed with uneven dubbing, featuring actors you had never heard of, when you could sit through the real McCoy, one that made sense *and* was spoken in plain old English, with the likes of Cushing, Lee and Price on hand, actors you could identify with and trust in. Most of my horror-mad pals avoided these films like the plague because of this reasoning. My own tastes being more hardcore, I tended to purposely seek them out *because* of this unconventional approach in presentation to the normal run of things. Once in a while, some fans wanted something a bit more spiced-up on their menu; Continental horror supplied that spice, in various shapes, forms and disguises.

Anton Giulio Majano's *Seddok, l'Erede di Satana* (*Seddok, the Heir of Satan*) is the classic case in point, a movie almost given the sign of the devil in movie compendiums and shunted to one side into a cobwebby backwater, perceived as being artistically bankrupt; low-grade Italian horror masquerading as the genuine article. First released in Italy in August 1960, Lyon's Films' original 105-minute running length was reduced to 87 minutes for the movie's U.S. premiere in Los Angeles in May 1963, where it was screened as *Atom Age Vampire*. The French, not known for their Puritan attitude toward the risqué, excised, against type, Susanne Loret's daring (for 1960) semi-nude strip (*Seddok*'s opening sequence), the film playing in a 97-minute version during February/March 1962, re-titled *The Monster in the Mask*. In England, it surfaced in April 1963 as *Seddok, Son of Satan*, classified "X" certificate, distributed by Topaz Film Corporation. The writer caught the badly dubbed 96-minute take of *Seddok* at the Regal cinema in Redruth, Cornwall on April 29, 1963, when it commenced a three-day run, double billed with the X-rated French thriller *Frantic* (Speve-Inter 1960; also released as *Double Deception*). It

Seddok, Son of Satan, released as *Atom Age Vampire* in America

left a mark on me then (despite the dire dubbing), and with the emergence of the Italian uncut DVD print in February 2011, it continues to leave a mark. *Seddok* has had an extremely lousy press over the years, rubbished without mercy for being overdramatic, erratic in technique, unpolished and downright corny, a poor man's take on *Eyes Without a Face*. These comments have undoubtedly stemmed from punters never having seen the original film in the confines of a half-empty cinema, viewing, in meager compensation, Alpha's atrociously butchered 1996 VHS issue, a whole 35 minutes edited out; the so-called "uncut" 2002 DVD knocks the running time up from 70 to 87 minutes but is still 18 minutes short of that essential 105 minutes; both VHS and DVD come under the heading of *Atom Age Vampire*. It was rumored in the early 1990s that a German tape existed of the complete 105-minute *Seddok*, but this never materialized to expectant fans. Now, with the opportunity of indulging myself in the unedited movie in letterbox format, Aldo Giordani's black-and-white photography restored to its former pristine glory, we can judge Majano's sole excursion into

mad doctor/surgical horror for what it really is, an Italian magnum opus brimming with glorious elements of schlock, camp histrionics, new-age science, old-style Gothic, good and bad acting, good and bad direction, eroticism, a dash of Italian Neorealism (yes, honestly!), *noir* and careful pacing over its very long 105 minutes, all topped off with a score veering from ominous to jazzy and featuring one of horror's most beguiling monsters, a freakish cross between Mr. Hyde and the Wolf Man. *Seddok, l'Erede di Satana* is a great horror/sci-fi picture, a one-off in many ways and a decisive addition to the cycle of European horror cinema. Let's discover why.

A thumbnail sketch of the plot is as follows: After a row with her sailor boyfriend, Pierre Mornet (Sergio Fantoni) demands, "It's either the nightclub scene or me." Stripper Jeanette Moreneau (Susanne [Suzanne] Loret) flounces away from the club in a distraught state of mind, gets in her car, drives like a maniac and spins off the road down an embankment, the vehicle going up in flames. Three months after the accident, her face still swathed in bandages, Monique Riviere (Franca Parisi) takes her from the hospital to Professor Alberto Levin's (Alberto Lupo) private clinic. Levin, a brilliant research scientist, has been experimenting with an advanced new formula called Derma 28 which has the power to repair

skin that has undergone genetic mutation caused by cancerous cell growths. He succeeds in curing Jeanette's facial disfigurement by the application of this wonder serum, rebuilding her ruined looks, but the effect is temporary; he requires fresh glands from female donors to concoct further quantities of the formula, thus preserving the stripper's beauty. Consumed with desire for the girl and callously doing away with devoted but clinging Monique, the doctor transforms himself into a hideous monster by injecting himself with the inferior Derma 25, killing women to obtain the glands necessary to make up fresh supplies of the more potent Derma 28. In the end, after several murders, he changes into his other, monstrous self in front of Jeanette without the aid of injections, is cornered in his greenhouse by the police and stabbed to death by perpetually browbeaten but faithful mute servant Sacha (Roberto Bertea). Jeanette, her features permanently restored, walks off with Pierre.

Seddok is composed of around 90 scenes, and a great number of the film's key scenes have failed to turn up in the 70-minute version seen by so many. The Italian DVD runs at 103 minutes but, allowing for transference and encoding of film to PAL, this equates to 105 minutes. Same with the Alpha issues—69 minutes equates to 70, 86 minutes to 87. It's little wonder that those viewing the 70-minute print will find much wanting; a third of the movie is missing, leading to sudden jumps in continuity and a total lack of

Alberto Lupo plays the evil surgeon Professor Alberto Levin, the man who created Derma 28 to fix scarred faces.

Professor Levin takes the inferior Derma 25 to turn into a monstrous beast, so he can kill women for their glands, to make more Derma 28.

narrative cohesion. The main sequences accounting for this lost footage are: Loret's opening strip scene (three minutes); Lupo finding Bertea drunk in his cellar and reactivating the generator prior to Loret's operation, also locating water seeping from a bricked-up entrance (three minutes); a nightclub dancer seductively wiggling her wholesome butt throughout her routine (two minutes); the operation on Loret (three minutes); the police and a pathologist discussing Parisi's sudden demise, standing over her dead body (two minutes); Loret writing a note to Fantoni and giving it to Bertea, who passes it on to Lupo (two minutes); Lupo killing a girl in the waterfront area, returning to his villa and becoming enraged at his dreadful visage in a mirror (three minutes); news of an escaped gorilla at large, a loony woman (Rina Franchetti) stating to the police and a reporter that "Seddok" is the killer, then strangled in her apartment by the monster, the police studying her corpse in the morgue (eight minutes); Bertea, drunk

again, pushed around by his master (two minutes); Fantoni on board ship, offered promotion (two minutes); and two minutes of closing credits. That's 32 minutes. The remaining three minutes is made up of various scenes that have been trimmed back to fit a 70-minute running time, particularly in the hospital and police station. There's also, at 26 minutes, a two-second "all over in a flash" glimpse of Lupo seated at his desk, awaiting transformation, yet the transformation itself doesn't occur until nine minutes later. Why this perfunctory fragment has been inserted is a puzzle; all it does is to highlight the overall sloppy editing work carried out.

The slightly improved 87-minute version omits Loret's striptease, parts of the Afro-Cuban dance, snippets of hospital footage, most of Loret's operation, the entire Franchetti segment, the ending credits and other loose ends. Okay, it's far more logical than the 70-minute hatchet job but still has an incomplete air to it. And the two shortened versions list Rina Franchet-

ti's name in the credits when, in fact, the respected Italian actress is conspicuous by her absence in both! If any horror fan has ever chanced upon a still from *Seddok* showing a startled woman with a pair of claws wrapped around her throat (it exists in at least two film books I've encountered) and wondered, "That wasn't in the movie I watched the other night," well, you're right, it wasn't! This forms part of the eight-minute Franchetti sequence of events that have been inexplicably cut from the two emasculated editions.

To once again illustrate the huge differences in all three edits of *Seddok*: In the uncut 105-minute print, Lupo's transformation from man into monster occurs at 48 minutes; in the 87-minute print, at 41 minutes; and in the 70-minute print, at 35 minutes. Therefore, to fully appreciate this picture, we must totally and without reservation disregard that drastically reduced 70-minute debacle and appraise the newly revamped print in detail with its new and extended scenes. The 87-minute edit of *Seddok* isn't all that bad, but the full-length cut is the definitive one, the one that shows Majano's much-maligned schizoid scientist B-gem to be an influential piece of Continental horror mayhem in its own right, a movie that, on three or four run-throughs, will have all those dismissive skeptics confessing, "Hey, this is actually pretty good!" In this writer's estimation, Majano's movie is not just pretty good, it deserves to come under the category of "flawed cult classic" status, a heady evocation of European New-Wave horror/sci-fi in its formative years, an expertly crafted mishmash of high octane theatrics, in-your-face surgical procedures, atmospheric photography and decent, old-fashioned monster thrills. *Seddok, l'Erede di Satana* is a landmark production just waiting to be rooted out and admired!

The Italian disc, as noted, is in letterbox format, has been beautifully brought back to vivid black-and-white life but, unfortunately, is hampered to a certain extent by a part-dubbed, part-Italian audio track, with Italian subtitles only. Basically, the additional 18 minutes added to the 87-minute edit are in Italian although, just to confuse the issue, several dubbed scenes existing in the 87-minute edit that were not shown in the 70-minute print have now reverted to Italian: Lupo in the cellar, charging up the generator and uncovering the bricked entrance; the dance number; parts of the operation procedure; the murder on the waterfront and its aftermath; and a few of the police/hospital segments. These are now included in their native language. In addition, a few short passages (Loret arguing with Fantoni after her striptease is a prime example) switch from English, back to Italian, back to English and back to Italian again with rapid ease, a marginal drop in clarity and volume noticeable from the Italian speech to English. Annoying to those looking for perfection, maybe, but audiences will quickly become use to it; the dubbing itself is not quite as crystal clear as in the 87-minute print; the Italian, on the other hand, is in a lower key and pitch perfect.

Atom Age Vampire's opening credits show a bat's wings morphing into the "V" of Vampire. The credits in the uncut *Seddok* set the tone better, displaying the unnatural outline of a man with claws and glowing eyes under the "Seddok" logo, top Italian film composer Armando Trovajoli's title theme ranging from a doom-laden clanging bell dirge to smoky jazz (Trovajoli racked up over 300 film scores in his long career). The action kicks off with Loret's saucy romp at the El Hoggar club, which may have been too racy for 1960, one reason why the sequence was chopped in every other country it was shown outside of Italy. Shimmying across set in a black bodice, stockings and suspenders to Trovajoli's jazzy score (a well-meaning customer has

Stripper Jeanette Moreneau (Susanne Loret) looks at her horribly mutilated face in a mirror, as a photo of her boyfriend appears in back.

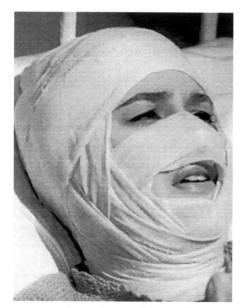

Susanne Loret immediately after surgery, as she heals in pain and frustration

unzipped her dress), the well-built peroxide blonde looks slightly ill at ease, especially when partly exposing her breasts and peeling off her nylons to a salivating clientele (Majano almost thrusts his lens up into the recesses of the actress' shapely thighs, an unsubtle moment of titillation guaranteed to leave every male member of the audience in a hot sweat!). Square-jawed navy guy Fantoni, annoyed at seeing his girl flaunting her assets to a bunch of ogling, middle-aged men, informs her in no uncertain terms that their romance is kaput if she carries on shedding her clothes for a living ("Oh please, don't treat me like this. You know your ship is about to sail," she sobs). After a blazing row, Loret, in tears, storms out of the club, gets in her car, speeds down the road and crashes through a wooden barrier, the vehicle bursting into flames. Three months later, she's still recovering in hospital, only her eyes and lips visible under wreaths of bandages (surely an acknowledgement to *Eyes Without a Face* here) and being offered a cup of tea to calm her nerves (the English dubbing, believe it or not, stays pretty faithful to the occasionally clichéd Italian script, written by Piero Monviso, Gino De Santis, Alberto Bevilacqua and Majano himself. Bevilacqua contributed

to the scripts of two Mario Bava movies, *Black Sabbath* [Galatea 1963] and *Planet of the Vampires* [Castilla 1965]).

When the stripper is confronted with the sight of her scarred features in a mirror for the first time, she smashes the windows of her room in anguish and rage, Trovajoli's orchestral music reaching a menacing crescendo. Then Parisi turns up in a white trench coat and matching beret, resembling an undercover agent for the French Resistance, with a tantalizing promise that her employer, Professor Levin, who has pioneered a revolutionary new treatment for scar damage, could give her back her beauty *if* she will allow him to experiment on her. What choice does the wretched girl have? Leaving the hospital in a cloak of secrecy, she arrives at his villa after a four-minute laboratory segment in which Lupo explains on tape (and for the benefit of the audience) how Derma 28, an anti-cancer vaccine, has grown out of Derma 25. "I'm not being immodest when I speak of a whole new era in the field of biology and therapy," says the far-from immodest doctor. To prove its restorative powers on abnormal cell growth (and her adoration for Lupo), Parisi injects herself with Derma 25 ("It can turn animals into monsters."), caus-

...BEFORE YOUR VERY EYES THE TERRIFYING TRANSFORMATION OF MAN INTO MONSTER!

ATOM AGE VAMPIRE

SUSANNE LORET
ALBERT LUPO
A TOPAZ FILM CORP. RELEASE

In this American lobby card, Alberto Lupo, transformed into the so-called atom age vampire, runs amok, knocking out Fantoni as Loret screams in the background.

ing unsightly scarring on her left arm. Crestfallen Bertea, the forever-hovering lapdog servant, is sent packing by Lupo, Parisi trying to calm the worried simpleton down. "When it's all over, you can bring me some roses," she coos to the poor sap. Treated with Derma 28, the tissue heals in the blink of an eye. "Let's stay home—together—with our records," is her enticing offer to the scientist, dragging him upstairs to her bedroom, her obsession for him mirroring the obsession that Lupo will soon feel for Loret.

Loret makes her grand entrance through the door like a drag artist, wearing a leopard-skin coat, the collar wrapped up high around her features to disguise her scars, Lupo ordering her to, "Show me your face! Show me your face, I said!" Removing her sunglasses, he gazes upon her puckered features and announces, without an ounce of sensitivity, "There's no doubt of it. Yes, she's disfigured forever! As if by a cancer that's beyond control—like leprosy!" "I will restore all your beauty," he hastens to add, trying to soften the blow, extolling the virtues of Derma 28: "The secret of spontaneous reproduction of living cells ... the secret of life—and also of death ... we can rebuild cells which have been destroyed. We have tamed the monster which once devoured us and made it serve our own ends." Loret, whimpering,

remains unimpressed. "I shall perform this miracle," proclaims Lupo. "I've never believed in miracles. I've even forgotten how to pray. Oh please let me go now," cries the stripper in distress. Lupo grows angry at her stubborn, even skeptical, attitude, but all Loret can do is weep hysterically and howl, "Let me kill myself right now," reaching for the gun in her bag. The irate doctor tells her that she can go ahead and use the gun on herself *if* his experiment doesn't succeed in getting rid of her blemishes, to which Loret slumps in a chair, mumbles, "No, no, I beg of you," and passes out. Lupo brushes aside her blonde locks, revealing the crisscross pattern of scars from cheek to neck, and observes to Parisi, "She's a beautiful human specimen," thus drawing to a close a scene of such towering rhetorical intensity (not helped by the clumsy English translation) that it's easy to understand adverse critical comments regarding the exaggerated method of role playing in Continental horror movies. Everything must be overstated to the nth degree—there's no room for subtleties in this fanciful setup.

Three minutes later, after the interlude with Lupo in his cellar, restarting the generator and stumbling upon another way in, we're back at the club and being treated to a provocative Afro-Cuban belly dance by a sexy wench wearing next

to nothing (sucking of fingers; leering at camera; rolling of eyes; pouting of lips; shaking of large butt—exotically named Glamor Mora), poor slob Fantoni drowning his sorrows in drink at the bar. Then we move on to Loret's operation in Lupo's utilitarian laboratory, Trovajoli's jazz-type leitmotifs coming into play as, following the operation, the scars quickly disappear from the woman's face. Loret is taken to her room and wakes, noticing that her facial deformities have faded from sight ("A miracle has happened to you!"); in gratefulness, she smothers her savior in kisses, much to Parisi's alarm. Alone together, the scientist declares his love (or should that be lust?) for the stripper, allowing his Latin temperament to get the better of him: "I'll tell you. You love me. I have snatched you away from desperation and from death. It is I who has restored your beauty. It is I who needs you." He kisses her hard. "You are nothing if not mine. You belong to me!" Unadulterated passion verging on tragedy of the kind the hot-blooded Continentals lap up so much! At first, that love (lust) is reciprocated, Loret's seductive come-ons (and one glass of wine too many) giving out all the right/ wrong signals, but it doesn't last that long; the scarring reappears, there's no more Derma 28 and Loret begins to feels like a caged animal, rejecting Lupo's amorous overtures. Radiation is suggested as a solution, or (heaven forbid) the transplant of glands from another human necessary to produce the drug becomes a thought. Far too dangerous, says Parisi, seething with jealousy at her lover's open craving for the girl and laying down a condition: She'll help with further operations if Lupo forgets all about any romantic liaisons with his patient. By forcing him into a corner, Parisi seals her own fate. Lupo murders her without batting an eyelid after admitting he's infatuated with Loret and calling her unreasonable, abstracting the glands from *her* body to produce the potion that will restore the stripper's face.

There follows a lengthy sequence in which the police and a pathologist arrive at the villa to report on Parisi's sudden death. Inspector Ivo Garrani spots three fused bottles on a shelf and is treated to a discourse on the effects of radiation on those sufferers caught up in the Hiroshima bombing. Lupo shows him shocking photos of Japanese burn victims, stating

Alberto Lupo's shaggy-haired hybrid of Mr. Hyde and The Wolf Man grabs a scalpel as laboratory rabbits cower.

that he is developing a cure to treat such deformities. "What you mean is exploit the horror by extracting its advantages. The bad that justifies the good, is that it?" asks Garrani. That last line sums up Lupo's subsequent actions to perfection, prophesying what will come next. With news of a gorilla escaping from a zoo, followed by the discovery of a girl's ravaged corpse, the Professor, out on a drive with Loret who suddenly complains of feeling unwell, decides to inject himself with Derma 25. ("Derma 25 can create a monster. A monster who doesn't fear killing. Who doesn't suffer as it kills?") Under the inhuman guise the drug will create, he can obtain those vital glands and the authorities will think it the act of a rampaging wild beast, not a man. That's the terrible dilemma facing Lupo. Like all scientists hell-bent on a mission, going back to the early years of *Frankenstein* (1931) and *Dr. Jekyll and Mr. Hyde* (1931), it takes him all of about 10 seconds to reach his

decision, ignoring the morality and medical ethics of what he is about to do in the name of scientific progress. In his lab, he pushes the syringe into his arm, pumps in the serum, sits at his desk and waits for the fluid to take effect.

Lupo's transformation, from scientist to a shaggy-haired hybrid of Mr. Hyde and Lon Chaney's Wolf Man, is achieved by an unusual but chilling combination of stop-motion and time lapse photography. Given depth by Trovajoli's creepy organ-based notes (the composer certainly chucks everything into this picture) and shot moodily in half-light, it's a splendid slice of man-into-monster filmmaking, sinister and atmospheric, as is the next few seconds; two caged rabbits in the laboratory twitch nervously as a hairy claw reaches for a scalpel. The first killing is a humdinger: A girl walks down a darkened street and is hailed by a hooded figure lurking in the shadows, promising her anything she wants in a gravelly voice. Ap-

proaching the figure ("What are we playing? Hide-and-seek?"), the creature turns, revealing grotesque features. Screaming for her life, the woman is dragged into an underpass to meet her end. Back in his laboratory, Lupo staggers into the radiation chamber, changes back and emerges in clouds of vapor, exhausted. From the initial transformation sequence to Lupo in his steam-filled atomic lab, Majano has fashioned over three minutes of mesmerizing sci-fi/horror worthy of anything that came out of America in the 1950s, demonstrating a genuine feel for the genre, each separate scene bathed in the kind of deep black-and-white imagery and artful backlighting that the Europeans were to become so adept at achieving.

When the scientist later talks to Loret, a virtual prisoner in her room, one hand is still in a claw-like state and he looks ill and ragged, signs that he has not fully recovered from his change from man to monster. Informing her that transplants may have to be necessary to preserve her tissue, he barks, "Why are you staring at me? I told you I'm tired and upset. I've spent the whole night working in the laboratory, so that you could wake up as you are." At this moment in time, audiences can't help feeling sorry for Lupo, despite his ghastly deeds—he's a man in torment, deeply in love, and that love is being spurned, despite his all-out efforts to save Loret from a life of ugliness by resorting to murder. After one more rejection from the stripper, who thrusts him away and backs off against the wall, he turns from her and the miserable expression on his face speaks volumes.

Loret then attempts to contact Fantoni by letter, but the missive is passed to Lupo by sneaky Bertea and burnt. Needing more glands, the next involuntary female donor is seated on the waterfront at night. A taloned hand emerges from behind the bench, an arresting shot complemented by Aldo Giordani's somber photography. Shrieking, the girl is pulled backwards and slaughtered, her bloody corpse glimpsed after Lupo has finished with it. Returning to the villa, the monster clambers through a brick opening into his cellar, gasping and snarling with exertion. Pushing back his hood, he observes his fearsome pitted countenance in a mirror, smashing the glass in blind fury, another rewarding moment for buffs to savor.

...BEFORE YOUR VERY EYES THE TERRIFYING TRANSFORMATION OF MAN INTO MONSTER!

ATOM AGE Vampire

SUSANNE LORET
ALBERT LUPO

A TOPAZ FILM CORP. RELEASE

Alberto Lupo looks at the beautiful results of his operation, as his assistant and lover Franca Parisi looks on from the background, in this American lobby card.

The next long interlude (eight minutes) is the one featuring Rina Franchetti that didn't make it in Alpha's 70 and 87-minute truncated versions or the U.S. theatrical release. For all those detractors who complain, "Who/where/what's Seddok?" The name "Seddok" is actually alluded to on the hour (therefore making sense to those U.K. punters who bothered to turn up and watch it as the Franchetti sequence was shown intact). The garrulous Franchetti reckons the butchering killer who slits his victims from throat to sternum isn't that escaped gorilla at all but a devilish monster with claws that she has had visions of for years, ever since she was a child. Yapping to the police, she then makes her views known to a reporter and a crowd of onlookers in a café, precipitating newspaper headlines in which "Seddok" replaces the gorilla as the chief murder suspect. Later, alone in her apartment with her caged birds (a cunning metaphor for Loret's own semi-captive situation), Franchetti receives a phone call from a prospective male escort and spruces herself up for a hot date. The doorbell rings, the door is opened and Majano manufactures a marvelous subjective shot, Franchetti, in full frame, backing away in abject terror from a snuffling presence that forces its way in (*not* a hot date!). A pair of gnarled hands encircles her neck,

choking the air out of her. As she lays sprawled on the floor, a shadow falls over her body, ready to perform surgery, the camera panning across the room to focus briefly on the dead woman's birds. Yes, by blabbing to the press, Franchetti's loose tongue has resulted in her paying with her life for gossiping, a spellbinding sequence conjured up by the director, composer Trovajoli introducing some eerie fairground tonalities to heighten the tension (a nod to Maurice Jarre's score in *Eyes Without a Face*, perhaps.)

Loret manages to arrange a clandestine meeting with Fantoni by the docks at night, but Lupo and Bertea tail her; Bertea whacks sailor boy over the head, Loret blacks out (not for the first time in this picture, and not for the last!) and she's dragged back to her prison. Meanwhile, Garanni, suspicious of Lupo's movements (he's been spotted in his car with Bertea and a comatose blonde female), settles on a plan of action, instructing his men to stake out the villa; with Fantoni posing as a police sergeant, the officer pays a visit to the scientist to sniff out more clues and determine whether or not Lupo is involved in these brutal slayings. It's here, in the 73rd minute, that a reference to the U.S. title *Atom Age Vampire* is made: Talking about possible radiation victims arriving from abroad (Japan is mentioned), and

whether this mysterious "Seddok" could be a mutation on the loose, Lupo offers a theory to the police: "The obsession of a vindictive-minded man who has been poisoned or disfigured forever by atomic radiation. One might even say a vampire of the atom age who wants to recover?" So, to all those who scoff, "Where's the vampire?" There *isn't* a vampire as such, but a vampire *is* referred to within the framework of the dialogue within the script.

After Garrani and company leave, Lupo gives vent to another prolonged shouting match with the trapped Loret (fetching in black stockings and see-through lingerie), the high-flown dialogue bellowed out, a verbal slanging match to top 'em all. "You want to go back to Pierre, but I'm going to save you now despite yourself," accuses Lupo. Loret moans, "Yes, I want to go back to Pierre. I don't care if I'm scarred for life because I know now that he'll love me anyway," an over-optimistic view from the blonde, as we've all seen the drunken lunkhead flirting with two women at the nightclub previously. "You think so?" Lupo roars sarcastically. "Well, your scars are already returning. Embryonic, still, and all but invisible, but if this action is not arrested almost immediately, you will turn into just what you were before. Yes, but worse, it will devour you, bit by bit. It will transform you into an animal like a monster under the very eyes of your Pierre." "I don't want to stay here anymore. I don't want to," groans Loret, going into her "little lost girl" routine, all ready to reach for the pistol in her bag. Lupo relaxes, promising again that he'll do all that he can for her and leaves. Then the ineffectual Fantoni returns to the villa, revealing to Lupo that he's Pierre, not a cop, but is haughtily dismissed as a stupid fool not worthy of the scientist's or Loret's attention. Lupo then sneaks into a cinema but sneaks out under the totally inept noses of a surveillance team, attacking another woman in her flat, unsuccessfully; she screams, a barking dog leaping to the rescue and taking a chunk out of the retreating killer's ankle. Back at the house, Lupo, now utterly demented, decides to take Loret away from it all and be damned. He's going to renege on his agreement to free her once the cure is permanent, waking her and staring at her face. "The treatment has taken effect at last!"

The climatic 10-minutes of Majano's outing is pure horror hokum, presented in true over-the-top Italian operatic-style cinema. Dressed up like a Barbie doll, Loret sobs and screams, "No! Help!" as the scientist slowly metamorphoses into his bestial other half in front of her, grunting, "I've unleashed a horrible force within me that I can no longer control. I've killed for you." "No, it's horrible. Let go of me," yells Loret in panic, Lupo, now fully morphed, growling, "You're mine. You are coming with me whether you want to or not!" Fantoni, loitering outside the gates, runs to her aid. A tussle with Lupo the monster on the stairs, to the tune of a barrage of screams from Loret, results in the seaman getting knocked senseless. Loret faints, Lupo carrying her into the greenhouse, pleading with Bertea to help in secreting her from the surrounding cops, who spray the greenhouse with machine gun bullets. Sickened by his master's wrongdoings, especially the murder of Parisi whom he adored, Bertea, his face crumpled in remorse, plunges a knife into Lupo's back. The scientist staggers backwards, one clawed hand held out to his servant's face in supplication. He then expires to the sound of a tolling bell, reverting to human form in front of Garrani, his death throes ending on a resigned note. Loret and Fantoni stare into each other's eyes and walk off, and the forlorn Bertea is taken into custody, Majano's camera tracking over a bed of roses which the servant used to tend for his beloved mistress.

A Spanish lobby card from *Seddok*

Seddok, l'Erede di Satana isn't all seriousness. Amid the showy melodramatics, there's a running gag concerning cop Garrani's repeated attempts to quit cigarettes, while those around him, including deputy Andrea Scotti, are inconsiderately lighting up at every given moment, blowing smoke into his face. Performance-wise, Alberto Lupo, dyed blond-hair brushed back *en brosse* style, is in commanding form as the committed Professor (a career best), bringing force and conviction to every scene he's in; a cold, clinical man of science, his will possessed (as so many before him in so many films) by his creation, which is how he views Loret; she's his plaything, and *his* alone. Speaking in mellifluous tones (in the Italian-only sequences), he dominates the narrative, a classy bout of acting equal to that of Vincent Price, Basil Rathbone and Peter Cushing in their heydays. As for Susanne Loret, the girl emotes like crazy (also a career best); brassily attractive in a *Dolce Vita*-type of way, Italian eye-candy of the blowsy variety, a feast for the front row dirty raincoat brigade. She's memorable for perhaps all the wrong reasons, her acting switching from sob-sob amateur dramatics to uncontrollable bouts of wailing, but give the actress her due, she puts her all into the role and does stand out, not content to simply fade into the background. In fact, Lupo and Loret form one of horror's more lurid doctor/victim pairings, such is their deliriously unhinged impact. Elsewhere, Sergio Fan-

toni is nice-ish but wooden-headed as Loret's boring boyfriend; dour Ivo Garrani's police officer with a smoking problem is gritty and amusing in turns; Franca Parisi looks darkly alluring (more so than Loret) playing Lupo's assistant-cum-mistress, suffering from a bad case of unrequited love; while timid mute servant Roberto Bertea skulks and cowers in the corners like an extra from a 1940s Universal horror picture, intoxicated for most of his screen time.

All credit must go to director Anton Giulio Majano and his technicians in managing to bring this macabre hodge-podge of differing styles and ideas to life. Skillfully blending the ham with the horror to produce a Continental monster opus unfairly derided over the decades, the film is now deemed by some to be a work of considerable significance and one that was, in hindsight, crucial in the evolution of this particular brand of Euro-horror.

So why do all the bad reviews exist? Apart from countless undiscerning fans catching that 70-minute *Atom Age Vampire* re-edited fiasco on tape and disc, 1960 saw the release of two seminal Continental horror flicks, Mario Bava's masterful *Black Sunday* and Giorgio Ferroni's elegiac *Mill of the Stone Women*, and by comparison, *Seddok* does come across in some respects like a trashy Italian B-movie of little merit, a tad one-dimensional, not multi-layered by any stretch of the imagination

(it's also, at one hour 45 minutes, rather lengthy for a 1960s B-horror film). True, it's short on the lyrical intensity that these two particular movies had in abundance. But on closer examination, it's clearly evident that *Seddok* is much more closely related to its American horror roots than Bava or Ferroni's archetypal foreign masterworks, becoming, in the process, more of an American-type horror film than an Italian-type one. This was the intention of Majano, to get a foothold on those lucrative overseas markets by rustling up a movie that resembled a black-and-white late 1950s American horror movie rather than an Italian horror one, yet, at the same time, retaining its Italian parentage. It wasn't Majano's fault that American distributors mangled his project in order to make it accessible to a non-Latin audience (at least in England the movie more or less stuck with its Italian title *and* was nine minutes longer), the outcome of which was a total misrepresentation of the director's original work and ideas. Lupo's unethical doctor, fixated with his creation/patient, his female assistant yearning for a more meaningful relationship but brushed thoughtlessly to one side in the name of scientific advancement, is no different than Colin Clive in *Frankenstein* or even Whit Bissell in [*I Was a*] *Teenage Frankenstein* (1957), both resolute, calculating scientists pushing back the boundaries of research at the expense of a deep, personal involvement of any kind. Lupo's domineering character also owes

a debt of gratitude to Pierre Brasseur's Professor Génessier in *Eyes Without a Face*, another fanatic oblivious to the feelings of his doting mistress (Alida Valli), his attention focused solely on his work. Also check out United Artists' *The Vampire* (1957); the similarities between this and *Seddok*'s noirish overtones are there for all to see, and that includes John Beal and Alberto Lupo's wrinkly monster makeup.

Yes, the accusation can be leveled (and has been) that *Seddok* is pulp in execution, loaded with fever-pitch verbal exchanges, over-mannered acting and trite dialogue, not worthy of serious critique, but that's all part of the film's oddball charm; it hoists itself admirably above its formulaic material and becomes something just that little bit special, warts and all. In addition, it's an undisputed fact, despite what the critics may think, that *Seddok*, like *Eyes Without a Face* and Jesus Franco's *The Awful Dr. Orlof* (1962), is one of the founding fathers of the Euro-splatter genre whose productions, many based on the taboo subjects of necrophilia, torture and porn/nude murders, reached a peak in the 1960s and continued until the early 1970s in a host of perverse productions such as Mario Bava's *The Whip and the Body* (1963) and *Blood and Black Lace* (1964), Antonio Margheriti's *The Virgin of Nuremberg* (1964) and *Web of the Spider* (1971), Antonio Boccacci's *Tomb of Torture* (1963), Dino Tavella's *The Embalmer* (1965), Sergio Garrone's *Lover of the Monster* (1974) and Riccardo Freda's *The Horrible Dr. Hichcock* (1962)

and *Tragic Ceremony* (1972). Majano's picture holds an important niche in Italian cinema, a pivotal cog in this cycle of depraved Gothic romance/sex/gore movies, and we must never forget or overlook that. Another fact is that this is one of those films that grow on you after repeated viewings, becoming hard to shrug aside with indifference. And if it *hasn't* left an impression after 50 years (very many haven't, vanishing without trace), why so much discussion about *Seddok, l'Erede di Satana*, or *Atom Age Vampire* on numerous Internet forums!

Rumors (never substantiated) have existed for years that none other than Mario Bava participated in *Seddok* in the role of producer. The film's credits list Elio Ippolito Mellino as "Production Manager," and Mario Fava as "Producer." It has been suggested that Mellino used the name "Mario Fava" as his producer's credit, but the question arises as to why this obscure character, who only featured as production manager in one other movie [Rinascita's *Le Avventure di Robi e Buck*, 1957], would use a pseudonym for the producer's role if he were already listed as *Seddok*'s production manager? It's an intriguing cinematic conundrum that may never be fully known, even though Bava knew Majano and had worked with some members of the cast and with scriptwriter Alberto Bevilacqua—so a link *did* exist.

Anton Giulio Majano concentrated mainly on TV work from 1956 to 1983, making *Seddok, l'Erede di Satana* his solitary venture into the world of Continental exploitive medical horror cinema. The director's early forerunner to this deviant new direction in horror represented a pooling together of differing rough-around-the-edges talents—Majano himself, Lupo and Loret—who went their own separate ways after the movie's completion, leaving behind them a project that is still talked about 50 years on, and one that was never repeated by those involved again. It's not perfect, far from it, but put into context against what had come before and what appeared after, Majano's contribution to the genre, in its original, unedited form, is an outlandish, once-in-a-lifetime beauty from sci-fi/horror's golden age, a real Italian X-rated guilty pleasure if ever there was one. Ridicule it at your own peril!

THRILLER'S
CLASSIC HORROR EPISODES
SEASON 2

BY GARY J. SVEHLA

Unlike today's unrelenting assortment of horror entertainment to be found on TV (including recent series such as *The Walking Dead, Penny Dreadful, Bates Motel, Hannibal*), television in the golden era of the 1950s and 1960s was basically sanitized and quite conservative. The world of *Leave It to Beaver* and *Father Knows Best* featured adults who wore coats and ties while unwinding at home and housewives donned frilly cocktail dresses to cook family meals. When fantasy or horror was approached, it was mainly done for comedy's sake, such as iconic series including *Bewitched, The Addams's Family* or *The Munsters*. Adult science fiction first appeared on the airwaves via series such as *Science Fiction Theatre* (where no monsters existed and most of the screenplay was spent talking about scientific oddities) and *One Step Beyond* (where once again the plots were fantastic but the imagery once again quite pedestrian). Which is the major reason why *The Twilight Zone* was such a spectacular and cutting-edge entry. For the first time actual aliens from outer space and even earthbound monsters were shown, and the external imagery of horror for once equaled the internal scripted ideas. Series such as *The Outer Limits* and *Thriller* took things one step further, but even then the worlds of horror and science fiction were sanded down to a safe buffered version of the more visceral horror and science fiction to be found in movie theaters at that time. American television of the 1950s and 1960s was considered family entertainment, and intensity and gore belonged in theatrical releases, not the child-friendly airwaves of NBC, ABC and CBS.

Thriller, perhaps the best showcase for horror on American television at the time, dared show haunted mansions at the crack of darkness filled with an axe killer or at least a few spirits of the dead, some of which even lived in a world of mirrors. Most of the horror was the horror lurking in the diseased mind, where even the fear of the supernatural was often linked to some variation of mental illness. *Thriller* never showed the world of vampires, werewolves or supernatural mythology, unless it involved some local serial killer who wielded a pitchfork as a murder weapon and became folklore created by the local community. Sometimes, as with movies such as *Mark of the Vampire*, the supernatural in a few *Thriller* episodes

In *The Premature Burial* series host Boris Karloff plays physician Dr. Thorne, who has electrical apparatus to raise the (nearly) dead.

is logically explained away and ghosts and goblins turn out to be the workings of fraudulent humans scheming acts of revenge. Or ghosts turn out to be psychopathic humans, demented and damaged. But a few episodes do feature actual monsters and ghosts, without trying to debunk the supernatural rationale.

Always imaginative and atmospheric, featuring a strong visual sense, *Thriller* allowed our nightmares to come to vivid life and to do so every week or two in a ritualistic and horrific manner. Perhaps this was the reason why the series alternated episodes of crime and mystery with the overt horror episodes … was this a compromise that the network demanded? And with the horror episodes only appearing sporadically, this only made the anticipation for the supernatural that much greater. Since the screenwriters and directors could not show the same degree of violence featured in the movie houses at the time, such creative television pioneers had to rely on well-scripted terror that got under the skin, that horrified the psyche and the soul without depicting too much violence, blood and mayhem. By having their creative hands tied by the standards of network television, perhaps this forced the innovative minds behind *Thriller* to be that much more creative and

to raise those short hairs on the backs of our necks in even more clever and insidious manners.

Sadly the second (and final) season of *Thriller* did not quite rise to the creative highs of its initial season, but the best horror-oriented episodes of season two once again become classic TV, and they still frighten and entertain over 50 years later, proving that censorship, subtlety and horror implied but left relatively unseen might still have its place in a genre that today has gone in the complete opposite direction … and might be worse off because of showing more and feeling less. This television series had to terrify audiences by interjecting creative cinematography, musical scoring, editing, acting and set design. Violent acts of murder had to be hinted (or partially shown) and blood splatter suggested. No easy way out, as *Thriller* had to involve audiences with fine-tuned scripting, well honed acting and a visual look that got under the skin. While not every episode totally succeeded, enough did in the series' two-year run that the show still remains a classic of horror film history.

While the better episodes of season one of *Thriller* stand out as the strongest, episode 3 of season two packed a wallop (first broadcast October 2, 1961), *The*

Looking like a spirit from *A Christmas Carol*, the zombie-like and speechless Stapleton roams the grounds of his estate, during the climax of *The Premature Burial*.

Premature Burial. Besides hosting the series with clever props and devilish background introductions, Boris Karloff plays a major supporting role in this episode, making it extra special. Directed by Douglas Heyes, one of the key players from season one (and who plays a far less important role in season two), the teleplay comes from Heyes and William D. Gordon, of course based upon the story by Edgar Allan Poe. And *The Premature Burial* becomes a standout horror episode from the second season.

Sidney Blackmer (Edward Stapleton) plays the victim of catatonic seizures that render him seemingly dead, and his fear of being buried alive (which is what exactly has been done in the horrifying pre-credits sequence) is masterfully conveyed. The coffin is carefully carried to his burial vault; the assembled mourners leave and sounds begin emulating from the casket. Soon it rocks violently to and fro, finally falling off its ledge and crashing to the ground below, the victim's hand breaking through the split wood and attempting to yank the handle open. Unfortunately, Edward Stapleton's good friend Dr. Thorne (Karloff) claims the "dead" corpse and applies an electrical contraction to jolt the life back into the not-actually-dead man. In a masterful performance, Blackmer suddenly sits up and starts to walk, at-

tempting to speak but unable to form the words, as he rushes around frantically trying to awake and verbalize the fact that he is alive. Karloff's compassion and Blackmer's horror are interwoven quite successfully.

If Stapleton can just manage to stay alive, as he is engaged to marry a much younger woman, Victorine (Patricia Medina), a beautiful femme fatale who only wants the old coot's money, as she is romantically involved with equally greedy Julian Boucher (Scott Marlowe). Preparing for another catatonic seizure, the wealthy elder has erected a new burial vault housing a casket that will fly open with just the slightest movement inside. Also, a rope will be threaded into the casket and placed in his crutching cold, dead hands. If he wiggles even a finger, loud bells will clang throughout the property. Also, he will always carry freshly minted necklaces and bracelets that proclaim: "I am Alive." However, shortly after their marriage, away from home with Victorine, Stapleton has another seizure, but instead of helping her husband, she takes the necklaces and buries them under a large rock. And instead of burying him, according to his wishes, in his newly struck burial vault, she buries her husband underground far away from home. Six weeks pass until Dr. Thorne orders

the corpse be exhumed and properly buried as he wished. And here the story kicks into overdrive.

Even though Stapleton has been in the dirt for six weeks, on the first night reinterred the bells start sounding from the vault, and the casket is found to be empty. Wearing his shroud and looking like a spirit from *A Christmas Carol*, the again zombie-like and speechless Stapleton roams the grounds of his estate, horrifying Victorine and her lover Julian, as they attempt to figure out a plan to escape her husband's wrath from beyond the grave. As the haunting apparition appears suddenly from outside a window, as the camera pans to the right, flowing past the guilt-ridden couple, *Thriller*'s strength at conveying another spooky mansion impresses. Before long it is revealed that Stapleton is in fact actually dead, that Dr. Thorne concocted a clever plan to create a death mask of his friend worn by a servant just to prove that Victorine did in fact knowingly kill her husband. But this final act of *The Premature Burial* holds its audience on the edge of its seat, as the ghostly corpse-like figure lumbers here and there, suddenly appearing out of nowhere, with that ghastly face conveying the horror of a living death. The teleplay must play loose with Poe, but the results are a nail-biting exercise in bad conscience and horror, made even more gripping with expert cinematography (by Bud Thackery) and direction. The episode is a slow burn— it starts by establishing characterization (the horror of one elderly man who fears being buried alive) but soon turns into a ghostly opera of the dead, where the re-animated return to haunt the living, or so it seems. And the sight of the white-shrouded corpse of Stapleton, with his ghoulish face, is not easily forgotten.

When it comes to season two's most memorable horror episodes, *The Weird Tailor* (teleplay by Robert Bloch from his own short story), episode four, directed by Herschel Daughterty, first broadcast Oct 16, 1961, becomes one of the most unsettling episodes of the series. Through a series of conflicting and conflicted moralities, told by the episode's various main characters, the deception of ultimate evil is displayed symbolically as spiders crawl around their webs, an image frequently repeated. In one disturbing image, the weird tailor Erich Borg (Henry Jones) is drinking shots

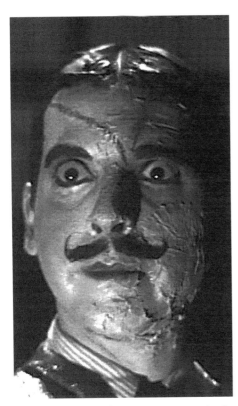

The haunting mannequin Hans (Diki Lerner) comes to life during the horrific ending of *The Weird Tailor*.

and beers at his local tavern, and when his intrusive landlord Mr. Schwenk (Stanley Adams) confronts Erich for past-due rent, the hazy face of Schwenk fades beneath the spider web, with a spider in the direct center of the web. Then the face of Schwenk morphs into the face of the man Erich has just murdered. Oh, what tangled webs we weave …

The basically unresolved tale of evil-begetting-evil begins when a wealthy Mr. Smith (George Macready), dabbling in black magic, a pentagram painted on the floor of his living room mansion, lit candles and smoke billowing up from the floor, is disturbed by his drunken, loutish son, who demands a bottle of liquor before he agrees to leave. Unfortunately, instead of walking *around* the pentagram, he walks through it, the smoke and fire briefly flaring, leaving Smith's son Arthur (Gary Clarke) dead. Mr. Smith now only lives to bring his son back.

In an eerie sequence, Smith visits fortune teller/spiritualist Madame Roberti (Iphigenie Castiglioni) to seek her help in bringing his son back to life. She speaks of her white magic (where she reads the future but does not dare interfere) versus his black magic (offering his entire fortune to change fate, defying heaven and nature, to bring his son back). She speaks of seeing all that is necessary in this world, even though the seeing-eye dog by her side conveys the fact that she is blind. But her vision is clearer than Smith's. Not able to help Smith, Roberti sends him to the "Honest Abe" used car lot to seek out the man who can help him. There he encounters Nick (aka Honest Abe), who offers to sell a rare, ancient volume of black magic to him for one million dollars. The wealthy Smith will have to liquidate everything in order to raise the money, but he is willing to become poor to have his son back.

His search finally ends up at the shop of tailor Erich Borg (Henry Jones), who abuses his beautiful wife Anna (Sondra Kerr), slapping her around and telling her to constantly shut up. Because of Erich's cruelty to his wife and her steadfast dedication to standing by her man, she fantasizes that the tailor's dummy (upon which new suits are sewn and fitted) is alive and the love of her life, even though the dummy has a half scarred and melted face. Anna sees Han's jet-black hair and full mustache as being matinee-idol handsome, and her fantasies of him compensate for Erich's abuse. Smith, reading from his black magic volume, gives Erich exact specifications for the tailor to make a suit for dead Arthur, to be made from metallic material that is described as having no color even though it glitters. In other words, the material would be perfect as a Vegas suit for Elvis Presley. The suit can only be sewn, hand stitching only, during specific hours at night. And Erich, who is constantly avoiding his landlord who wants his rent, will be paid upon delivery, or so Mr. Smith promises (even though he is now penniless, having paid Honest Abe/Nick his money immediately).

While most *Thriller* episodes avoid the heavy irony of the typical *Alfred Hitchcock Presents* episode, *The Weird Tailor* ends with absolutely disturbing imagery that makes its narrative shortcomings forgotten. When Smith demands the suit, Erich (who has come to Smith's low-rent apartment) wants payment as promised. Smith promises to deliver the money soon, but that's the very excuse that Erich has been giving his landlord, Mr. Schwenk, throughout the episode. A fight erupts, both men reaching for a knife (by the way, Arthur's body remains frozen in the upright freezer, ready for his father to slip the Elvis jacket on his frozen corpse), but the far luckier Erich kills his adversary. Returning home to Anna, the tailor is comforted by his wife, who tells her husband that she cannot remain with a murderer. Declaring he will solve her problem, Erich attempts to strangle the poor woman before she is saved in the oddest way pos-

Hans, who moves in slow herky-jerky movements, saves his beloved Anna (Sondra Kerr) from the violent attack of her husband Erich.

sible. Instead of burning the jacket as Erich requested, she instead places it on the mannequin that she loves. And in one of the most disturbing sequences in television, the dummy, Hans, comes to life as a human (played by an unbilled Diki Lerner), whose face is still burned/melted with huge stitching running across the top of his face. Hans moves in slow herky-jerky movements, resembling a wind-up toy that scurries across the floor, unbalanced, almost falling. Off screen Hans strangles Erich and returns to confront Anna, speaking in a high-pitched German-accented screech, declaring the two of them will remain together forever. On this unsettling note of unnatural love, the episode ends.

Perversion of morality becomes the dominant theme of *The Weird Tailor*. First we have a father who dabbles in black magic and allows his son to enter the unholy pentagram. Then we have Smith's unnatural request of the fortune-teller to bring his son back, at any price. Then we have Smith willing to pay his last dollar to Honest Abe for a demonic book that describes a method of bringing the dead back to life (ironically, the used-car dealer states that his actual name is Nicolai or Nick, a name frequently associated with the Devil). And finally Smith tricks a poor tailor into making him a special suit that will return his son to life, but Smith never intends to pay the man for his efforts. And finally Erich the tailor's abused wife Anna accidentally uses the suit to imbue her male fantasy mannequin with unholy life, in the ultimate perversity. In the worst example of the trickle down theory of serving the black arts, everyone touched by black magic dies a violent death or experiences an even more perverse life. At the episode's end, nothing has been resolved, nor is a lesson learned by any of the participants. This downward spiral offers no possibility for redemption or salvation. It remains one of the darkest individual episodes of the series, simply because both the evil and the less-than-evil are all destroyed in this satanic maelstrom.

The Herschel Daugherty-directed *God Grante That She Lye Stille*, adaptation by Robert Hardy Andrews (based upon the story by Cynthia Asquith), Episode 5, first broadcast October 23, 1961, borrows sequences and one major character from the barely year-old Italian horror classic,

Elspeth Clewer (Sarah Marshall) is being burned as a witch and vampire, from *God Grante That She Lye Stille.*

Black Sunday/Mask of the Demon, directed by Mario Bava. Of course Bava's inspired cinematography combined with the riveting performance of Barbara Steele cannot compare to this quickly-produced television episode, yet this installment of *Thriller* becomes one of the most haunting entries from season two. *Thriller* always managed to do wonders with creepy old mansions, and when ghosts were added to the mix, *Thriller* always excelled. The story begins in 1661 with Elspeth Clewer (Sarah Marshall) being burned as a witch and vampire (shades of *Black Sunday*). As the dazzling black-haired beauty vents her curses most enthusiastically, she damns her entire ancestral-line-to-be with curses of lives unloved, childlessness and painful deaths … until her promised return to the living. The overseer of the execution is the stone-faced Henry Daniell, in his final appearance on the series. While the location and witches' execution are cut-rate when compared to *Black Sunday*, the performance by Marshall both resembles the energy and evil exuded by Steele, and both actresses even resemble one another. It is interesting to note just how influential *Black Sunday* became in so brief a time.

Almost 300 years to the day of the witch burning, the final Clewer heir returns to her ancestral home, her father

having recently died at sea, and in a few days, on her 21st birthday (the actual 300 year anniversary), Lady Margaret (also played by Sarah Marshall, but now sporting a blonde wig) will receive her family inheritance. But Elspeth's curse leaves Lady Margaret alone and unloved. Her oldest and best friend, her terrier dog, acts fearfully when arriving at the dank mansion and quickly runs away and disappears. Even the two pet birds act oddly. And how convenient that Margaret's bedroom balcony overlooks an overgrown and neglected graveyard (with uneven mud and rock, billowing fog, gnarly trees and the burial site of her relative and vampire witch, Elspeth). Sarah, Margaret's maid, does not last very long in the household, as she is scared off by the horrific course of events, and her replacement is a psychiatric nurse hired by her new doctor, Dr. Stone (Ronald Howard), so we know immediately that Margaret's situation will not end up well. The excellent Victor Buono plays Dr. Van de Velde, a psychiatrist who predicts Lady Margaret's eventual demise. Her first night settled in, Margaret finds the translucent presence of the ghostly Elspeth visiting her, the witchy-woman approaching her in a deliciously threatening manner. Sequences such as this one are *Thriller*'s forte, always managing to get

Three hundred years after the witch burning, Elspeth's ghostly spirit visits last heir Lady Margaret (blonde), both played by Sarah Marshall.

under the skin to chill the blood. Just like in *Black Sunday*, the witch Elspeth desires to possess her twin's body. But here the raven-haired evil one wants to possess her virtuous blonde counterpart by first driving her insane through fright and finally stopping her weak heart at the moment that their souls exchange bodies.

A haunting Jerry Goldsmith musical score creates atmospheric buildup, accentuating the horrific mood of the witches' appearances amid thunderstorms and the blackness of night. As the possessions increase in intensity, Margaret reverts to locking herself in her bedroom, screaming and treating her attendants with nasty intent (momentarily, for brief periods, becoming Elspeth at her most arrogant and evil). Before long Dr. Stone is sleeping in the vacant bedroom down the hall. But her nurse, sleeping in another bedroom, is stabbed in the arm after Margaret rises in the middle of the night wielding a long knife. Far less subtle, Margaret's poor little lost dog is found in the eerie graveyard with its throat slit and her pet birds are found dead in their cage, with their heads torn off. By day Margaret seems calm and under control, but at night all Hell breaks loose. The local Vicar (Henry Daniell, as a descendant of the original executioner) attempts to share the history of Elspeth Clewer with Dr. Stone, and Daniell's entire purpose is mainly one of

suddenly appearing behind Stone in the graveyard and knocking on the ancestral home's door at the oddest of hours. He says little but simply appears as Gothic window-dressing to amp up the unease. But, my-oh-my, Henry Daniell's countenance is simply terrifying under spooky make-up and even spookier because of costume and cinematography.

Under Daugherty's inspired direction the episode creates an aura of slow-rising chills, with the young innocent unable to fight off the evil assault by Elspeth from beyond the grave. Lady Margaret is an orphan, cared for only by servants, not a lover or friend in sight to lean on for comfort. Even though Dr. Stone has love-interest potential, after he hires a psychiatric nurse to watch over her, the viewer comes to realize that Stone's interest is strictly professional. And so Margaret's predicament becomes very sad and even more tragic as the relentless haunting initiated by Elspeth quickly drives the delicate girl over the brink of sanity, and with her defenses shattered, it is far too easy for the witch to possess Margaret's body at will, if even at first for short durations.

The episode's ending is both fitting yet, at the same time, dramatically an emotional letdown. Margaret eventually accepts her defeat and even her own death (her weakened heart and the witch's mental barrage are simply too much for

her to continue to fight) with peace and acceptance. Her final words to Dr. Stone are that she has won as she dies, and the spirit of Elspeth leaves her body and returns to her grave where she disappears beneath the soil. Since Lady Margaret is the final heir in her family line, when she dies she denies the witch the final opportunity to return to the living world by invading the body of a living family member. Margaret's self-sacrifice by accepting her own death becomes heroic and she becomes the only force preventing the witch/vampire from resurrection. In a sense the audience wishes Margaret to prevail and become the heroine that survives after defeating evil. But the poignancy of her death might well be the episode's strongest aspect.

The Return of Andrew Bentley reminds audiences immediately of the intensely horrific episodes from season one, such as *Pigeons from Hell* and *The Hungry Glass*. Episode 12, broadcast December 11, 1961, the original story by August Derleth and Mark Schorer, features a teleplay by Richard Matheson. Besides starring in the episode, John Newland (famous for the TV series *One Step Beyond*) also directed.

The script's simplicity allows Newland's stark direction and the creepy cinematography of John F. Warren to weave its magic. The cast features a mute Reggie Nalder as the ghost of the long departed Andrew Bentley, and his performance is horrifying. Without muttering a sound, Nalder stands erect outside the haunted mansion, waving his arms frantically, calling forth his Familiar (or personal demon) to do dastardly deeds. In one sequence the camera is tight on Nalder's face, his eyes half-closed in a virtual squint, but suddenly he opens both eyes wide and beams forth his malevolent power. Down in the family vault he appears and disappears at will, his quivering optically-created Familiar disguising the fact that actor Tom Hennesy is performing the role with a sack of some kind over his head. But as an effectively translucent glowing demon, the Familiar, along with Nalder, creates a tandem of terror.

In his small role of Uncle Amos, Terence de Marney is over-the-top but still effective as the dabbler in the Black Arts, who fears dying and having his rival Bentley possess his body (or rather, Bentley's Familiar possess his body). Thus he reluc-

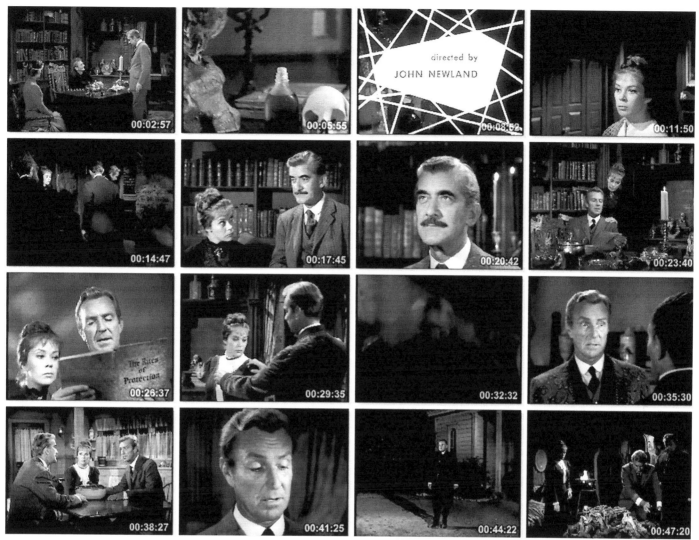

A photo montage of various frame grabs from *The Return of Andrew Bentley*

tantly (he even says so) leaves everything to his nephew Ellis Corbett (John Newland) if Ellis agrees to live in his ancient mansion (with his new bride) and protect the burial vault from ghostly interference. The eccentric uncle calmly talks to Ellis and yet barks demands, his paranoia causing him to constantly look over his shoulder and out the window, making sure he is safe from the powers of darkness. In another standout sequence, after Ellis and wife agree to the terms, Amos drinks poison and dies while playing his organ, eventually expiring and falling upon the keyboard, which maintains the unnerving, monotonous chord.

What makes this episode especially powerful is the means by which the plot is revealed, piece-by-piece. The household servant Jacob (Ken Renard), fearful and slow to reveal any family history, turns in his resignation immediately to Ellis, but is made to feel guilty and stays on for the short term, fearful for his life. The man's

demeanor and the small tidbits of plot concerning him just ratchet up the suspense to a higher level. Unfortunately Jacob dies before he is allowed to leave. As the mystery is finally revealed, one final letter from the late Uncle Amos stresses that the Rev. Burkhardt (Oscar Beregi) must be brought down to the burial vault and be protected by prayer and a crucifix. Bentley's corpse has been moved from its original burial spot in the vault and his corpse must be found and burned, but the mansion is huge and the secret nooks and hiding places are many. However, in the frightening finale, a secret passage is found behind Uncle Amos' giant pipe organ and the skeletal remains of Andrew rot behind the moveable wall. Before the Familiar can strike to protect its master Bentley, Bentley's corpse is torched in a cauldron and the Familiar too is returned back to Hell, ending the curse.

The only negative to this particular episode is the overwhelming musical

score by Morton Stevens. During specific sequences his music enhances fear as expected, but too often his music swells, rumbles and overstates the obvious. Moments exist where I had to turn the volume down, as the stingers were too much.

Basically *The Return of Andrew Bentley* is so effective because of the direction by John Newland and the haunting cinematography in and around the mansion. Newland demonstrates that a mute performance by Reggie Nalder can be masterfully unsettling because of his quirky body movements and masterfully crafted photography (a menacing steel bar held over his head; expressive arms waving his demon onward; a haunting facial close-up). The episode is at its absolute best when the dialogue stops dead, or at least becomes intermittent, allowing the visuals and sound to take over and create an ominous mood that chills the blood.

Equally effective and again one of the better horror episodes of season two

The wax figure of Annette is set on fire and slowly melts away, revealing the human skull beneath the waxy surface, from *Waxworks*.

is *Waxworks*, episode 16, first broadcast January 8, 1962, the teleplay by Robert Bloch, adapted from his own short story. The episode shines by the nature of its stellar cast, its outré plot (actually the story gets pretty darn convoluted at the end but such ambiguity serves the horror elements well) and its masterful direction, again by Herschel Daugherty.

The plot involves a series of murders that occur within a traveling wax museum that tours Europe. The operation moves to the United States and the murders continue. It seems that victims see any one of the 50 wax figures of fiendish murderers at the museum and, then later, that *one* wax figure of greatest intensity comes to life, stalks and kills that person. The first victim is a young art student who is sketching a hatchet murderer who has a clubfoot. After the museum closes and the patrons exit, the camera focuses on the trapped female as she cries out for help, with the lumbering legs and feet of the wax figure (shot from low-angle, looking upward) suddenly coming to life, ambling toward the girl who screams and is later found dead, the victim of an axe murder. A police sergeant Dane (Alan Baxter), investigating the first murder and the museum overall, forces the owner's niece Annette (Antoinette Bower) to open a side door that contains a wooden coffin, resting vertically hidden inside, with a strange

new wax figure, an intense-looking man with a beard, resting inside. Later, outside the museum along a narrow avenue, the same bearded wax murderer, now fully alive and driving an automobile, runs the trapped policeman down, killing him instantly.

The museum owner and sculptor of the wax figures, Pierre Jacquelin (Oskar Homolka), is squat and quite serious, a man who appears to be helpful and jovial with the police investigation, but is actually subversive and a little too careful in revealing the information he does. His strange niece Annette, according to Pierre, frequently dates but breaks men's hearts a little too often, devoting her life entirely to art and the museum. When rugged young cop Hudson (Ron Ely, soon to be TV's Tarzan) takes her out on a diner date, she is polite yet anxious for the date to end and to be returned home. And just as Hudson returns her home at the waxworks, the stranger in the shadows, Colonel Bertroux (Martin Kosleck), makes a sudden appearance, claiming to be investigating the murders that originated in Europe, but a cop who appears a little too cool and detached.

The plot, taking on the guise of a police procedural whodunit, is colored by the eeriness of the densely photographed museum and the hovering, silhouetted wax figures within, those menacing subjects with hoisted murder weapons, staring eyes and threatening stances. When such figures appear to come to life, the whodunit takes on another level of complexity.

The episode's climax does not simplify the situation. After Hudson is stabbed in the back while walking only a few feet

behind Lt. Bailey (Booth Colman), Bailey confronts Pierre (after Pierre, a few minutes earlier, got the drop on Bertroux and dumped his corpse into a barrel of boiling wax) and another door is opened to reveal a wax figure of niece Annette. However Pierre now announces that Annette is his wife, that she was convicted of murder and executed 30 years ago. He keeps her "alive" by covering her rotting flesh in wax, but the wax contains the blood of all the murder victims which, because of a magic spell, returns his wife (who has not aged, so she is now his "niece") to life. With wigs and wax body parts lying on the table nearby, Pierre says he disguises himself as his murderous wax figures and commits the crimes, but the pear-shaped Pierre does not always resemble the body types of the wax figures he supposedly becomes. So the suggestion exists that such a "curse" also returns the other wax figures to life, just as Annette lives for extended periods of time. Instead of solving the occult mystery, Pierre's explanation just makes the plot that much more weird. Soon Pierre gets a bullet in the gut and dies, and the wax figure of Annette is set on fire and slowly melts away, revealing the human skull beneath the waxy surface. Annette was indeed a corpse covered in wax and brought back to life via human blood and a supernatural spell. Yet somehow the audience must find it difficult to

Beautiful witch Meg Peyton (Pamela Searle) gladly helps her executioner place the noose around her neck, as thanks for being allowed to wear her wig, from *A Wig for Miss Devore.*

accept the fact that Oskar Homolka disguised himself as wax murderers to carry out the resurrection of his wife Annette.

Even with such plot improbabilities, *Waxworks* is basically terrifying and the cinematography by veteran Benjamin H. Kline emphasizes the shadows, the spooky lighting and the odd angles of murderous wax figures and the intensity of the killings. *Waxworks* contains a plot as inky black as its wax museum setting, yet the horror carries the audience on its shoulders and succeeds in its ambitions.

The season two *Thriller* episodes followed a formula. The supernatural episodes typically involved a witch, vengeful demon or an evil spirit returning from the dead. The crackle of thunder and the flash of lightning became the soundtrack of a deserted house at night, or preferably a decaying mansion filled with cobwebs. Characters might appear to be inviting and polite, but generally a self-serving motive lied just beneath that surface gloss. Burial grounds and disturbed graves became a signature image of evil and fear. Thus, when an episode cut through such standard baggage to create something a little different and innovative, *Thriller* shined even brighter. Episode 19, broadcast January 29, 1962, was one of those special episodes. *A Wig for Miss Devore,* directed by veteran John Brahm, based upon an August Derleth short story adapted by Donald S. Sanford, in many ways became a spectacular low-rent version of *Sunset Blvd.*, but with supernatural and horrific overtones.

In one of the most unsettling pretitle sequences, shot on the expansive set

A Wig for Miss Devore begins by filming an execution sequence on the expansive set first used in season two's earlier episode, *Guillotine.*

Studio head Max (Herbert Rudley) is about to be pushed into a fountain and drown by the monstrous hands of Miss Devore (Patricia Barry).

of season two's earlier broadcast *Guillotine*, a hangman's gallows replaces the steel blade. Beautiful witch Meg Peyton (Pamela Searle), guilty of witchcraft and the death of six citizens, wishes her executioners a good morning and greets them with a smile. When one of the executioners tells her that she must remove her wig, Peyton becomes unhinged for a brief moment, but her flirtatious manner results in the other executioner allowing her to keep it on, at least until after her demise. Peyton, sensing the trembling hands of her hangman as the noose approaches her neck, happily assists him in fitting the rope in the proper manner. Soon the lever is pulled and Meg Peyton dies quietly. It is only after her death that the hangmen see her now withered and monstrous hands and arms grasping the wig, which was the source of her beauty and youth.

Now in the swinging 1960s washed-up movie star Sheila Devore, bleach-blonde and over-the-hill at age 39 (the studio head stated she was done at age 32 and she has not worked since), wants to make her movie comeback playing Meg Peyton, using all the actual dialogue from the execution. And to top it off, she wants the studio to acquire the historic Peyton wig, now on display in an English museum. In this initial sequence with Devore (Patricia Barry), the aging actress, her eyes hidden behind large black sunglasses, stares off into the distance, her fantasy of wanting to stage a star-turn comeback being totally devoid from reality. Speaking to her meek agent (and former studio accountant, who has proof that the studio head Max and her major director George have stolen payments due Devore, and he is using the threat of exposure to orchestrate Devore's comeback), she wants the starring role in the Meg Peyton project and all the accruements of her Hollywood past life as a star. And of course Max (Herbert Rudley) and George (John Baragrey) are forced to readily agree to the agent's (John Fiedler) demands or risk financial exposure.

Intermingled among the thunderous applause welcoming Devore back to the set and her prima donna expectations (but not in a nasty way; rather she is pictured sympathetically and delusional), we have the supernatural horror that is worked in so perfectly. After the wig arrives, it transforms Devore into the dazzling beauty of eight years previously, but a letter follows a few days' later informing her agent of the curse associated with the wig and, more specifically, the wearer of the wig. Even though the milquetoast Herbert tries to warn Devore of the danger, she does not have time to face such reality. While everyone appears to be kind toward Devore,

everyone except her agent is attempting to manipulate her. And her one obvious enemy, a Hedda Hopper gossip columnist Arabella Foote (Linda Watkins), wants to get to the bottom of the supernatural secret of the wig (she steals the letter that offers the warning).

First studio head Max makes a romantic play for Devore, but he is merely protecting his financial interests by manipulating her. Alone in his extravagant mansion, near an indoor fountain, Max wants the star to take off her wig, since they are no longer working. But after the wig comes off, Devore transforms into an aging hag, but we the audience only see her gyrating arms and hands against a black background and then we see these withered hands push Max into the fountain and hold his head beneath the water until he drowns. The make-up here appears to have come from Universal's recent *The Leech Woman*, released about two years earlier. Later when director George makes a romantic play for her, the wig once again comes off and the startled man falls off a high-rise balcony to his death. Finally, during a studio party, held on the set, Arabella confronts Devore and pulls the wig from her head, and Devore's Mummy-like hands scratch the woman to death (fright might also be a factor, as her wounds appear to be superficial).

In a very unsatisfying conclusion, Devore, wearing a heavy head scarf and rushing past the assembled onlookers, runs past several stone columns stored on the studio lot, but one of them mysteriously falls (without reason), crushing Devore underneath. Screaming to not turn on any lights, a man still turns on a car's headlights and we can see the wretchedly withered head of Devore, her sparse white hair mostly gone, tumors growing on her cheeks and neck, as she shortly expires with her bulging eyes registering shock and fear. Devore's agent suddenly remembers the wig, and before he can get back to the party, Devore's devoted maid, who loves to hold up and admire her mistress' clothing, puts on the wig, and looking glamorous and star–like, she passes among the crowd of party-goers, as the camera freezes on her smiling face, a fresh victim of the witchy curse of Meg Peyton all those generations ago.

A Wig for Miss Devore reminds the viewer of *Sunset Blvd.*, *The Leach Woman*

Boris Karloff, Dick York and Carolyn Kearney from *The Incredible Doktor Markesan*

and any number of movies (*Black Sunday; Horror Hotel*) where a witch, at the moment she is to be burned at the stake, declares a curse that will carry down through a blood line allowing the witch to return to life and continue her evil reign generations later. This *Thriller* is different from most, merging a very modern sensibility with an ancient curse from hundreds of years ago. The acting by Patricia Barry is marvelous and her character dominates our attention. Her motivating force is revenge for the Hollywood that abandoned her and kicked her to the curb during what she envisioned to be her artistic prime. Of course the viewer can tell that Devore is delusional and truly a legend in her own mind. She is also dedicated to her work and career and certainly deserved better treatment at the hands of those who molded her career. The viewer feels sorry for Devore and we are pulling for her to make some sort of artistic comeback, even if that means starring in an independent movie production. But unfortunately, Devore's vanity and her over-inflated sense of talent and beauty ultimately destroy her, as she murders all those who dynamited her career and used her (and her money) for their own greedy purposes. In a cruel manner, *A Wig for Miss Devore* exposes the cesspool that Hollywood had become and the manner in which talent that never reached the top was often disposed of like last week's trash. In other words, what have you

done for me lately is the battle call that all movie stars face, and once the bottom falls out of a career, it is time to move on. But people such as Miss Devore are blinded by false perceptions, and men of declining power with evil intentions prey upon poor souls such as Miss Devore, and their evil seems so much more duplicitous than any curse concocted by witch Meg Peyton, who stood beautiful, kind and polite on the gallows that bright morning, com-

forting the hangman whose hands shook. Modern evil is far less kind as this episode demonstrates.

Finally what many consider the zenith of the season two horror episodes appeared February 26, 1962, as episode 22 of *Thriller*. Based upon an August Derleth and Mark Schorer story, adapted once again by Donald S. Sanford, *The Incredible Doktor Markesan* stars Boris Karloff in the title role, with direction provided by veteran horror film director Robert Florey (*Murders in the Rue Morgue*, 1932, Universal Pictures). This would be the horror hurrah of season two, even though the episode is flawed and suffers as a result. But when people remember (from season one) *The Hungry Glass*, *The Purple Room* and *Pigeons from Hell*, *The Incredible Doktor Markesan* elicits cheers as the hero of season two. It just goes to show that the best horror episodes of season two are generally a peg or two lower than the best of season one.

One of the strengths of this episode is the spooky characterization that Boris Karloff brings to the role of Markesan, his one monstrous performance in the series. Also, the episode features one of the best-dressed decaying mansions (haunted or otherwise) ever featured in any *Thriller* episode. Perhaps the plot being reduced to a sidebar with too much emphasis

Dr. Markesan flashes his evil smile, as animated corpse professor Billy Beck hovers in back, contrasting Karloff's formerly gloomy corpse portrayal with this more animated one that surfaces near the end of the episode.

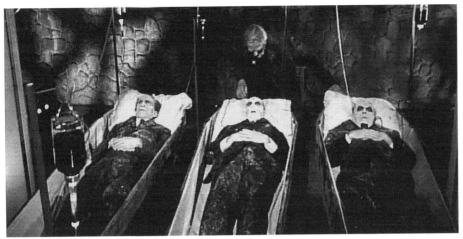

The living corpses of the three dead professors in Markesan's basement laboratory

placed on atmosphere and fright underscores the actual horror created. While a sense of mystery constantly drives the plot forward, too much time is spent with our modern couple locked away in the mansion's master bedroom, ultimately escaping, but then simply wandering up and down dank corridors and coming across people who wish to remain unknown. Fred Bancroft (the generally comical Dick York) and wife Molly Bancroft (Carolyn Kearney) are married graduate students, broke (they have $12 between them), who are looking for jobs at the local university. Even though Fred has not seen his Uncle Konrad Markesan in 20 years, he feels the old man will allow them to stay for free in the huge mansion (strangely, now crumbling and in a state of disarray) until they find jobs.

But in these first sequences, Karloff plays Markesan as a gloomy walking corpse, dust, dirt and cobwebs on his jacket and head. Dark circles frame his eyes and Markesan's fingertips are black and appear dead. He moves slowly in a herky-jerky manner, his dead eyes never registering any emotion. Even when Fred cracks a joke or asks a question, Markesan's face is a blank slate. We later learn that the old man is in fact dead, so his performance is wonderful and truly evocative of the living dead (but in a far more subtle sense than a zombie in today's cinematic universe). Karloff allows his character to utter about as many words as the Monster spoke in *Bride of Frankenstein*, but with the dramatic effect that less is more. He tells Fred that he can take any money he needs but that he cannot stay in the house. Soon giving in, Markesan tells Fred that he can

stay up in the master bedroom from sunset to dawn, but that he and his wife must not come outside their room for any reason (and the old man locks them in, just to make sure). With a hangdog expressionless performance, Karloff was creating something subtly horrific.

But later in the episode, when we learn that Doktor Markesan has used a mold from gravesites to re-animate the dead (three professors who worked at the university with him and who died scoffing at his work), the three corpses kept hidden in wooden coffins in his basement lab, tubes and wires running from their bodies; they look more than dead, with pale white faces and spots of decaying flesh on their faces. However, during these times, Markesan sometimes seems more animated, more energetic, and he sometimes flashes an evil smile that seems counter to his established character as displayed early on in the episode. It is as if Karloff played Markesan one way in the earlier sequences and differently in the end-of-episode ones. One might say that once his secret was out, he did not have to remain so secretive and death-like, but it seems to me that the character of Markesan does vary uncomfortably too much from beginning to end.

And that darn ending for me becomes an outright failure. Wandering around the house alone, Molly comes across Karloff and his small army of corpses wandering mindlessly toward her, with Karloff flashing his sly and evil smile as the corpses approach. She soon screams and the sequence cuts away, with Fred now searching for her. In a sequence far too brief and silly, a huge light structure overhead falls

and crushes Markesan beneath (but the medic is already dead, right?). Fred wanders into a side room where he finds the ghastly corpse of Molly (yes, the undead army killed her), with a focus on her absolutely stupid 1960s hair-do, as she slowly leans back down to rest in her coffin, and slowly closes the coffin lid as a scream erupts from within. To me too much too soon and what we see is rushed and silly. Robert Florey has crafted the perfect sense of dread and the undead, but in the final minutes of the episode, this incredible mood becomes silly and almost laughable. The episode suffers from such a hodgepodge approach.

The Incredible Doktor Markesan is ultimately one of the best horror episodes of the series, simply because of the mood of dread generated throughout. Karloff and his private army of living corpses is creepy and well lit, but the ultimate ending just does not maintain this quiet subtlety of classic horror. Too many scenes with York and Kearney occur, and far too little Karloff is featured. Still, for network television, this episode is chilling, atmospheric and unnerving. And any episode that shows Boris Karloff as a re-animated living dead is worthy of serious attention.

Thriller, perhaps for the best, disappeared from the screen far too quickly, ending its run at the creative peak and not the valley, and Karloff continued acting in features, right up until the end of his life in 1969, mostly in American International movies that milked his horror film persona. Just like Alfred Hitchcock did in his intros for *Alfred Hitchcock Presents*, Boris Karloff played up his horror persona to perfection, blending an atmosphere of creepy horror persona laced with a light dose of humor. And when Karloff actually appeared in an episode, so much the better. It is not that *Thriller* broke the glass ceiling or created something brand new and profound, it was just that for television the series dared to push the envelope and bring a tad of the unnerving, the unsettling and the horrific to American living rooms via network TV. For a short time this series managed to merge good writing, good acting and good direction to horrify baby boomers throughout the land (and their parents as well).

And the memory of hiding our eyes through fingers pressed tightly over our faces remains to this day.

THE MUMMY'S SHROUD
HAMMER'S DUSTY SECRET

BY NICHOLAS ANEZ

By 1967, the glory days of Britain's famous Hammer Film Productions was on the wane. Hammer's ascendancy began 10 years earlier (or 13, if you include the Quatermass entries from 1954 and 1956) with the release of *The Curse of Frankenstein* (1957) and continued its peak years with *Horror of Dracula* (1958). Among the many excellent films that Hammer produced during this time included *The Mummy* (1959). However, unlike the Dracula and Frankenstein movies, Hammer didn't make a sequel to their original mummy film, despite its success. Five years later, Hammer did produce another mummy film, though it was not thematically connected to the earlier film. *The Curse of the Mummy's Tomb* (1964) played on a double-bill with another Hammer entry and committed the cardinal sin of being boring. After this disappointment, Hammer waited three years to make another mummy movie. The title was *The Mummy's Shroud* (1967) and it attracted even less attention than the second movie. Hammer released it as a supporting feature with the company's *Frankenstein Created Woman*, and those critics who

bothered to see it gave it scathing reviews. Contemporary reference books give it little if any respect. Even the director of the movie, John Gilling, seemed to have disdain for it. In Wayne Kinsey's book, *Hammer, The Bray Studio Years*, the director states that he wasn't proud of the movie and considered it one of his worst. In the book, *Hammer, The House of Horror*, Howard Maxford calls it "a less than routine affair." And in his annual *Movie Guide*, Leonard Maltin gives it his lowest rating and calls it a "bomb."

The Mummy's Shroud admittedly pales next to Terence Fisher's 1959 movie, which had the advantage of starring Peter Cushing and Christopher Lee, both of whom had already reached the status of Hammer's reigning horror icons. Its low budget is obvious and the plot is a retread of previous movies in which a mummy is brought back to life to wreak vengeance upon the blasphemers that desecrated its tomb. Also, this mummy's make-up seems somewhat bland and misses the mark. However, to counter these deficiencies, it has some assets, among them Hammer's typically fine attention to period detail,

some clever departures from the familiar plot, well-developed characterizations and fine ensemble acting.

The Mummy's Shroud begins in ancient Egypt, 2000 BC. Palace intrigue drives the Pharaoh's young son Kah-to-Bey and his loyal slave Prem into the desert. When the boy dies, Prem places a sacred shroud over his body and buries him. In 1920, an archaeological expedition financed by wealthy industrialist Stanley Preston searches for Kah-to-Bey's crypt. Sir Basil Walden leads the expedition which includes Preston's son, Paul, along with linguist Claire de Sangre and photographer Harry Newton. After the expedition is reported missing, Preston and his wife Barbara arrive in Cairo. Preston organizes a search party, which he reluctantly joins, to find the expedition and orders his local flunky Longbarrow to accompany him. Meanwhile, Sir Basil and his party discover Kah-to-Bey's grave just before Preston and his party find them. They ignore the threats of Hasmid, the keeper of the tomb, who warns of death to anyone who desecrates the grave. When a snake bites Sir Basil, this seems

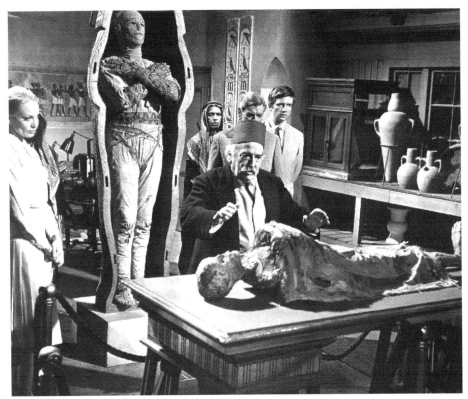

A cast group shot surrounding the majestic mummy of Prem (Prem is played by Dickie Owen, while the actual mummy is played by Eddie Powell)

to be the first indication that they should heed Hasmid's warning. Nevertheless, they unearth the body of Kah-to-Bey along with the sacred shroud that covers him. Though Claire anxiously refuses to decipher the words on the shroud, they take their discovery back to Cairo where Prem's mummified body lies in his coffin. Preston secretly has Basil committed to an asylum and assumes full credit for the expedition's success. But Hasmid and his fortune-telling mother, Haiti, have their own plans. He steals the shroud and reads the words of death, which brings Prem back to life. One by one, the mummy exacts his vengeance against the four desecrators, until the last two survivors desperately try to stop the curse.

This brief summary of the plot must have a ring of familiarity to it for anyone who has seen previous mummy films, including Universal's movies from the 1940s. The lengthy prologue elicited some criticism for its exposition, but it is necessary to fully understand the tragedy of the ill-fated boy and his loyal slave. Evil triumphs in ancient Egypt; the benevolent pharaoh is murdered and his son, the rightful heir to the throne, dies soon afterward. Prem's devotion to his young master assumes a tragic component

because he was unable to protect the boy and restore him to his throne. Thus, his desire for vengeance after death is totally unselfish. In view of this, it is possible to view Prem as the film's only noble character. The members of Sir Basil's crew possess the hubris of many Europeans of the era, whose assumption of moral superiority automatically disregarded the culture of people whom they consider inferior. This is their only sin and most of them will be punished for it. The irony is that only those who beg forgiveness of Prem will be spared a horrible death.

The characterizations, for the most part, are interesting. Stanley Preston is an arrogant, pompous braggart who has concern only for himself. He is accustomed to getting his way, usually by means of bribery or force. As his fear mounts, he will even relinquish his wife and son to escape death. Barbara Preston never expresses any feelings for her husband, but her expressions at key moments signify her contempt for him. Indeed, the pleasure with which she enjoys his mounting fear and impending death is chilling. Paul Preston also displays some unexpected backbone when he turns against his father. Sir

Basil appears to be a kindhearted person whose consideration for his colleagues takes precedence over his own ambitions. Among his colleagues, there is no hint of romance, which is a welcome twist. Claire is just another member of the expedition, whose linguistic skill is needed. Claire is also somewhat different from the usual heroine in that she instinctively senses from the beginning that there may be more than superstition to the sacred shroud. It is this respect for other cultures that will save her and Paul from a grisly fate. This same respect will allow her to restore the shroud to Kah-to-Bey, which signifies the culpability of the expedition. Inspector Barrani, the local police officer in charge of the investigation, is initially an insensitive detective but, after many deaths, he reveals his humane quality by telling the survivors to leave Egypt immediately. And then there is the pitiable and harassed Longbarrow, whose meek subservience to Preston will eventually doom him. His fate is particularly sad because Preston, to satisfy his own ego, forces him to join the search party and, consequently, become a victim of the curse.

The movie has its share of thrills. Prem's mummy looks somewhat different than the usual cinematic mummy, perhaps because the filmmakers based his appearance upon actual mummies in the

Eddie Powell, who was Christopher Lee's stunt double in many of his Hammer films, takes a comic break while filming *The Mummy's Shroud*.

Egyptian Rooms of the British Museum. He perhaps doesn't look as threatening as Christopher Lee's incarnation, though when he opens his crusty eye lids for the first time it is quite unsettling. This mummy is inspired in his manner of disposing of those who dared to defile his master. He crushes one person's skull. He breaks a bottle of acid upon another victim. And he wraps another victim in a curtain and throws him out of the window. Prem's motivation for vengeance is devotion to his master. He is not evil but is only seeking justice against those that he perceives as evildoers. In contrast, Hasmid has only hatred in his heart, so his murderous actions are less excusable. And then there is Haiti, whose cackle and accompanying glee at predicting deaths are quite chilling. Here is a woman who really enjoys her profession. Also adding to the film's excitement are the realistic fight scenes. Harry puts up a valiant defense against Prem, and the climactic battle with the mummy against Paul, Claire and Inspector Barrani is quite thrilling and edited with great craft.

As usual with Hammer, the entire cast of British actors approach their roles in a totally professional manner, with as much diligence and preparation as they would do for a Shakespearean play. Andre Morell gives his customary fine performance as Sir Basil; through his expressions and tone, he makes it clear that he is seeking neither fame nor fortune, only knowledge. John Phillips, with his disdainful tone and assumption of superiority, makes Preston totally despicable, but he also skillfully

Sir Basil (Andre Morell) is about to have his skull crushed by Prem.

conveys a trace of fear beneath the bluster. Elizabeth Sellars as Barbara doesn't have that much dialogue, but the camera often dwells on her expressions, which adeptly transmit repressed emotions of hatred and resentment toward her husband. Maggie Kimberly as Claire has an exotic look that creates an air of mystery, which is appropriate for her enigmatic character. David Buck as Paul and Tim Barrett as Harry fulfill their requirements more than agreeably. Richard Delgado is perhaps a bit over-the-top as Hasmid, but he is supposed to be a fanatic and fanatics by nature tend to be hysterical. Catherine Lacey's performance may be even more exaggerated, but this makes Haiti a truly frightening character. However, with due respect to the other fine actors, it is Hammer regular supporting player Michael Ripper as Longbarrow who deserves special praise. He projects pitiable subservience not just by his words but by his perpetually obsequious manner. His eagerness to please the haughty Preston initially appears to be just typical of his character, but it eventually becomes evident that he is hoping that his timid submission will get him back to his beloved England. When it seems that his wish will be granted, it is one of the few joyful moments in his life. This makes his subsequent disappointment and violent death truly lamentable. Ripper's performance is award-worthy and would probably have been recognized as such if it were not in a Hammer B-movie.

This was the last film John Gilling directed for Hammer. He had begun writing scripts for the company in the late 1940s but left after a falling out with production chief Michael Carreras over authorship of a script in 1951. He returned in 1960 and directed his first film for Hammer (although technically the film was never credited as a Hammer Film Production), *The Shadow of the Cat*. He subsequently directed for the company a pair of swashbucklers, *The Pirates of Blood River* (1962) and *The Scarlet Blade* (1962), which were commercially successful. He wrote the screenplay for the horror film *The Gorgon* (1964) and directed *The Reptile* (1966). He based his script

Prem admires the golden hair of Claire (Maggie Kimberly)

for *The Mummy's Shroud* upon a story by John Elder (a pseudonym for Hammer's executive producer Anthony Hinds). Hammer considered him a good director but Kinsey's book reports that Gilling had "questionable people skills" and that "his bad temper was legendary." Perhaps Gilling was in a foul mood when he denounced the movie because it is better than he may have realized.

An atmospheric score by Don Banks is also an asset. Born in Australia, Banks established a reputation as a composer of concertos while also achieving fame as a jazz composer. He joined Hammer in 1962 and subsequently scored eight films for the company, either in the thriller or horror genre. This was his fourth score for a Gilling film, including one non-Hammer, and his final score for Hammer. The florid main theme, with a full chorus and orchestra, vividly recreates an ancient world.

In view of its terrible reputation, *The Mummy's Shroud* is a pleasant surprise. There are worse ways to spend 90 minutes. And it's difficult to not like a movie with the tagline: "Beware the beat of the cloth-wrapped feet."

The iconic Allen K., famed for his small ink portraits, here combines many of them to create a classic horror film montage.

BY ERNIE MAGNOTTA

THE FEARSOME FOURSOME:

UNDER-APPRECIATED HORROR OF THE '70S AND '80S

If you happened to be a horror fan during the 1970s and 1980s, you probably remember what a glorious time it was. The amount of sheer creative talent that existed during these two decades is mindblowing. Up and coming writers and directors such as George Romero, Dario Argento, Wes Craven, Tobe Hooper, Stephen King, David Cronenberg, John Carpenter and Sam Raimi would soon become horror filmmaking icons, producing classic works such as *Dawn of the Dead, Deep Red, Suspiria, The Hills Have Eyes, A Nightmare on Elm Street, The Texas Chain Saw Massacre, Carrie, The Shining, Scanners, Halloween, The Thing* and *The Evil Dead.* Two amazing lists. And they aren't even definitive. Horror film buffs really had it good. These amazing films would not only terrify generations, but they would also instantly change the landscape of the horror film universe.

Unfortunately, this time period wasn't exactly 20 years filled with five-star classics. The 1970s drive-in circuit had its fair share of inept and incoherent horror films, while the video stores of the 1980s suffered from a barrage of amateur, shot-on-video disasters. Amidst

the excellent and the terrible were many solid and well-made horror films that, for various reasons, failed to ignite a spark with its target audience. Many of these films suffered because they didn't follow the popular formula of the time, were promoted poorly or were overshadowed by their more mainstream counterparts. To me, many of these films are as good as or, in some instances, greater than some of the better-known horror output of the time. To prove my point, I've picked four films—two from the '70s and two from the '80s—that I believe should have gone on to greater critical acclaim and, in some cases, been accorded the sequel treatment.

My first pick is 1974's often-neglected *Captain Kronos: Vampire Hunter,* a wonderfully original vampire adventure from legendary Hammer Film Productions. The film focuses on Kronos, a brave warrior who, with the help of his loyal hunchbacked assistant Professor Hieronymus Grost, has dedicated his life to eliminating the plague of vampirism from the world. Aiding the duo on their quest is the lovely Gypsy girl Carla, as well as Kronos' old friend, Dr. Marcus.

After looking into several unexplained deaths at a nearby village, Kronos' investigation leads him to suspicious siblings Paul and Sara Durward, but when the Captain and his goodhearted group of vampire slayers arrive at Castle Durward, they find, to their horror, that they are in for much more than they bargained. Sounds like the usual Hammer vampire formula with Kronos substituting for Professor Van Helsing, doesn't it? It's not. In fact, it's much more complex than that.

As much as I love vampire movies from this time, including Hammer's *Dracula A.D. 1972* and its sequel, *The Satanic Rites of Dracula, Captain Kronos: Vampire Hunter* is much better than either of those films, but is, unfortunately, lesser known to horror movie fans. Perhaps the absence of an iconic genre star such as Christopher Lee or Peter Cushing resulted in the film being relatively ignored. Also Paramount's distribution for B-productions was very hit-and-miss at the time.

Written, produced and directed by the talented Brian Clemens, the entertaining film, which expertly balances horror and adventure, not only takes the usu-

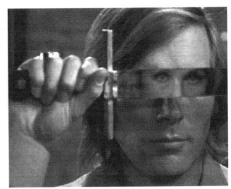

Captain Kronos turns the evil vampire's hypnotic gaze back upon itself.

al vampire lore and stands it on its head, but also combines it with a hero who is an amalgam of several different genres. These innovations would make the film exciting while, at the same time, help it to rise above the tired and conventional horror fare of the day. For instance, the movie opens in a forest on a sunny afternoon. Within the first few minutes we see a beautiful young girl being menaced by a mysterious figure in a dark-hooded cloak. Moments later, when the young girl's friend comes looking for her, she finds that the lovely lass has been drained of all her youth. With one scene, Clemens has already rejuvenated a formula that, by 1974, had become very stale. The welcome changes continue as the filmmaker shows the cloaked menace, resembling the Grim Reaper, creep past a flowerbed and, in the process, kill off all the blossoming foliage. These vampires do not only suck blood, they suck the life out of their young victims in order to remain young themselves. They also seem able to roam freely in the daylight, as long as they remain cloaked beneath the sun's rays.

Another very original addition to vampire mythology is the "Toad in the Hole" sequence. Grost and Carla place a dead toad into a wooden box and bury it on a dirt road. They wait for a coach to ride by and then they dig up the box and open it. If the toad is alive, it means that a vampire has passed over it. Add-

ing original mythology to the established vampire canon adds interest. Another bit of inventive undead tinkering comes when we learn that a vampire only bleeds at the moment of its death. Although these changes breathe fresh life into the hackneyed formula, they are only part of what makes *Kronos* such an original film.

A major reason that this movie works so beautifully lies in Clemens' ingenuity combining a story involving original vampires with an innovative adventure hero. Clemens eliminates the old man of science, academia or religion, as seen in characters such as Professor Van Helsing

and various priests and doctors, replacing them with a very unique adversary for his just-as-unique undead. Captain Kronos embodies many different types of action hero. With his tights and mastery of a sword, he resembles the swashbuckling hero Robin Hood. Kronos is also constantly smoking, much like Clint Eastwood's Man With No Name, and the film very much feels like a Spaghetti Western in spots. There's a bit of the Kurosawa samurai in there too. Although he is a hero, the character of Kronos seems a bit cold at first. He also has some anger management issues in him, due to the fact that, after they were unfortunately turned into vampires, Kronos had to kill his own mother and sister. However, we soon see that he is a goodhearted hero, who will always help a friend. These traits are most noticeable in the scene where Kronos defends Grost from a gang of bullies, led by the late, great Ian Hendry. This is the

Captain Kronos (Horst Janson) and the loyal Grost (John Cater) are on the hunt in *Captain Kronos: Vampire Hunter*.

Caroline Munro relaxes during the shooting of *Captain Kronos*.

Carla (Caroline Munro) and Horst Janson share a warm moment

scene that most recalls the Western genre, and it's quite humorous as well.

Speaking of that, Clemens does a great job mixing humor with drama while, simultaneously, adding depth to his characters and advancing the plot. In the scene where Kronos' old friend Dr. Marcus becomes a vampire, the good doctor begs Kronos to kill him. The problem is that there are many ways to kill a vampire, and different methods work on different creatures (and do not work on others). Kronos and Grost try a stake in the heart, hanging and burning before finally realizing that a silver cross will do the trick. The captain is clearly frustrated at the sight of his friend having to endure such agony, but the scene actually becomes a little intentionally funny. The humor helps to offset the horror while, at the same time, it shows Kronos' empathy toward his friend.

In addition to Clemens' excellent screenwriting, the film is also helped immeasurably by his solid direction. Clemens' prowling camera creates a sense of dread and uneasiness, especially in the scene where the vulnerable Carla waits alone on a couch in the vampire's castle. In contrast to the horror is a very tastefully photographed love scene between Kronos and Carla, as well as some excellently edited fight sequences. Several iconic images appear, such as Kronos holding a mirrored sword up to his eyes,

which turns the vampire's hypnotic gaze back on itself.

Acting-wise, all of the performances in the film are effective, especially Horst Janson as the heroic Captain Kronos, John Cater as the loyal Grost and the lovely Caroline Munro as Carla the Gypsy. The film also features John Carson as Dr. Marcus, Shane Briant as Paul Durward, Lois Dane as Sara Durward and Wanda Ventham as Lady Durward, all of whom add immeasurably to the movie. Like many of Hammer's best films, *Kronos* has an almost fairytale quality to it, and the production values are superb. Besides containing gorgeous cinematography, the film also boasts beautiful locations, impressive sets, elegant costumes and a magnificent musical score by Laurie Johnson.

The movie was set up as the first of a potential series, but due to poor promotion and distribution, combined with Hammer nearing the end of its glorious run, this was, unfortunately, not to be. At one point in the movie, a character mentions there being many different species of vampire, so I'm assuming that had the series continued, audiences would have been treated to even more original takes on the vampire myth. If any one of the four movies reviewed here required a sequel, this was the one.

All in all, this is a top-notch production that, although it has gained in popularity over the years, still hasn't garnered the recognition it so richly deserves. Bottom line: If you enjoy Gothic horror, action, Westerns, swashbuckling heroes,

ONCE THEY WERE ALMOST HUMAN!

Beneath the living...
Beyond the dead...
From the depths of Hell's Ocean!

JOSEPH BRENNER PRESENTS

SHOCK WAVES

The Deep End of Horror!

starring **Peter Cushing** · with Brooke Adams · Fred Buch · Jack Davidson
Luke Halprin · D.J. Sidney · Don Stout · and **John Carradine**
A Zopix Presentation · screenplay by John Harrison, Ken Wiederhorn
music by Richard Einhorn · produced by Reuben Trane · directed by Ken Wiederhorn
Released by JOSEPH BRENNER ASSOCIATES, INC. · in EASTMANCOLOR [PG] PARENTAL GUIDANCE SUGGESTED

In *Shock Waves* the Nazi zombies sport short blonde hair, dark goggles and wrinkled features.

clever plot twists, good humor, grand adventure, Hammer films or all of the above—*Captain Kronos: Vampire Hunter* is a fun ride that is not to be missed.

My second underrated pick, although not a Hammer film, features one of that legendary company's greatest stars, the immortal Peter Cushing. Released in 1977, the independently produced *Shock Waves*, a chilling tale about underwater Nazi zombies, is a wonderfully creepy and overlooked horror film.

This is one of the first films to deal with undead zombie Nazis (*The Frozen Dead*, made in 1966, might well be the first one made during the modern era). However, the theme has continued in horror films, such as Jess Franco's *Oasis of the Zombies* (1981), Jean Rollin's *Zombie Lake* (1981) and, more recently, 2009's *Dead Snow* and its 2014 sequel. Although these films all have their moments, I find *Shock Waves* to be the scariest of the bunch. Inspired by the novel *The Morning of the Magicians* by

Louis Pauwels and Jacques Bergier, *Shock Waves* tells the story of a hapless group of vacationers who, after being shipwrecked, seek refuge on a remote island inhabited by murderous Nazi zombies. Now, I'm sure you're saying to yourself, "Except for the Nazi part, we've seen this a million times," right? Well, much like *Kronos*, this film takes what's expected and does something a little different with it. And that makes all the difference.

The most obvious change is in the zombies themselves. If audiences are expecting shambling, brain dead, George Romero-type cannibals, forget it. With their short blonde hair, dark goggles, wrinkled features and Nazi uniforms, these eerie creatures bear no resemblance at all to the classic zombies we've come to know and love. Not only are they fast moving when needed, but they can survive in water as well as on land. They also have no desire to consume human flesh. All these things want to do is find and kill you. And scariest of all, they're quite intelligent.

Another reason the movie works so well is due to director Ken Wiederhorn, who takes the very simple premise and creates an extremely unsettling film by

The immortal Peter Cushing plays the man responsible for the zombie threat, in *Shock Waves.*

The ship's crusty old captain is played by John Carradine, in *Shock Waves.*

avoiding an over-abundance of gore and, instead, infuses the film with not only suspense and atmosphere but fearful imagery as well. One of the best visuals in the movie is of the silent Nazi zombies slowly rising out of the sea, one at a time, until we notice that there are at least a dozen of them. There's also an amazing shot of a lone Nazi walking along the ocean floor. Another frightening scene comes when the ship's crusty old captain (played by the late, great John Carradine) shoots a flare into the darkness and the dim light partially illuminates the Nazi ghost ship, which sits out in the ocean just a short distance away. Also, the director films many of the zombie attack scenes in broad daylight. This may have been intended, or it may be due to more economical concerns. Whatever the reason, it's a refreshing change of pace. Another nice aspect of this film is the pacing. Although Wiederhorn doesn't rush things, the film never seems dull. The talented director takes his time, establishes his characters and slowly builds up a real sense of dread.

Speaking of the characters, our small group of doomed vacationers are a pretty believable and, with the exception of nerdy complainer Norman (Jack Davidson), a mostly likeable lot. (However, in the best Harry Cooper/*Night of the Living Dead* tradition, the thoroughly-irritating

Norman also happens to be correct in his views.) The immortal Peter Cushing, as the scar-faced man responsible for the zombie threat, is marvelous as always, especially in the scene where he explains how the Nazi zombies came to be. The talented actor really sells this scene and totally makes us believe his story. As the heroine, the beautiful Brooke Adams gives an excellent performance. She's terrific in her scenes where she flees in terror from the Nazi threat and, just as Cushing made us believe that the zombies are real, Brooke's extreme fear of them makes us that much more afraid. The rest of the cast does a more than adequate job and, combined with a well-written screenplay, wonderful make-up, isolated locations and a very eerie electronic musical score, helps to create a sense of inescapable doom. The film also has a ghoulish E.C. Comics feel to it and really sustains its tension, because these zombies can be lurking anywhere, either in that ocean or on that island.

Why this film never got the recognition or success it deserves is a mystery to me. It was released at a time when Satanic hits such as *The Exorcist* and *The Omen* were all the rage, and the mega-budgeted *Star Wars* was box-office king. Not following either one of these popular formulas, perhaps this low-budget fright fest just got lost in the shuffle. Whatever the reason, *Shock Waves* remains a suspenseful

and unique piece of 1970s horror, whose haunting images will leave a lasting impression on its viewers.

As we move into the 1980s, I've chosen two somewhat neglected classics, ones that would make for perfect viewing on a rainy Halloween night. First up is 1981's superb made-for-TV movie, *Dark Night of the Scarecrow.* Released to CBS on October 24, 1981, *Dark Night of the Scarecrow* tells the story of Bubba Ritter, a mentally challenged man who, after being wrongfully accused of murdering a little girl named Marylee, is hunted down by angry townsfolk Otis Hazelrigg, Skeeter, Philby and Hocker and then murdered, vigilante-style, while hiding inside of an old scarecrow. When the four men are acquitted by the court just days before Halloween, someone or something hell bent on revenge begins killing them off, one-by-one.

Expertly written by J.D. Feigelson and masterfully directed by Frank De Felitta, *Dark Night of the Scarecrow* is, without a doubt, the best made-for-TV horror movie of the 1980s. There are many reasons for this, but let's start with Feigelson's script. Boasting amazingly detailed and, in some cases, quite complex characterizations, added to a simple but enthralling story, and relying on suspense and atmosphere, the teleplay is downright perfect.

Complementing this is Frank De Felitta's lyrical direction. The director first establishes his setting with nice wide

DARK NIGHT OF THE SCARECROW

"Mar-vel-ous! I was terrified!"
— Vincent Price

Charles Durning delivers an incredibly multi-layered performance as postal worker Otis Hazelrigg.

shots of the gorgeous countryside. Later, this comforting environment will turn ominous, as the camera slowly prowls through it at night. De Felitta also has a knack of juxtaposing joy and fear. In the pub scene where the newly acquitted men happily party together, the wind outside begins to pick up. It whistles through the trees while blowing garbage around and suggests that something dreadful is coming. The director also rightfully avoids any extreme gore, which was popular at the time. This is evident in many scenes, starting with the attack on young Marylee. While playing with Bubba, a vicious dog

attacks the innocent girl, but instead of focusing on this grisly sight, De Felitta cuts away to a series of garden gnomes that Bubba and Marylee had been admiring seconds before. The scene is quite unsettling as we hear the awful attack and poor Marylee's cries for help. Of course it must be remembered that this is a television movie and extreme gore was not allowed, but this only forces the filmmakers here to be that much more creative. Later, Hazelrigg brains someone over the head with a shovel. Rather than showing the impact and spurting blood, the director makes this death even more effective

by filming it just out of frame. When Hazelrigg raises the shovel back up, the poor man's hat is stuck to it. It's a wonderfully ghoulish touch. De Felitta doesn't lack a sense of humor either. When the first act of revenge takes place and we are about to see the deathblow, instead of showing the blood, the director cuts to a breakfast table and shows us strawberry jelly hitting a plate. De Felitta also goes for chills. One of the most hair-raising scenes comes when one of the soon-to-be victims happily rounds the corner of his home just in time to see a tall dark figure shut off all the lights inside. The director films several haunting images as well. The scene of Bubba's terrified eyes beneath the scarecrow's mask is a chilling sight and not easily forgotten. Also, after Bubba's execution, the men learn that not only was he innocent, but he was a hero who saved his best friend Marylee's life. At this point, the guilty men just stare at the lifeless, bloody scarecrow before them and, suddenly, the wind picks up ferociously, as if an angry supernatural force has been unleashed. The final image of the film has not lost any of its power. It's still just as frightening and revealing as it was back in 1981.

I can't go on about the greatness of this movie without mentioning the cast. Everyone in this film does an impeccable

"Bubba didn't do it!" Larry Drake portrays the mentally handicapped Bubba Ritter, who carries the mutilated body of young Marylee (Tonya Crowe) home.

job, especially the late Charles Durning, who gives an incredibly multi-layered performance as postal worker Otis Hazelrigg, an evil man whose many traits include being cold-hearted, somewhat sleazy and sinisterly charming. He's also a liar, a boozer and a bully, not to mention he's completely two-faced. (The hypocritical Hazelrigg puts on a great show in front of his fellow townspeople, who believe him to be a pillar of the community, but only a select few know the real man hiding within.) We get some insight into his unnatural obsession with Bubba and Marylee when we find out that Hazelrigg also fancies the young girl, only not in the innocent way Bubba does. Also, it's almost as if Hazelrigg is praying for Bubba to do something wrong, so that he'll have an excuse to punish the poor man. Charles Durning makes you feel as though this is the most important component to his character and, like all the great actors that have played villains, he truly makes us hate him. Durning conveys all this and more, and he not only does it brilliantly, but also subtly. His performance never seems campy or over the top. It's absolutely perfect. In a career spanning 60 years, it's one of the actor's best performances.

Although Durning carries much of the film himself, he sure has some incredibly talented help.

First and foremost, Larry Drake is amazing in his brief but pivotal role as the good-hearted but mentally handicapped Bubba Ritter. Performed flawlessly by Drake, there isn't a second where audiences are not convinced that he is truly mentally challenged. One of his most memorable scenes comes after a dog attacks Marylee. A frightened, distraught Bubba carries her home to her mother and cries, "Bubba didn't do it!" Drake gives a beautiful and somewhat heartbreaking performance, very similar to Peter Cushing's heart-felt sympathy as Arthur Grimsdyke in 1972's *Tales from the Crypt.* Tonya Crowe as Marylee does a top-notch job as the happy and innocent little girl who, after Bubba's murder, begins acting a bit strange and mysterious. Crowe plays her role as if Marylee could now be slightly unbalanced. It's a terrific performance, especially considering that she was only 10 years old at the time. Jocelyn Brando is wonderful as Bubba's mother, the only one who can see through Hazelrigg's façade. She also gets to recite one of J.D. Feigelson's very quotable lines: "There's other justice in this world besides the law!" And last, but certainly not least, are Hazelrigg's three cohorts: Hocker, Philby and Skeeter. Played by Lane Smith, Claude Earl Jones and Robert F. Lyons, respectively, these three talented and immediately recognizable faces are terrific as Hazelrigg's not-too-bright and easily manipulated posse. Each man's character is different from the others and, due to their talented portrayals, we totally believe that these people are not only real, but that they have lived in this small town all their lives. Lane Smith is extremely convincing as the smarter and tougher of the three, and nobody plays terrified

"There's other justice in this world besides the law!" Durning and his not-too-bright posse, played by Claude Earl Jones, Lane Smith and Robert F. Lyons

like Claude Earl Jones. Rounding out the gifted threesome is Robert F. Lyons, who shines as the dimwitted one who is constantly being lied to and influenced by the devious Hazelrigg.

If there's one other component that must be mentioned, it's the awesomely haunting musical score by Glenn Paxton, which perfectly complements the visuals as well as the story and helps immeasurably with the movie's creep factor.

So, why wasn't this near-perfect film a success? I'm not totally sure. I think the time of release may have had something to do with it. The movie premiered just six days before the much anticipated release of *Halloween II*, a highly publicized sequel, which would go on to be one of 1981's biggest hits. I believe this horror blockbuster may have overshadowed the modest little TV movie.

Although it certainly has its fans, *Dark Night of the Scarecrow* is still unknown to many. If you haven't seen it, I highly recommend doing so. However, don't take my word for it. Here's what legendary horror icon Vincent Price had to say about the film: "Marvelous! I was terrified."

Yep. That's right. I bet you're already trying to track down a copy.

Happy, happy Halloween,
Halloween, Halloween.

Dan (Tom Atkins) and Ellie (Stacey Nelkin) meet The Halloween Three.

Happy, happy Halloween,
Silver Shamrock.
It's almost time, kids. The clock is ticking. Be in front of your TV sets for the horrorthon. And remember the big giveaway at nine. Don't miss it. And don't forget to wear your masks. The clock is ticking. It's almost time.

That jingle and those words are familiar to anyone who has seen my final pick. It's a really entertaining film that has been hated by many horror fans ever since its release in 1982. Over 35 years later, the movie is finally beginning to get

some of the recognition it deserves, but it still has a ways to go. I'd like to help it along by explaining why it was so wrongfully despised and, also, why it is essential viewing for genre fans.

The film's title: *Halloween III: Season of the Witch.*

The film's only real fault: It's title.

1981's *Halloween II* was a major hit for Universal, but a decision was made afterwards to drop the immensely popular but already repetitious Michael Myers storyline and, instead, create a series of original horror films that would focus on

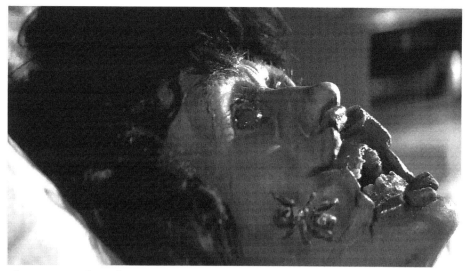

The ominous shot of a huge insect crawling out of the mouth of a woman's horribly burnt and distorted face will stay with the audience.

Conal Cochran (Dan O'Herlihy), always dressed in a black suit, shows one of his rare chilling facial expressions.

the holiday of Halloween without featuring "The Shape." *Halloween* creators John Carpenter and Debra Hill commissioned the great Nigel Kneale—creator of the legendary Quatermass character and series—to pen a screenplay based on an original idea by Hill. After rewriting some of Kneale's material, Carpenter hired talented filmmaker and friend Tommy Lee Wallace to direct. Wallace, who had been an editor and production designer on the original *Halloween*, as well as being the man responsible for creating Michael Myers' iconic mask, wound up rewriting Carpenter's draft shortly before filming began.

The story centers on Dr. Daniel Challis, who sets out to uncover the mysterious murder of one of his patients, with the help of Ellie Grimbridge, who is the daughter of the murdered man. Their investigation leads them to Santa Mira, California, where they find out that Silver Shamrock Novelties, a corporation which manufactures Halloween masks, has very sinister plans for the children of America.

Sounds kind of different, doesn't it? It is. Let's start with the screenplay. With the exception of being influenced somewhat by 1956's magnificent *Invasion of the Body Snatchers*, the story is not only completely innovative, but very different from the zombies, werewolves and slashers that were currently populating the 1980s horror scene. This movie stands alone, not only including an original villain, but the film also features a brand new protagonist as well.

Dr. Challis, played by the always-welcome Tom Atkins, isn't the typically young, squeaky-clean hero audiences expect. The middle-aged and recently divorced doctor smokes, drinks and doesn't spend as much time with his kids as he should. In his defense, he doesn't want to neglect his children, but long work hours prevent him from seeing them as often as he should.

On the upside, he seems to be a very caring doctor and when Ellie's father, who he's only known for a few hours, is murdered, he feels terrible and attends the man's funeral. Like the distraught Ellie, Challis seems to become obsessed with finding out exactly what happened to the poor man, and this obsession sets him on a quest for answers. He uncovers the fact that Halloween mask manufacturer Conal Cochran is not only the fiend responsible for Mr. Grimbridge's death, but also has a ghoulishly sinister plot of epic proportions brewing just below the surface.

Played by the talented Dan O'Herlihy, Cochran is always dressed in a black business suit and, because he takes great delight in his evil plan, is rarely seen without a smile on his face. There is one facial deviation, however. When Cochran realizes that Challis and Ellie have found Mr. Grimbridge's station wagon hidden in the mask maker's factory, the look on O'Herlihy's face is chilling. The actor is extremely convincing in a *Goldfinger*-style scene, where he not only explains his diabolical plot to a captive Challis, but speaks about the Celtic origins of Halloween as

well. O'Herlihy is perfect and the fiendish fun he has in playing this marvelous villain is noticeable throughout the film.

Stacey Nelkin also gives a great performance as Ellie. She plays her as smart, tough and determined, and she totally holds her own against Atkins and O'Herlihy. Three fine actors play very well written and somewhat original characters.

Director Tommy Lee Wallace does a fantastic job of guiding these characters through the film and his stylish visuals tell a unique story. For instance, the glowing electronic pumpkin we see in the opening credits isn't there just to be stylish. It will have great significance later on. Wallace also shows his ability at building fear by filming shots of several empty hospital corridors which, when edited together, create a sense of uneasiness. Later, he films Cochran's point-of-view looking through the closed window of a limousine, and we really get the feeling that something eerie and supernatural is approaching. Wallace, as previously stated, is no slouch in the image department either. At one point, Dr. Challis is frantically looking around for Ellie. When he peers out the motel room window, Wallace shows us five of Cochran's henchmen

An iconic image of three trick-or-treaters that create a feeling of absolute dread in *Halloween III: Season of the Witch*.

standing there, staring directly at Challis. One of the film's scariest images comes in a wide shot at dusk, where we see a group of innocent mask-wearing trick-or-treaters silhouetted against a gorgeous but ominous orange sky.

There's also a creepy shot of a huge insect crawling out of the mouth of a woman's horribly burnt, distorted face. It's a very effective visual that will stay with the audience, and it's just a taste of the gruesomeness to come. Tom Burman was responsible for the film's effective make-up. Another fantastic Burman effect comes at the beginning of the film, when one of Cochran's henchmen grue-

somely pulls a man's face apart with his bare hands. It's an almost 40 year-old effect that still completely holds up to this day. Burman wasn't the only make-up artist on board here, however. Mask-maker extraordinaire Don Post was brought in to contribute witch, pumpkin and skull masks to the film. Always accompanied by that extremely catchy jingle (you'll never get it out of your head) when promoted on TV, these masks, dubbed "The Halloween Three," become huge parts of Cochran's evil plot.

Complementing all these wonderfully ghoulish images is the gorgeous cinematography by Dean Cundey. Wallace

and Cundey use the widescreen Panavision frame effectively, and along with Cundey's masterful lighting techniques, give the movie a very polished look. Especially terrific are the night scenes. They're expertly lit and always sharp, as well as being atmospheric. We can really understand why Cundey has been nicknamed "The Dean of Darkness."

Another creative aspect that contributes to the movie's success is the futuristic synthesizer score by John Carpenter and Alan Howarth. It perfectly fits this film and greatly enhances the extremely striking visuals.

If this movie were not called *Halloween III* and simply titled *Season of the Witch*, I think it would have done much better business, been better loved and would be considered a minor classic today. As it stands now, many people still dislike the movie because they felt fooled into thinking that they were going to see a Michael Myers *Halloween* sequel and, instead, got something completely different. I can understand being upset in 1982 (I was disappointed at first too), but not over 35 years later. Audiences should take a look at it again, with fresh eyes. We now know that it was an in-name-only sequel (for marketing purposes), so just view it as the stand-alone film.

For those who haven't seen *Halloween III: Season of the Witch*, don't only read the negative reviews. It would be silly to let a minor detail like a misleading title keep fans from enjoying a wonderfully creepy horror film that, along with *Dark Night of the Scarecrow* (and the original *Halloween*), should be required viewing every October 31. Grab a copy and give it a try. And don't forget to wear your Silver Shamrock masks. The clock is ticking. It's almost time …

Well, there you have it. Four original horror films that unfortunately get lost among the horror herd of the 1970s and 1980s. The good news is that they're not lost at all. All four films are not only currently available on DVD, but have also been given re-mastered Blu-ray transfers as well. If you're looking for unpretentious and scary horror flicks that contain, among other things, amazing writing, acting and direction, then track down this fearsome foursome, turn off the lights and have an enjoyably frightening time. Make every night Halloween!

Dr. Challis is tied up and forced to wear a Halloween mask.

A Planet Film Production
A HISTORY OF PLANET FILM PRODUCTIONS

BY CHRISTOPHER GULLO

Hammer Film Productions dominated the British horror film industry from the mid-1950s through the middle 1970s, with colorful takes on Frankenstein, Dracula, the Mummy and other classic Gothic characters. As goes the old saying, "success breeds success." Once other production companies saw the money Hammer was bringing in, it was not long before competitors entered the lucrative market. Hammer's biggest competitor was Amicus Productions, which carved its own piece of the pie with a focus on anthology/portmanteau horror films starting with *Dr. Terror's House of Horrors* and using some of the same talent employed by Hammer. Tigon British Film Productions came a little later to the game and also created some well-known chillers, including *The Conqueror Worm* and *The Blood on Satan's Claw*. Besides the big three, a few smaller British production companies hoped to cash in on the popular horror film genre, including Tyburn Productions and another company with a rather small

output (although boasting a long connection to the film industry)—Planet Film Productions. Run by Tom Blakeley with his partner William Chalmers, Planet was initially a distribution company for Mancunian Films before turning to production. They completed one crime noir, *The Marked One*, and three genre films, *Devils of Darkness*, *Island of Terror* and *Night of the Big Heat*, before folding.

The Blakeley family had a long connection to the film industry, dating back to its very beginnings, starting with Tom's grandfather, James Blakeley, who owned several cinemas and was an early film distributor in English northern mill towns in 1908. Tom's father, John E. Blakeley (affectionately known as "Dad" or "Pop" to those he worked with), worked for his father James as a distributor before endeavoring to produce film shorts starting in 1927 under his then company, Song Films Limited, for which he filmed condensed versions of various operas for moviegoers. John E. Blakeley was also a fan of music

hall comedy and convinced many of the comedians to be filmed for a wider audience. His biggest star was Lancashire comedian Frank Randle, whom he directed in eight low-budget comedies. Besides directing, John E. Blakeley also worked as a writer under the pseudonyms Anthony Toner and Roney Parsons. Tired of bringing his cast and crew to London to film, in 1947 John E. Blakeley decided to build Manchester's first sound film studio and, at the time, it was the only British film studio outside of London. Nicknamed "Jollywood" for its many comedies, the studio was crafted from a converted church in Rusholme, which is where Tom Blakeley and his younger brother John, Jr. would get their start in the business. John started as a camera operator, while Tom directed some of the films and would eventually work as a cinematographer (as would Tom's own son Mike, many years later). Mancunian was eventually sold to the BBC in 1954 and became a television studio. Tom Blakeley took over Mancu-

Brian Nissen and William Lucas in *The Marked One*, the first film that Planet Film Productions distributed

nian after his father retired and continued to produce second features in the early 1960s. The last comedy Mancunian made was *Trouble with Eve*, which Tom produced in 1960.

William Chalmers was a traveling salesman for Butcher's Film Service and met Tom Blakeley while he was distributing films, including the aforementioned *Trouble with Eve*. Blakeley and Chalmers joined together and, after distributing films such as *The Marked One* and *The Break* (1963) for their joint ventures Planet Film Distributors and Doverton Film Distributors, they decided to take the next step and start producing films on their own. An early Hammer connection for Planet Film Productions was that *The Trouble with Eve* and *The Marked One* were both directed by Francis Searle, who was responsible for a number of Hammer's early efforts, including *The Man in Black* (1949), *The Lady Craved Excitement* (1950), *Cloudburst* (1951) and *Whispering Smith Investigates* (1952). Searle was responsible for helming Planet Film Productions' initial 1963 production, *The Marked One*. The crime noir told the story of an ex-con forger turned lorry (truck) driver, Don Mason (William Lucas), who is targeted by gangsters in the belief that he knows the whereabouts of a set of counterfeit bank note printing plates. When his wife and daughter are

threatened, Mason must go back to his criminal roots to find the culprits responsible. The resulting film fit neatly into the British traditional noir genre.

Planet Film Productions next foray would take them into the Gothic horror genre, which Hammer had revived in England with *The Curse of Frankenstein* in 1957. Although featuring the promising sounding title *Devils of Darkness*, Planet Film Productions 1964 production was an

awkward mix of horror themes that paled in comparison to Hammer's output. One of the main differences that set *Devils of Darkness* aside from other horror genre efforts at the time was the decision to set most of the story in present day France—making it the first British horror film set in modern times. While Hammer would eventually also go this route in the 1970s with *Dracula AD 1972* and *The Satanic Rites of Dracula*, the look of a modern culture really takes away from the Gothic atmosphere that a Victorian backdrop provides. As if to emphasize this point, the prologue to *Devils of Darkness*, set in the late 1800s of Brittany, France, was actually quite effective. Set amid an ancient graveyard, Count Sinistre's stone coffin breaks open and he, in bat form, puts a curse on a beautiful Gypsy girl (Carole Gray) and takes her as his immortal bride. These scenes were bold and colorful, much like a Hammer production, but this ends abruptly when the plot fast-forwards to modern day France. Once set in modern day, the entire plot slows down to a snail's pace with dialogue-heavy scenes that don't lead anywhere. Modern beatnik/hipster party scenes are also out of place and create a disjointed feel to the plot.

While bats are a staple of the horror genre, in films of this era they tended to be a distraction due to poor special effects, which was the reason Hammer used them sparingly (and to the detriment of

Count Sinistre's accomplice in evil, Tania, played by Carole Gray

Brides of Dracula). The bat incarnation of the Count in *Devils of Darkness* (the actual transformation is never shown) resembles the rubber artifact it most certainly is and the creature is not as threatening as it should be. Later in the film, when the hero Paul Baxter (William Sylvester) visits a scientist (Edward Judd), real bats are shown which unintentionally provide a stark contrast. A bigger and less forgivable distraction is the Count himself. Arman du Moliere, aka Count Sinistre, is played by Hubert Noel—in his first of only two horror films, the other being the even more inferior *Cathy's Curse* (1977), in which he did not play a villain. Noel is not even an effective poor man's Christopher Lee; he is not imposing in the least, looking less like a vampire than a suspicious French politician. Even more disappointing is that his victims are seen with bite marks on their necks but he is never shown to have manifested fangs. Sinistre does have a hold over the townspeople, who are members of his cult of red-robed Satanists, an interesting take, but his prolonged search for a gold bat talisman that he lost while claiming a victim is a subplot not needed. Every good horror film should have some sort of exciting confrontation, but in *Devils of Darkness* Count Sinistre practically does himself in while trying to escape from Baxter, his death

a poor copy of Christopher Lee's disintegration in Hammer's *Horror of Dracula* (1958).

One of the brighter spots and key performances in the film comes by way of Sinistre's Gypsy bride Tania, played by Carole Gray. Gray did not have a long film career, although she did appear in a few other genre films, most notably the underrated *Curse of the Fly* (1965), which gave her a much more satisfying role. In *Devils of Darkness* she starts out with a wonderful dance routine for her fiancée before Sinistre decides he wants the vixen for himself. Then she becomes Sinistre's accomplice in evil, although the vampire's decision to take Baxter's new girlfriend (played by Tracy Reed, cousin of Oliver Reed) as his next bride strikes deserved jealously in Tania. Gray's performance then allows her a little room to expand her character, especially when arguing with Sinistre and trying to warn Baxter in order to keep her status. With her sultry looks and acting chops, Gray must have impressed producers as well, for she was back in Planet's next feature, *Island of Terror*.

Blakeley acquired a script from Edward Andrew Mann and Alan Ramsen entitled *The Night the Silicates Came*, which would become Planet Film Productions' second horror film under the shooting title, *Island of Terror*. To get the needed capital for the production (a budget of £70,000), Blakeley brought in producer Richard Gordon, a Brit who relocated to the U.S. and formed Gordon Films, a company that distributed British films. Gordon was also a veteran of producing his own genre films including *The Haunted*

Count Sinistre (Hubert Noel) conducts a ceremony with the red-robed Satanists in *Devils of Darkness*.

ASTOUNDING! FROM AN EXPERIMENT ON LIFE— CAME A DEVASTATING DEATH!

PLANET FILM PRODUCTIONS presents

STARRING
PETER CUSHING
EDWARD JUDD

ISLAND OF **TERROR**

EASTMAN COLOUR

co-starring
CAROLE GRAY   EDDIE BYRNE
SAM KYDD   NIALL MacGINNIS

Directed by TERENCE FISHER
Produced by TOM BLAKELEY

RELEASED BY PLANET FILM DISTRIBUTORS LTD

Strangler, Corridors of Blood (both starring Boris Karloff), *Fiend Without a Face, First Man Into Space* and *Devil Doll*. He had also previously worked with Chalmers co-producing the 1956 British crime thriller, *Assignment Redhead*. Gordon's initial connection to Planet Film Productions had been distributing *Devils of Darkness* in the U.S. for the company. Having him on board for *Island of Terror* wound up to be a real blessing, as Gordon was on good terms with Hammer head Jimmy Carreras, who offered up star Peter Cushing and director Terence Fisher, who both at that moment were not working on a Hammer production. Fisher was the creative force behind most of Hammer's early horror films, although for a brief spell in the mid-1960's he broke away to direct three science fiction alien invasion films—*The Earth Dies Screaming* (1964) for Lippert Films, and *Island of Terror* (1966) and *Night of the Big Heat* (1967)—for Planet Film Productions. Fisher's use of filming in close quarters at various sets at Pinewood Studios contrasted with his shots of the rural wooded island, filmed at Black Park in Buckinghamshire, and this helped create a claustrophobic feel that adds greatly to the suspense. The film's assistant director was Don Weeks, who also had a long association with Hammer as a production manager.

The 1950s was a golden age for science-fiction films involving mutated monsters running amok and attacking helpless humans. Most of the fascination of these films came from the World War II dropping of two atomic bombs on Hiroshima and Nagasaki, thus ushering in the atomic age. The general public worried about the possible disastrous effects of atomic bombs and radiation mutations and film producers were only too glad to provide nightmarish scenarios. *Them!* (1954), *Tarantula* (1955), *The Amazing Colossal Man* (1957) and *Fiend Without a Face* (1958) are only some of the monster movie examples. By the 1960s these types of science-fiction movies were making way for more traditional horror productions, although examples of mutated monsters could still be seen in Planet Film Productions' *Island of Terror*. Interestingly, *Island of Terror* addressed the real life studies of cancer treatment and radiation therapy currently dominating the research fields. Although not the most visually impressive creatures, the silicates resembled giant green brains sporting octopus tentacles and managed to produce real chills due to their disposing of victims in a most horrid way. The attack on a victim is followed by a horrible sucking noise as the silicate liquefies the bones. Barry Gray, who was also serving as composer for several of producer Gerry Anderson's "Supermarionation" productions, including *Thunderbirds*, created the eerie electronic sounds to accompany the silicates' attacks. Virtually unstoppable, with bullets, petrol bombs and grenades having no effect, and multiplying rapidly on an island with no phones or a quick way to escape, the silicates are a true claustrophobic horror and provide unrelenting suspense for

Carole Gray finds herself under attack by a roving tentacle of a silicate from *Island of Terror*.

Peter Cushing, Edward Judd and Eddie Byrne confer in *Island of Terror*.

the team of scientists and locals. Not to mention the silicates manage to turn up where you least expect them, like high up in a tree! Everything comes to a head in the village hall as the scientists and locals are boarded up inside with nowhere left to run, surrounded by the silicates who lay siege to the building and everyone within.

Filmed from August to September of 1965, the completed film proved quite popular in England (released in 1966) under distribution by Planet Film Productions. Universal picked up the U.S. distribution rights where it was paired on a double-bill with another British science-fiction film, *The Projected Man*, which Richard Gordon also co-produced. The theater posters for the double-bill announced: "Together … The Horrifying Terror Twins!"

One of the strengths of *Island of Terror* was its fine British cast. Among the leading players was Edward Judd (*The Day the Earth Caught Fire*, *First Men in the Moon*, *Invasion*) as Dr. David West. Handsome and believable, Judd was at the height of his popularity in the 1960s and displayed leading man charisma, so evident in *Island of Terror*. So notable was Judd's role as the hard drinking, burnt out newspaper reporter in Val Guest's *The Day the Earth Caught Fire* (1961) that he was considered to play James Bond in the original 1962

film, *Dr. No*. Two other actors in *Island of Terror* had previously appeared in Planet Film Productions' *Devils of Darkness*: Carole Gray (*The Curse of the Fly*) as the damsel in distress Toni Merrill and Eddie Byrne (*Jack the Ripper* and *The Mummy*) as Dr. Reginald Landers. Fans will remember the attractive Gray from a rather shocking opening to *The Curse of the Fly*, in which she jumps through a broken window in only her bra and panties, all before the opening credits! Sam Kydd (*The Quatermass Xperiment*, *The Projected Man*) played

Constable John Harris and had one of the best lines in describing the body of the first silicate victim: "Aye, there was no face. Just a horrible mush with the eyes sittin' in it." The entire cast provided solid acting, which added a realistic human element into a shocking science-fiction tale.

The biggest coup of *Island of Terror* was the inclusion of Peter Cushing. Cushing starred as Dr. Brian Stanley, a character both brave and intelligent and able to deliver a good joke or two. In a 1966 review for *Variety*, Cushing's performance in *Island of Terror* was singled out: "Peter Cushing, whose performances in this type of role are always above average, is properly brusque and has a wryly objective point of view. He also varies between heroism and cowardice, creating a character with natural, not exaggerated fears and hesitations." By 1966, Cushing was a bonafide horror star whose name alone could pack theaters. His role in *Island of Terror* certainly elevated the film above other standard B-genre efforts.

Although *Island of Terror* left open the opportunity for a direct sequel, a year later Planet Film Productions instead optioned John Lymington's novel *Night of the Big Heat*, which shared many similarities with *Island of Terror*, from its alien invasion and island locale, as well as the use once more of actor Peter Cushing and director Terence Fisher. In *Night of the Big Heat* (aka *Island of the Burning Damned*) another island alien invasion is taking place with the stranded heroes forced to fight to the death to save civilization. However, unlike

One of the blob-like silicate monsters from *Island of Terror*

Christopher Lee inspects his equipment from *Night of the Big Heat*.

the man-made silicates, the creatures of *Night of the Big Heat* are true aliens whose intense heat incinerates anything in their way. Terence Fisher, back in the director's chair, benefited the pace and plotting. Also back was Peter Cushing, this time in a smaller guest star role and not as lucky

Christopher Lee plays aloof scientist Godfrey Hanson, sweating along with axe-wielding William Lucas.

as his former character in *Island of Terror*. The aliens are also somewhat similar in looks and movement to the silicates from the previous film, this time resembling glowing masses of gelatin and their deadly heat attacks consist simply of the entire screen fading to a brilliant white. In fact, the first alien encounter in the film seems to be lifted from *Island of Terror*, with another local trapped in a cave with an unknown terror.

The big difference this time out was that Planet Film Productions was able to also snare Cushing's favorite co-star Christopher Lee to star in the film. Lee, appearing as the aloof scientist Godfrey Hanson, portrays his character as a factual man of science who does not easily relate to the island's populace. However, he rises up to the occasion as a leader in order to make a stand against the alien invasion. It is great to see Cushing and Lee working together on the same side to fight against the outer space monsters, however brief their interactions may have been.

Another comparison between Planet Film Productions' final two films is the ro-

mantic subplot. While *Island of Terror* had its romantic angle between Edward Judd's Dr. David West and his wealthy girlfriend Carole Gray, in *Night of the Big Heat* a torrid affair exists between Jeff Callum (Patrick Allen) and his steamy secretary, Angela Roberts (Jane Merrow). In fact, Merrow's character brings quite a lot of her own heat to the island as evidenced by some of the men ogling her, so the film's title winds up being a double-entendre. In a strange real life twist, Allen's actual wife Sarah Lawson played his screen wife. This subplot affair carries on for a good portion of the film but it does add some extra human tension to the otherworldly one the island is facing. *Night of the Big Heat* would be Planet Film Productions last production, as the company folded after this production (which failed to make an impact at the box-office). While Hammer, Amicus and Tigon were dominating the market, Planet Film Productions offered a viable cinematic offering of their own, worth a revisit. The company put its own unique spin on vampires and science-fiction films.

Jane Merrow Interviewed by Christopher Gullo

CG: What was it like working with your *Night of the Big Heat* co-stars Peter Cushing, Christopher Lee and Patrick Allen?

JM: Peter was a lovely gentleman, intelligent, kind and it was a real pleasure to work with him, a privilege as well. He was a wonderful actor and person. He was so famous that I got goose bumps meeting him and I'm very glad that I had the opportunity to work with him.

As with Peter, Christopher was a lovely man. I was a bit afraid of him to begin with and thought he was rather grand. But after getting to know him, I found him very helpful and kind, and again, a consummate professional.

Patrick was another nice man. I was playing a rather tawdry girl who had a thing for his character, and his real-life wife was playing his film wife, so I felt a little strange in our more torrid scenes, but it was all good fun and we had a good time.

CG: What was it like working for director Terence Fisher?

Bottom left: Jane Merrow grabs the wandering hand of Patrick Allen; Top right: A revealing shot of Jane Merrow on the beach, both photos from *Night of the Big Heat*

JM: Working for Terence Fisher was a most enjoyable experience. He was a consummate professional, always happy to discuss ideas, and he communicated very well with the cast and crew, and he also moved quickly. So the set always had energy and excitement.

CG: In a previous conversation with Cushing he noted that, while it was supposed to be extremely hot on the island, in fact they were filming in the winter and it was very cold. Could you elaborate on this?

JM: How right Peter was. We all had very thin clothes on and were shivering with the cold. But we were all sprayed and smothered in glycerin at the start of every shot and had to act like we were in fact very hot and sweaty!

Mike Blakeley Interviewed by Christopher Gullo

Tom Blakeley with his parents, John E. Blakeley and Martha Isobella

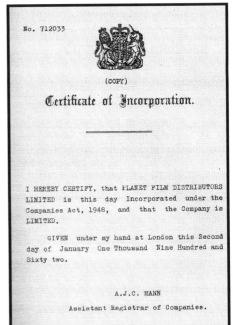

Planet Films' Certificate of Incorporation

CG: Your family has a long background in the film industry. Can you fill us in?

MB: It all started with my grandfather John E. Blakeley and what became Mancunian Films. The family business began in 1908 with film distribution. My grandfather distributed Charlie Chaplin's first feature-length comedy, *Tilly's Punctured Romance* (1914), in the U.K., which kicked him off. Following this success, my grandfather purchased several cinemas. He made several silent operas, which he distributed as 20-minute shorts, all shown with musical accompaniment provided by musicians and singers.

In 1932 he met Stan Laurel and Oliver Hardy at a convention at the Midland Hotel in Manchester and Stan asked him why he did not go into sound movies? When my grandfather replied that the equipment was too expensive to purchase, Stan replied back that he could hire a studio. Mancunian Films (the name Mancunian means a native of Manchester) was thus born and my grandfather produced *Boots! Boots!* in 1934, with music hall artist George Formby, at the Albany Studios in London (a space above a taxi garage), followed by *Off the Dole* the following year. After the great success of these films he contracted music hall entertainers from Blackpool (the entertainment capital of the North) to appear in films produced by F.W. Baker and him from Butcher's Film Services, Ltd. in London and Net-

tlefold Studios, Riverside, being the most relevant. Artists they employed included Frank Randle, who was famous for his outlandish behavior and risqué sexual implications.

By 1947 my grandfather converted an old church in Manchester into a film studio. The first films that my dad produced were under the Mancunian banner for my grandfather. Mancunian Films diverted when they sold the studios to the BBC in 1954. By that time my grandfather was getting old and weary and he retired shortly afterwards. Mancunian still provided film units to Granada television in Manchester and also made some feature films from 111 Wardour Street in London.

CG: Do you have any favorite films from the Mancunian cannon?

MB: Well, my dad started producing with the film *Trouble with Eve*, so that one gets a nod. Another film that my dad produced, *Tomorrow at Ten*, brought quite a famous actor, Robert Shaw, into the limelight. I thought this film was a very good thriller. The film was actually remade as a television release about 20 years ago and I got a few thousand dollars for it, so that was all right (laughs).

CG: How did Planet Film Productions come to be?

MB: My dad partnered with Bill Chalmers, and after distributing some

Top: John E. Blakeley at work; Bottom: Tom Blakeley, founder of Planet Film Productions

The legal contract establishing the partnership between William Chalmers and Thomas Blakeley

MB: I visited a few of my father's sets, though I was quite young at the time so I don't remember a lot of details. I remember my dad making *Devils of Darkness* for Planet. Unfortunately I think the film had a crap ending; I think my dad ran out of money (laughs). I recall meeting Terence Fisher—he was very short, quite squat, with a high-pitched voice. He obviously knew what he was doing as he directed two films for Planet. I never met Peter Cushing but I know that he always sent my mum a Christmas card for some 30 years after filming *Island of Terror*, which goes to prove that he must have enjoyed working with my dad!

Besides Planet Film Productions, I remember meeting a few people and seeing filming done at nearby Shepperton Studios; Roger Moore immediately comes to mind. Also I recall seeing Bing Crosby and Bob Hope doing *The Road to Hong Kong* and also remember another film being made, the science fiction *Day of the Triffids*. I was in the business as well and was a quite well-known cameraman in my day. And my kids are in it too; they joined on their own, so it is a family business really.

films together, they decided to take the step into forming a production company. Then came Planet Film Productions, whose offices were at 111 Wardour Street in London. Their first feature was *Devils of Darkness*, then *Island of Terror* and finally *Night of the Big Heat*. Planet Film Productions folded after *Night of the Big Heat*. My dad's plan was not to only produce horror films with Planet, but he was open to any project with a good script. One project which didn't work out was a big feature film with possibly Burt Lancaster in

the lead role. It was to be called *Long Run South*. However, the British film financing company screwed up the project for my father when they ran out of money after making David Lean's *Ryan's Daughter*. And so my dad ran out of money and he could not do the film. It was eventually made under the book's original title as *Von Ryan's Express*, although at that point the production no longer involved my dad.

CG: Did you ever get the chance to visit any film sets that your dad worked on?

John E. Blakeley (left) produced *Boots! Boots!* in 1934, starring music hall artist George Formby (right). The movie was filmed at the Albany Studios in London.

CG: How would you describe your dad as a producer?

MB: My dad as a producer was a very fair man, and I think he did a pretty good job as an independent one. He was not very prolific in making films, but the films that he did make seemed to make money.

CG: What about your dad's partner William Chalmers?

MB: Bill Chalmers was a charming man, short and dapper. He used to work for Rank as a salesman, which is how he met my dad as he was working for Butcher's Film Service that was distributing Mancunian films at the time. Butcher's also had a long connection to Mancunian. F.W. Baker was the director early on and my grandfather made some films with him.

CG: It has been noted that your dad was offered distribution rights to the Spaghetti Western classic *A Fistful of Dollars* and its sequels. What happened there?

MB: I can tell you exactly what happened. My dad had seen the original film and asked if I could come and take a look. I was about 14 I suppose and we went to a little theater on Wardour Street. I watched this film and thought, bloody hell, that's good. My dad told me yeah, we've been offered the exclusive rights. I said I think you should go for it. But Bill Chalmers didn't like it; in fact he hated the film. So my dad turned the film package deal down.

On a somewhat related note, I did meet Clint Eastwood on the studio lot in Hollywood. I always remember Clint drove this old Morris Minor woody station wagon and that he had these three camper vans together, which he used as his offices.

CG: Were there any other films that your dad was offered that didn't work out?

MB: Another film my dad turned down was *A Hard Day's Night*. The Beatles asked if he could make the film for them as he had experience with music hall comedies, but my dad said he wouldn't know what to do for a pop group, so he passed on it.

My dad unfortunately did nothing professionally after Planet Film Productions folded. He was so disappointed after the knockback from the film-financing corporation that he just lost heart in filmmaking. He did do a bit of charity work afterwards, but he was pretty much retired from the industry. He faded away from the business basically.

CG: Are you involved in keeping up the history of your family's film connections?

MB: Yes indeed. In fact, in 1980 the Mancunian Film archive was destroyed in a fire and I have been working on re-gathering all the films my grandfather previously produced. The Northwest Film Archive has been quite helpful in my quest.

One film my grandfather made in 1926 that I tracked down recently is called *La Traviata*. It is a 20-minute silent short of an opera production. My grandfather used to send an orchestra out with the film for showings. He filmed something like 20 silent operas. People liked to go to the theaters to get warm and see the stars of the day. He fulfilled this need by bringing music hall personalities onto the stage to film, so people could watch them. And this new medium was soon taking off to blossom as the business it is today.

[Text copyrighted © by Christopher Gullo, 2017. Blakeley family photos from the Mike Blakeley Collection; studio photos from the David McConkey Collection]

A CINEMATIC PRIMER TO JESS FRANCO

BY TROY HOWARTH

Jess Franco. The name strikes a definite chord with cineastes the world over. For some he is a genius and one of the true mavericks; for others, he is a talentless hack who peddled pornography in the guise of "art." Few opinions seem to fall between the two extremes, though exceptions are inevitable. Over the course of approximately 55 years, he directed somewhere in the neighborhood of 200 films. Of these films, a hefty percentage of them exist in alternate edits, often prepared with his input, which can be considered unique in themselves. To say that Franco was prolific would be an understatement; to suggest that his output was erratic would be putting it kindly. And yet, despite his many missteps, Franco retains a loyal cult following. Fans argue the merits (or lack thereof) of his many films; some titles are more popular than others, but even among the fans there is no consensus on which film is his "masterpiece." Of all the so-called "European cult cinema" filmmakers, he is far and away the most unpredictable. But this is part of his charm. To test a cinematic cliché, "life's a lot like a Franco film … you never know what you're going to get."

My own introduction to Franco's cinema was a bit complicated. As a kid growing up in the VHS boom of the 1980s, I encountered a lot of odd films on bargain bin cassette releases, often having no clue ahead of time what I was letting myself in for. The presence of a favorite actor like Christopher Lee often seemed like a solid seal of approval, but seeing the likes of *Howling II: Your Sister is a Werewolf* (1985) and *The Keeper* (1976) soon cured me of this delusion. On the other hand, sometimes staying inside to watch the afternoon horror film on "Commander USA's Groovy Movies" while my friends were outside playing in the sun could yield an unexpected treasure; I'll never forget my first exposure to the films of Paul Naschy and Amando De Ossorio in this context. With regards to Franco, I certainly read about him before I actually saw one of his films. When I dove into Phil Hardy's *The Encyclopedia of Horror Films* in 1985, I was too young to comprehend its intellectual approach to film criticism, but I loved reading the plot synopses and salivating over the sensational images. Franco was one of the directors I read about whose films sounded … interesting. The fact that so much of his work seemed fixated on sex wasn't of interest to an 8 year old, but that aspect would certainly become more interesting later on … at the time, however, he seemed to have had a hand in a number of horror films with familiar genre staples (Fu Manchu, Dracula, the Frankenstein monster) and actors I was already enchanted with, including Christopher Lee. The odds of actually seeing one of his films seemed slim to nil, however; they never seemed to air on television and VHS editions, not easily obtained at the local department store, may as well have not existed at all. Then one fine day I found myself perusing the racks at a local thrift store and my eye was caught by the title *Kiss and Kill*. As it turns out, this was the re-titled (and heavily edited) version of Franco's *The Blood of Fu Manchu* (1968). I was pumped, to say the least, and begged my mom to buy it for me. It was only the second of the series that I had seen (*Brides of Fu Manchu* used to pop up on channel 9's late movie, while *Face of Fu Manchu* would finally surface on Cinemax a few years later), and at the time it struck me as a perfectly respectable movie; bear in mind, of course, that critical faculties in children aren't all that highly developed and so long as a film hits the basic points of interest, it's easy to win them over. Not long after that, I managed to find a rental cassette of *Count Dracula* (1970), Franco's notorious attempt at bringing Bram Stoker's novel to the screen in a faithful manner. I had read some nasty things about the film, but that didn't sap my enthusi-

Christopher Lee wanted to get closer to Bram Stoker's concept of the vampire king in Jess Franco's *Count Dracula* (1970).

asm for finally having a chance to see it. Predictably, it won me over—big time. Christopher Lee as Dracula was always a sure-fire recipe of success for me, and the film struck me as a great deal of fun. That was more or less it for Franco for the next few years, but as my critical faculties began to sharpen and I developed into a fine young film snob, I began taking the word of the critics in Hardy's seminal tome to heart. Clearly Franco really was a hack and a pornographer, so why should I bother taking him seriously?

Flash-forward to the mid-1990s … for reasons too complex (and frankly, rather boring) to get into here, I was becoming more and more immersed in the world of European cult cinema. I voraciously devoured all the Mario Bava, Dario Argento and Lucio Fulci films that I could. I explored the work of Riccardo Freda and Massimo Dallamano. I dabbled a bit in Jean Rollin. And a realization hit me: Jess Franco was one of the major names and, critics be damned, I felt it was time to give the devil his due and explore a little further. I had long been intrigued by the likes of *Succubus* (1967) and *Venus in Furs* (1969), so these were the titles that I selected to begin my journey into the universe of Jess Franco. I'd be lying if I said that they won me over right away, but they clearly weren't the work of a no-talent hack, just

the same. The time had finally come to dig deeper and deeper … and the further I dug, the more I felt compelled to keep going further. It's important to understand that when you begin dabbling in the works of somebody like Bava or Argento, you're generally assured a certain consistency of quality—well, this was certainly true of Argento up until that point in the mid-'90s, anyway—but when you begin exploring Franco's work, there is no such safety net. The worst films of Bava are flat and listless, but they're still done with a certain amount of polish and skill. The worst films of Franco, by contrast, will have you clawing your eyes out by the time they limp to their final fade to black. It's not easy being a Franco fan for this reason, among others, but again it is an undeniable part of what makes him so very unique. Anybody who sets out to really become educated on his work has to be equipped with a certain measure of tenacity and patience—to say nothing of a heaped helping of blind faith. Those who continue on the journey are invariably loyal to the man;

those who bail early on are quick to write him off as incompetent. Neither side is "right" per se, but the more zealous and vociferous naysayers are arguably a little too eager and prone to hyperbole … just as some of the more adoring and open-armed fans are as well.

Franco was born in Madrid on May 12, 1930. He took an early interest in composing music and was reportedly dabbling in writing his own compositions as a young child and was something of a prodigy on the piano. By the time he was in college, however, Franco had become a devoted cinephile. He was not interested in the new wave of European art house cinema that was flooding screens by this time however; his tastes lay in the mainstream of Hollywood. He loved *noir*, horror, comedy, and fantasy—anything that served to take his mind away from the drudgery of his day-to-day existence. He was also a devoted fan of comic books and pulp fiction and would later claim to have written a number of thrillers himself, under the name of David Khune; like so many claims made by the witty raconteur; however, this would eventually be revealed as a … little white lie. In any event, Franco was able to combine his two passions—film and music—when he

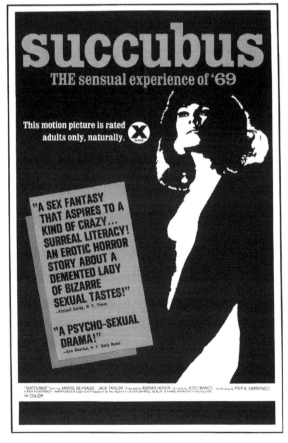

entered films in the early 1950s as a composer. He would work his way through the ranks as an assistant director before finally directing his first film, the 1957 documentary *El árbol de España*. He would direct his first feature, *We Are 18 Years Old*, in 1959. Franco's early works are polished and refined, showing a firm grasp of (and respect for) accepted cinema technique. Franco would bring this sense of craftsmanship to his breakout hit, *The Awful Dr. Orlof* (1961). The story (reportedly based on a novel by … David Khune) is a pretty standard rehash of Georges Franju's masterpiece *Eyes Without a Face* (1959), with elements of Edgar Wallace thrown in for good measure. The appeal of the film rests in its stylish execution. Franco's love of the Universal horror classics is evident in the film's elegant black and white *mise en scène*, but he takes the material to bold new extremes by introducing elements of sadism and even a brief flash of nudity, at least in the French print. The film's success opened the floodgates to a new genre of cinema in Spain, but Franco, annoyed by the censorship regulations imposed by the dictatorship of Generalissimo Francisco Franco's regime, would soon depart and adopt the persona of a traveling nomad. Suitcase at the ready, he would hop from one country to the next, wherever the next producer was willing to take a chance on him and bankroll another project or hire him to helm a less personal assignment.

Franco's career can be divided into various phases or periods. Following his initial tenure in Spain (which climaxed, notionally, with his collaboration with Orson Welles on the latter's magnificent Shakespearian drama *Chimes at Midnight*, 1966; Franco was hired to be Welles' assistant and would be entrusted with directing the second unit material, including the justifiably revered battle scenes), he would go to Germany and work for producer Adrian Hoven on a trilogy of films, including *Succubus*. The success of that film landed him a contract with British producer Harry Alan Towers, who was based in London but was producing films cut rate in various European cities; this in turn led to another tenure in Germany for producer Artur Brauner. From there, Franco would relocate to Paris, where he worked for producer Robert De Nesle; after this, he began a busy association with

the company Eurociné. Swiss producer Erwin C. Dietrich hired him and oversaw a series of films directed by Franco throughout the latter half of the 1970s. After that, the death of Generalissimo Franco resulted in a gradual relaxation of censorship standards, which spelled greater creative freedom for the arts. He would then return to Spain, where he took a gamble (and lost) with his own production banner (Manacoa Films) and was given creative freedom by the producers at Golden Films Internacional; following a flurry of creativity, his output began to slow, though he was given an opportunity of making a comparatively big budget horror film called *Faceless* (1987) by producer René Chateau. The experience was generally positive, and Franco followed up with a few similarly budgeted action and adventure films, which proved to be more and more unfulfilling. In the 1990s,

fans rediscovered his work and the cult of Franco began to proliferate around the world. As fans hunkered down in front of their TVs to watch badly panned-and-scanned and heavily censored or reworked versions of *A Virgin Among the Living Dead* (1971) or *Female Vampire* (1973), the filmmaker found himself on the cusp of a major comeback. He garnered a few good notices for his agreeably goofy mixture of gore, horror, soft-core and punk rock titled *Killer Barbys* (1996), but this led to a series of films shot on video, many of which were produced by American-based One Shot Productions. These films were good for one thing and one thing only: They allowed Franco to continue making films, even as his health began to deteriorate. Most of the films he made for One Shot are unspeakably awful, though they predictably have their fans. One can't help but get the feeling while watching them

REDEMPTION

"One of the most erotic and transgressive works in the horror genre."
— Tim Lucas, Editor of *Video Watchdog*

Lina Romay in Jess Franco's
FEMALE VAMPIRE

INCLUDES THE COMPLETE ALTERNATE VERSION: **EROTIKILL**

JESS FRANCO'S
THE AWFUL DR. ORLOF

2008. Franco took the loss hard, but he determined to push on making films as a means of keeping his mind sharp. His body was failing, however; confined to a wheelchair, he did his best to continue his work, but he simply was in no shape to continue the kind of ultra-prolific work-load he had once enjoyed. The news broke on April 2, 2013 that Franco had finally succumbed to a stroke, leaving fans the world over shaken. For many of us, it was like losing a favorite crazy uncle; his best days as a filmmaker may have been behind him, but his outspoken, opinion-ated presence on DVD and Blu-ray in-terviews was a constant joy and besides, there was always that ray of hope stub-bornly clinging to life that, maybe, with the right project and the right tools at his disposal, Franco could have delivered one final gem. Sooner than mourn what has been lost, however, it helps to keep things in perspective. For many of us, there are far more Franco films out there (especially when one factors in the variant edits of so many of them) than there is time in which to fit them all in. As such, it helps to have a subjective guide when viewing some of the more interesting ones. Chances are if you've seen any of Franco films you've seen at least a few of the films covered here—it could be that they didn't do any-thing for you. If so, the chances are good that Franco simply isn't the filmmaker for you. On the other hand, one never knows when that one film will crop up which will serve as something of a key to unlocking the hidden pleasures that can be derived from his oeuvre. Those of you who are ready and willing to undertake the jour-ney may well find these titles worthy of consideration; those who have already tried and didn't like what they saw may hopefully feel inspired to give it another go … or not. In any event, this should hopefully serve as something of a helpful guide to some of the more interesting and rewarding pit stops in Franco's labyrin-thine filmography.

The 1960s

The Awful Dr. Orlof (1961)
Inspector Tanner investigates the kidnapping of several young women from the streets of Paris. In time it is revealed that they have been abducted by the mysterious Dr. Orlof, a brilliant surgeon who has succumbed to insanity while attempting

that they are everything his best films were not. They're strained and self-conscious in their arty pretensions and aspirations to become "cult classics." Franco's best work of the 1960s and '70s worked because they were so "stream of consciousness" in their approach—there is an inher-ent purity of intent at work, while these later films seem designed to confound the viewer. With their nonexistent production values and generally awful performanc-es, they offer only sporadic evidence of

Franco's talent and passion. Sadly, even as public recognition of his abilities began to emerge (culminating with his winning the Honorary Goya, Spain's equivalent of the Lifetime Achievement Oscar, at the 2009 Goya Awards), his personal fortunes began to decline. On February 15, 2012, his longtime companion/muse Lina Romay succumbed to cancer at the too-young age of 57. She had been by Franco's side since the 1970s, though they were only finally married in April

Morpho (Riccardo Valle) is confronted by his master Dr. Orlof (Howard Vernon).

to restore his daughter's beauty, by using the skin of unwilling "donors."

The Awful Dr. Orlof was the film that ushered in a new era of horror films in Spain. It was also the film that would become Franco's calling card, much to his later consternation. The director was not in the habit of speaking well of his films, but he grew tired of hearing nostalgic comments regarding this one in particular. He would later dismiss the film as a museum piece, but its impact on his career and the development of the Spanish horror film cannot be overestimated.

At the time the film was made, the specter of Generalissimo Francisco Franco loomed large over the Spanish film industry. Films of a horrific or fantastic nature were frowned upon and the only way they could be assured to pass through the censor without being confiscated was by setting the story in another country—it didn't matter if the action was centered in Transylvania or London, just so long as it wasn't set in Spain. Franco therefore invented a fictitious locale of Hartog, presumably located somewhere in Europe. A co-production arrangement with France allowed for more salacious material to be filmed for inclusion in the French print, while the Spanish version was very chaste indeed.

The story is nothing to get excited about. Franco drew from a well of influences that included German Expressionism, low-budget mad scientist program-

mers of the 1930s and '40s (one can easily imagine Orlof being played by Bela Lugosi or Lionel Atwill) and, above all, Georges Franju's art house horror classic, *Eyes without a Face* (1960). It's not the story that matters, however; it's Franco's treatment of it. The opening scene announces the arrival of a bold new stylist, a canted camera angle offering a cock-eyed view of a prostitute staggering home, giddy and drunk; the situation is comic, but the aggressive soundtrack and moody light-

ing announce that something sinister is afoot. The action cuts indoors, where the girl's laughter and singing soon give way to shrieks (the original Spanish title, *Gritos en la noche*, translates as *Screams in the Night*), as she is attacked and abducted by Orlof's blind assistant Morpho, who tracks his victims by sound. The story wastes no time in dispensing with the necessary exposition, and, if it is burdened with too many police procedural sequences, Franco's mastery of the form is evident whenever he cuts back to the scenes involving Orlof and his obsessive experiments.

Orlof is well-played by the Swiss actor Howard Vernon, who had already worked with directors like Fritz Lang and Jean-Pierre Melville and would go on to appear in films by the likes of John Frankenheimer, Woody Allen and Jean-Luc Godard. Vernon and Franco became fast friends during the production, and the actor would soon become part of his unofficial "repertory company." It speaks volumes about Franco's charisma on set that he was able to attract the loyalty of a classy actor like Vernon, who would appear in some of the strangest and sleaziest films of his career under Franco's direction. The late actor (who passed away in 1996) would later speak of Franco with great affection: "Franco is an impossible person! As I said, we are very, very good friends … the best. I really love that guy,

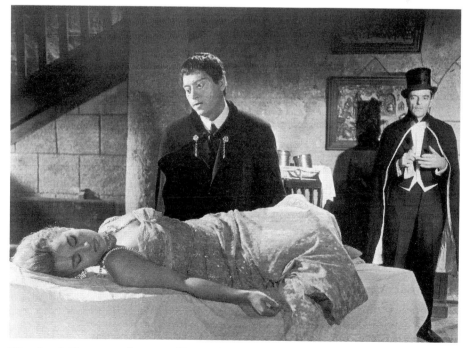

Morpho delivers another unwilling subject to Dr. Orlof, looking dapper in his top hat at the right.

A French newspaper ad for Jess Franco's breakout hit

but he's impossible. You can't imagine how talented he is. He knows everything there is to know about the cinema, moviemaking and camerawork. […] Franco is also exceptionally good at telling a story. He knows way before he starts shooting exactly what he wants to see on screen. He is also a very funny and eccentric person."[1] Vernon's career would be nothing if not eclectic as he moved from the art house to the grindhouse with alarming regularity. For Franco, he would become a close friend and a reliable performer, one who was capable of playing just about any role, be it large or small. Dr. Orlof is certainly the actor's best showcase for Franco. He plays the role with the sly humor and devilish twinkle one would associate with actor Lionel Atwill, without lapsing into camp overstatement. He almost succeeds in making Orlof a quasi-tragic figure, which was no easy feat.

As for the character of Orlof, he would return to Franco's filmography time and time again. The spelling would later be changed to Orloff and the role would be filled by actors young and old, in both a heroic and villainous context. The same can be said of the good doctor's sidekick, Morpho, played here by Riccardo Valle (or as he was Anglicized on some prints, Richard Valley), and the intrepid Inspector Tanner, played by Conrado San Martín. These character names would appear over and over again in Franco's universe, though part of the reason was simply one of frenetic productivity on Franco's part; they were names that had a certain appeal for him and he would revive them and plug them in as if he were revisiting an old friend. In essence, the Dr. Orlof we see here isn't the same Dr. Orloff we see in *Faceless* (1988), just as the Morpho presented here is not the same Morpho seen in *Vampyros Lesbos* (1970); they are simply variations on a theme, a notion that informs Franco's cinema as a whole.

Ultimately, *The Awful Dr. Orlof* is not Franco's best film, but it is one of his most polished and is certainly the most significant in terms of its impact on his career. He would use it as a launching pad to explore the genre in progressively more experimental and personal ways as the years went by.

Notes:
1. Balbo, Lucas and Peter Blumenstock (ed.), *Obsession—The Films of Jess Franco* (Berlin: Selbstverlag Frank Trebbin, 1993), p. 200.

Venus in Furs (1969)

Jazz musician Jimmy discovers the mutilated body of a beautiful woman on the beach in Istanbul. He becomes fixated on her and flees to Rio De Janiero to lose himself in the fun and frivolity of Carnival. While there, he meets Wanda, who bears an uncanny resemblance to the woman on the beach …

Following a stint in Germany, where Franco directed the extraordinary *Succubus* (1967), in addition to a couple of fun pop art spy thrillers, legendary exploitation guru Harry Alan Towers signed Franco. Towers' base of operation was in England, but he would set up film shoots wherever it was the most convenient and economical for him to do so. One of Franco's earlier films for the producer was *99 Women* (1968), which marked his debut in the "woman in prison" genre; while on location in Brazil, he grabbed some footage of the Carnival and used it as backdrop for this altogether more personal film. Such improvisations were becoming more and more common in Franco's filmmaking by this time. The story related by Franco in his interview included on the Blue Underground DVD

Dennis Price (see his face in the mirror) is seduced by the vengeful Wanda (Maria Rohm) in Jess Franco's masterpiece, *Venus in Furs*.

release is that this film originated with a conversation he had with jazz legend Chet Baker; whether this is true or simply another Franco flight-of-fancy is open to debate. Even so, he maintains that he was so struck by Baker's obsessive yet destructive persona that he decided to devise the story of a black trumpet player who falls in love with a white woman; Towers was reportedly not keen on the idea and had Franco change the character to a white trumpet player who is involved with a black love interest—these were different times after all. In any event, Franco would suffer some post-production interference, but this did not prevent him from making his most impassioned and imaginative film to date. Originally titled *Black Angel*, it was changed to *Venus in Furs* because of the success that greeted Massimo Dallamano's adaptation of the Sacher-Masoch classic of erotic fiction. In order to make sense of the title, some inserts were filmed with leading lady Maria Rohm dragging a mink stole behind her as Barbara McNair croons on the soundtrack, "Venus in Furs will be smiling!" If it all sounds a bit daft, never fear. The film is anything but, and it shows the director at the top of his game.

Franco's evolving cinematic style is evident throughout, which alternates between the elegant and rough-and-ready. The director's early works leave no doubt that he was perfectly capable of delivering

a polished, conventionally "well-made" picture, but as time went on he became more and more bored with the conventional and adopted an approach which proved alienating for many viewers. Some have suggested that the director more-or-less "lost it" at that point, but a familiarity with his body of work reveals that he was still capable and willing to deliver a more polished product when he felt it was in the best interests of the movie. *Venus in Furs* boasts some beautiful cinematog-

raphy from Angelo Lotti, but Franco's use of stock footage and crash zooms are sure to irritate some viewers. The overall approach is still far more "professional" compared to so many of his subsequent projects, but there are definite signs that a change was in the air.

The film is arguably Franco's most moving and emotionally involving, but it also has an enticing air of mystery about it. The cast is just right, even if the central characters had to be adjusted to suit the climate of the late 1960s. James Darren brings unexpected depth and pathos to the role of Jimmy. Darren had been a fixture in inane teenage fare, like *Gidget* (1959) and *Gidget Goes Hawaiian* (1961), and the director was none too convinced in the beginning that he was right for the role. Franco had envisioned an actor like Roddy McDowall but he soon found that Darren was committed to the part and the director was impressed with the actor's determination in mastering the art of appearing to play the trumpet on film. Wanda is played by Franco's go-to "fetish actress" of the moment, Maria Rohm. The beautiful, Viennese-born Rohm had married Towers in 1964 and was understandably a prominent part of the films he produced. It wasn't sheer egotism that prompted him to use her, however; she was a genuinely talented actress and the camera loved her. Not all of the roles that she played for her husband were worthy of her talents, but *Venus in Furs* would pro-

In this U.S. lobby card, Dennis Price enjoys the long legs of Maria Rohm.

also adding in layers of pathos; Price's big scene with Rohm is arguably the best set piece in Franco's filmography, which is saying quite a lot. The other major player in the scenario is singer-actress Barbara McNair, who had already provided a rip-roaring theme song for the aforementioned *99 Women*. McNair is the heart and soul of the film. She plays the role of Jimmy's devoted girlfriend Rita, who tries desperately to drag him away from his fixations without success. McNair's gently affecting performance helps to complete the love triangle, and she more than holds her own against her more experienced costars.

One of Franco's masterstrokes was in securing the services of British pop icons Manfred Mann and Mike Hugg to collaborate on the music. Music is something of a character in the film. Jimmy and Rita are musicians who use their art to express themselves and vent their pent-up frustrations and heartache. Franco spends a lot of time in the various night clubs and other venues as they perform; this fixation on performance is nothing new in Franco's work, but it would become even more marked in the 1970s. The music is entrancing and helps to make these sequences a vital part of the film. Some of the music was also recycled from earlier compositions by Bruno Nicolai, who had scored *99 Women* and would go on to work with Franco on a number of other significant films. Liberal use is also made of library tracks by the likes of Syd Dale (notably the haunting main title theme) and Keith Mansfield, while quite a few cues were pulled from Stu Phillips' score for *The Name of the Game is Kill!* (1968).

Franco would later complain that the film was compromised in the postproduction, with Commonwealth United (a subsidiary of American International Pictures) introducing its own editor to prepare the English-language version. Commonwealth saw fit to impose some psychedelic effects, which were definitely not in keeping with Franco's style, but even with the tinkering, *Venus in Furs* remains a remarkable work. The narrative is complex and developed with confidence; the measured pace suits the dreamlike ambience perfectly. The performances are just right, and if some of the "hip" '60s dialogue sounds a little stilted nowadays, it always pays to look at films with a sense

vide her with an exceptional showcase. She makes the enigmatic Wanda into a soulful and moving presence. Rohm is a genuinely sensual presence, and her elegant beauty and willingness to reveal herself both physically and emotionally makes her into one of the most memorable figures in all of Franco's work. The unsurpassable trio of Klaus Kinski, Dennis Price and Margaret Lee play her tormentors. Kinski's notorious behavior on set made him into a legend, but he and Franco got along well and he gives an intense but pleasingly understated performance here. Price had been one of the

top stars of the British film scene of the 1940s and early '50s, but alcohol abuse and a longstanding battle with personal demons had derailed his career; by this stage professionally he was game for appearing in anything, provided it paid. Franco found him to be charming, malleable and completely professional, even while hitting the sauce first thing in the morning. Lee, like Rohm, was an actress exploited for her exceptional looks, but the two shared another thing in common: They were both good actresses. The three performers bring just the right touch of decadent sleaziness to their roles, while of the context in which they were made. Alternately eerie, mysterious, gently erotic and even a little perplexing, *Venus in Furs* is Jess Franco's masterpiece.

The 1970s

Eugénie de Sade (1970)

Eugénie lives a quiet, secluded life with her beloved stepfather, the author Albert Radeck de Franval. Albert's writing explores the notion of pain and pleasure, much like that of the Marquis de Sade, and eventually Eugénie begins to take inspiration from it. The two enter into a pact whereby they become lovers determined to explore every extreme fantasy that comes to mind ...

Franco began exploring the work of the Marquis de Sade on film with the Harry Alan Towers production of *Justine* (1968). The film sought to offer competition to AIP's ill-conceived mini-epic *De Sade* (1968), which featured a fatally miscast Kier Dullea in the role of the author. Franco's version at least offered a properly wild Klaus Kinski in the role, but his screen time was limited and the film suffered from a fractured, episodic narrative written by Towers himself. The two men subsequently collaborated on *Eugénie: The Story of Her Journey into Perversion* (1969), which was infamous for years as Christopher Lee's so-called "blue movie." It offered a much better distillation of de Sade's themes and obsessions, but Franco would top himself with *Eugénie de Sade*.

The film was produced on a shoestring budget and appears to have been largely improvised, setting the tone for much of Franco's subsequent work. Franco and his small but gifted ensemble remained faithful to the theme of the destruction of innocence, while allowing the material to breathe thanks to many well-chosen *longueurs*, which would also become more prevalent in his subsequent work. The emphasis on mood over plot would become a sore point for some viewers, but it is arguably one of the key facets of his work, which makes it so fascinating (and indeed, rewarding) for his fans.

All of which should not suggest that *Eugénie de Sade* doesn't have an interesting story. Far from it! The narrative unfolds as a lengthy flashback told to the character of author Attila Tanner (played by Franco, in one of his more serious performances) by the mortally wounded Eugénie, as she lies dying in a hospital

room. The story that unfolds details the mutually destructive relationship between Eugénie and her father, Albert. Franco resists the urge of making Albert into a total monster by implying very strongly that Eugénie is every bit as guilty in the big scheme of things. Eugénie senses her father's weakness and exploits it, just as surely as Albert crosses the line by breaking a major taboo; they may not be related by blood, but even so, Albert served as Eugénie's parental figure and the notion of them entering into a sexually charged relationship is understandably unsettling. Franco details their relationship with detachment, suggesting that he is not interested in passing moral judgment on them. He merely observes as they progress from one extreme to the next, ultimately working murder into their repertoire of kinky thrills.

This connects into one of the most interesting facets of Franco's work: the empathy he displays for his characters. Very few of Franco's films have overt villains or heroes, but other screenwriters generally crafted those that do. Franco's own take on his characters is to accept them for what they are, without making excuses and reducing them to broad stereotypes. There are exceptions to this, of course. His pulpy women-in-prison films, for example, make a point of contrasting the brutalized prisoners with their perverse (and often affluent) oppressors. On the whole, however, Franco is among the least judgmental of European genre film-

makers, especially where sex and sexuality is concerned. His films showed interracial relationships long before this was deemed generally acceptable (*Venus in Furs* comes to mind); they depict homosexuality and lesbianism without suggesting that such things are perverse or morally suspect. In short, he displays a very open-minded perspective that steers clear of hypocritical moral posturing. Not only does this make him the ideal sexploitation filmmaker, but it also makes him the ideal artist to translate de Sade's writings to the screen. Of course, Franco was never concerned with remaining true to the letter of de Sade or any other writer for that matter; this may well have been one of the major shortcomings of his proposed "definitive" take on Dracula (*Count Dracula*, 1970). Instead, he distills the essence of de Sade's fevered fantasies and explores them again and again in an appropriately obsessive manner. Eugénie would become one of his most oft-revisited sources of inspiration, sometimes openly so (*Eugénie*, 1980) and sometimes in a more concealed manner (*How to Seduce a Virgin*, 1973).

Eugénie de Sade also offers the finest collaboration between Franco and his most beloved "fetish actress," Soledad Miranda. Franco first worked with the actress in 1960 when she made an unbilled early appearance in *The Queen of the Tabarín Club*. She then reappeared on his radar when she was cast as Lucy in *Count Dracula*; her magnetic presence was said to have impressed Christopher Lee, and

Jess Franco's favorite "fetish actress," Soledad Miranda, from *Eugénie de Sade*

Franco recognized that she had a unique potential which had never been properly exploited. Franco talked the young woman into coming with him to Germany to make a series of films with erotic content; Miranda worried what her family would think, so she agreed on the condition that she could be billed under a pseudonym. Thus, "Susan Korda" would top *Vampyros Lesbos* (1970), *She Killed in Ecstasy* (1970), *The Devil Came from Akasava* (1970) and *Eugénie*, and she appeared in a rather gratuitous subplot in the dreamy but uneven *Nightmares Come at Night*. *Vampyros Lesbos* is their most iconic collaboration, and there's no denying the film's many charms, but it doesn't work its way under one's skin like *Eugénie de Sade* does. *Vampyros Lesbos* is more stylish and benefits from a slightly healthier budget, but *Eugénie de Sade* is more emblematic of Franco's cinema as a whole, with its hasty surface and clever improvisations. It may be crude and a little awkward, but it has real heart and a burning intensity at its core. It also offers Miranda her most complex role. She changes from naïve, bookish and shy to self-assured, sexually voracious and cruel without missing a beat. She also plays very well off her screen stepfather, played by Paul Muller. Muller made his first foray into Franco's universe with a small uncredited role in *Venus in Furs* (he plays the rather fey impresario, who employs Jimmy and Rita) and he would become one of the director's most reliable "mascots," along with Howard Vernon.

Albert is almost certainly Franco's best role. He is a credible, intellectual type, but he has an expression that can change from the benign to the chilling at the drop of a hat. Franco plays the other major role and gives a very good account as the voyeuristic Attila Tanner. (What a name! Tanner, of course, was one of the names that would keep cropping up in his films.)

Special note must also be made of Bruno Nicolai's music. Given the very cheap and rough-and-ready nature of the production, Franco wasn't able to afford hiring Nicolai to compose an actual soundtrack for the film, so he picked through some of the composer's back catalogue and selected some excellent cues with which to score the picture. The main theme is a variation on a theme written for *99 Women* (1968) and was actually composed for the Italian miniseries *Geminus* (1969), directed by Luciano Emmer. Titled *Tema Barocco (con voce)*, it sets a haunting mood and becomes so much a part of the fabric of the film that it's hard to believe it wasn't written specifically for this film. The music associated with the various killing set pieces was written for Sergio Martino's *giallo The Case of the Scorpion's Tail* (1970), while various other cues were used from that film as well.

A Virgin Among the Living Dead (1971)

Christina returns to her family home for the reading of her father's will. While there, she meets a number of bizarre relatives and is plunged into a nightmarish scenario where dream and reality are hopelessly intertwined ...

On his audio commentary for the Kino Blu-ray release of *A Virgin Among the Living Dead*, critic Tim Lucas spends a lot of time emphasizing the impact of Soledad Miranda's death on her adoring director, Jess Franco. It's a point well worth pondering, for the specter of death and grieving looms large over this most elegiac of Franco's films. There is nothing to suggest that Miranda and Franco were ever lovers, but he was most certainly very taken with her; it seems more likely that his interest was paternal in nature, as she was happily married and he was also still married to his wife Nicole during this period of time. Even so, Miranda was the muse his work had been waiting for. Meaning no disrespect to such beautiful (and talented) actresses as Maria Rohm, Estella Blain and Janine Reynaud, but Miranda was the ideal presence for his deeply personal genre films: ethereal and beautiful, with an air of sadness and mystery. She made a powerful impression on producer Artur Brauner as well, who phoned the young actress on the morning of August 18, 1970 to notify her that he wanted to sign her to a long-term contract. Later that day, flush with her new-found success, Miranda was en route to her home in Lisbon when she was involved in a terrible car crash; she died a few hours later. Soledad Miranda was just 27 years old. The news hit Franco hard and, as Tim Lucas emphasizes in his commentary, *A Virgin Among the Living Dead* saw him pouring his heart out into a film, arguably for the first time ever. Certainly he had made films that were personal, even obsessive, but there is a nakedly emotional quality in this film that would not be matched until he made *The Other Side of the Mirror* (1972).

Above all else, *A Virgin Among the Living Dead* is a meditation on death and loss. It is also an exploration of the hold the dead continue to exert over the living. Franco does not mean this in a literal sense—the advertising campaign which made it appear to be a zombie movie misses the point by a mile, though it undoubtedly attracted many viewers who might otherwise have given it a miss—but rather in the way that the losses we suffer in life will guide our subsequent actions. In the plot, Christina was somewhat estranged from her father, yet she retained a deep devotion to him.

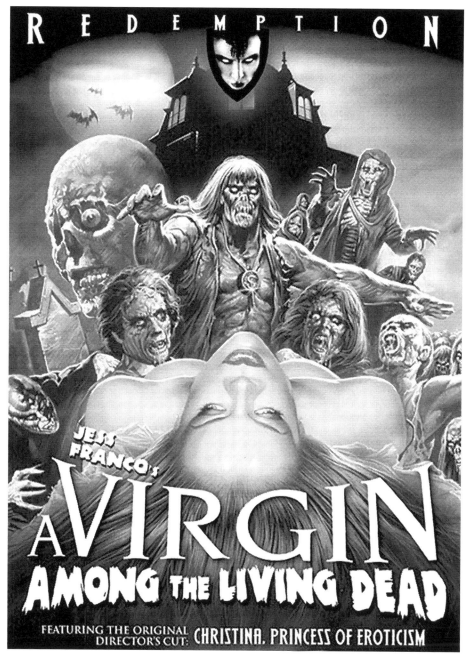

REDEMPTION

JESS FRANCO'S

A VIRGIN
AMONG THE LIVING DEAD

FEATURING THE ORIGINAL DIRECTOR'S CUT: **CHRISTINA, PRINCESS OF EROTICISM**

When she discovers that he has not only died, but also died as a result of a suicide, the loss affects her deeply. The relatives she encounters are in fact shadows of a distant past, but she does not recognize this on her own. Lost in a sea of melancholy, Christina—borrowing a page from *Alice in Wonderland*—goes down the rabbit hole to an alternate reality where it is still possible to communicate with her dead father. The idyll she enjoys is disrupted, however, when it becomes apparent that the spirits of her "loved ones" do not have her best interests in mind. The film ends on a note of ambiguity as everybody appears to return to the elements, but the lingering question remains: Is this a positive thing for Christina or is she throwing

her own life away in search of something she is not meant to find? Franco does not provide any answers, and that is part of the film's power and appeal.

The film again shows signs of haste in its production, and critics who bemoan Franco's use of zooms are not likely to be won over here. Truth be told, there is nothing "incorrect" about the use of the zoom lens, though it is very much identified with '60s/'70s filmmaking and people have been brainwashed into thinking that it's merely a sign of bad taste or indecent haste on the part of the filmmaker. On the other hand, revered filmmakers like Robert Altman, Luchino Visconti and Stanley Kubrick all indulged in zoom shots, while genre filmmakers like Mario

Bava were also eager to explore their possibilities. Franco's use of the zoom is admittedly sometimes a little clumsy and ill judged, but how is it possible to dismiss its usage altogether as being somehow "wrong"? If 10 directors were handed the same scene and asked to describe how they would stage and cover it, there would be 10 different approaches. Some would play it on a single shot; others would favor montage. Franco's decision to go with the zoom lens is therefore a matter of personal taste. Quite apart from that, it's obvious that he utilizes it in a deliberately stylistic fashion. Many of the zooms in his films probe into the scenery and seek to explore the inner-workings of the characters and their psychological makeup. Without wanting to get too highfaluting about it—after all, the device is also an admitted timesaver, and there are definitely instances in his filmography where this seems to have been the motivating factor—there's no denying that Franco had a deep affection for the zoom shot and his use of it should not be too quickly or arbitrarily dismissed.

A Virgin Among the Living Dead is not likely to appeal to hardcore horror buffs; it's too slow, too ethereal, too arty and too elliptical for that. However, its dreamy images, powerful Bruno Nicolai soundtrack and appealing performances (Howard Vernon and Paul Muller both appear here, with Franco in one of his more typical "weirdo" roles, while Britt Nichols and Anne Libert impress in their roles and serve as the director's transitionary "fetish actresses," until the arrival of Lina Romay) combine to make the film one of his most rewarding experiences. Perhaps more so than any other film in his sprawling oeuvre, it is the one that best encapsulates the peculiar, offbeat vibe that typifies Franco at his most inspired; as such, it's an ideal title to weed-out the potential fans from the diehard naysayers.

The 1980s (and beyond ...)

The Sexual Story of O (1984)

Mara and Mario seduce the innocent Odile, with the intention of "giving" her to a debauched aristocratic couple with a fetish for young girls. Unfortunately, Mario develops feelings for Odile, and things do not turn out well ...

In the interview included on the Severin DVD release of this film, Franco ad-

DISTINCTION FILMS. INC.
PRESENTS

Eugénie

...the story of her
journey into perversion.

To reach the
ultimate in
pleasure she
must experience
the ultimate
in torture!

Starring THE "INGA" GIRL MARIE LILJEDAHL, JACK TAYLOR, MARIA ROHM, And Guest Starring
CHRISTOPHER LEE • Screen Play By PETER WELBECK • Music By BRUNO NICOLAI • Produced By HARRY ALAN TOWERS • Directed By
JESS FRANCO • A VIDEO-TEL INTERNATIONAL INC. PRODUCTION • COLOR   NO ONE UNDER 18 ADMITTED Ⓧ

The Sexual Story of O, which deals with the destruction of innocence, is closest in spirit to Jess Franco's earlier Eugénie ... The Story of Her Journey into Perversion.

mits that *The Sexual Story of O* was inspired by the success of Just Jaeckin's 1975 adaptation of Dominique Aury's novel *The Story of O*. Franco was less than impressed with Jaeckin's films (which he dismisses as a still-life with no real passion) and set out to develop his own very personal take on the material. Truth be told, the end result is far closer in spirit and plot particulars to his 1969 de Sade adaptation *Eugénie: The Story of Her Journey into Perversion*. As in that earlier film (and its many variations in his cluttered filmography) it is about the destruction of innocence. It is also one of the few truly successful straightforward sex films he ever made.

The film continues the director's exploration of a more abstract manner of filmmaking. Franco focuses on seemingly innocuous details in an almost fetishistic manner. Long languid shots of the landscape and intense close-ups of flowers and other sexualized images of raw nature alternate with various sexual trysts. The plot is slight and takes a while to get underway, but Franco's control over the material is absolute throughout. Unlike so many of his sex-oriented films, this one is legitimately erotic and the sex scenes actually add to the film's impact.

Actors who were foreign to the director's milieu dominate the cast. In the

accompanying interview on the DVD, Franco confirmed that this was deliberate, as he wanted to experiment a bit instead of relying on his usual cohorts like Lina Romay or Antonio Mayans. Leading lady Alicia Príncipe was already a veteran of the Spanish erotic film scene. With her doe-eyed visage and attractive figure, she proves to be an ideal substitute for Marie Liljedahl and Soledad Miranda, who played the comparable roles in the 1969 and 1970 versions of *Eugénie*. Franco is typically candid in his recollections, describing her as game but not very bright. Despite his protestations that she comes off as dimwitted in the film, she is actually very good in the role. She is a likable actress and doesn't seem to be shy about exploring the more sordid aspects of the character. The stunning Mari Carmen Nieto, who appeared in several of Franco's films around this time, including her debut role in the erotic noir *Blood on My Shoes* (1983), plays Mara. Nieto isn't nearly as intimidating as Maria Rohm had been in a comparable role in *Eugénie: The Story of Her Journey into Perversion*, but she is good enough in context and she certainly makes a vivid impression with her fearless sensuality in the various sex scenes. It's easy to understand why Franco was more comfortable working with people with

whom he had a better rapport, but the amazing thing about the small ensemble in this film is that they all work together very well as a unit. The unease Franco apparently felt in working with this new group of actors does not show onscreen, and the end result shows him working close to the top of his form.

The film benefits from some elegant camerawork and compositions, which Franco accomplished in collaboration with Juan Soler. Franco's approach to filmmaking had been very "hands-on" for quite a few years, but the experience of working in Spain for the company Golden Films Intercational would allow him to work on an even more intimate scale. The crews became smaller, the interference from the front office became a thing of the past and the films he would make during this time would be among the most experimental and interesting of his career. So long as the end result delivered "the goods" (i.e., sex, and lots of it), he was more or less free to experiment as he saw fit. *The Sexual Story of O* is not necessarily the best of these films (*Gemidos de placer*, 1983, would offer another variation on de Sade, and is undoubtedly a more technically adventuresome work, comprised of long intricate takes similar to what Alfred Hitchcock experimented with in *Rope*, 1948), but it is arguably the most elegant.

Faceless (1988)

A model named Barbara Hallen disappears, and her wealthy father hires private detective Sam Morgan to find her. Morgan's quest leads him to the clinic of Dr. Frank Flamand, whose work in the field of plastic surgery has been grabbing headlines. Soon Sam discovers that there is a sinister side to the doctor's work ...

Following a dispiriting decline into the world of hardcore pornography, Jess Franco was gob-smacked when wealthy independent producer René Chateau sought him out to direct a (relatively) prestigious film with the healthiest budget he had seen since the late 1960s. The union between Franco and Chateau would not be without its ups and downs, but *Faceless* made it clear that the director's flair for genre cinema remained intact, and it injected his flailing career with a much-needed dose of adrenalin.

The film can almost be seen as a summation of Franco's career in genre film-

Helmut Berger (left) and Brigitte Lahaie (right) add star power to Franco's classiest project in many years, *Faceless*.

making. It brings things full circle back to *The Awful Dr. Orlof*, with its tale of face grafting, but it works in elements of the kinky, subversive elements, which would come to typify his later work. Amazingly, some fans would dismiss the film as a gun-for-hire assignment. If one insists on Franco's films being rough around the edges, then yes, the slick, polished look of the production may come as a shock. But to suggest that it was an impersonal project is to ignore the evidence to the contrary. While it is true that Franco didn't get to develop the picture from the word go, he would impose his quirky personality on every aspect of the production. As co-stars Christopher Mitchum and Caroline Munro recall in the extensive supplements included on the Shriek Show/ Media Blasters DVD release of the film, Franco would often be taken with a moment of inspiration and improvise little bits of business, which had nothing to do with the plot. The end result may threaten to burst at the seams as a result, but that is part of the film's charm. The plot is generic and old-fashioned, it's true, but with Franco injecting weird touches on such a regular basis it certainly never becomes boring or stale.

On the downside, the film's emphasis on gore results in some rather unfortunate special effects. Truth be told, Franco was never at his best when it came to effects shots. Either he simply didn't really understand how to make them work or he simply didn't care. No matter the reason, this problem rears its head during the film's various murder scenes, which seem indebted to the stylish kills found in many an Italian *giallo*, while also acknowledging the trend toward slasher fare. Tighter editing and more judicious camera angles would have helped, but Franco lingers for too long on various images, thus robbing them of their potency. It could be that this was his perverse joke at the film's expense; if it were, it doesn't really help the film any.

That caveat to one side, the film is impeccably executed. The cinematography by Jean-Jacques Bouhon and Maurice Fellous is slick and stylish. Franco makes good use of mobile camerawork and more casual fans will be relieved by the comparative lack of zoom-shots. The score by Romano Musumarra is an undiluted '80s delight, capped off by a marvelous theme song ("Destination Nowhere"), which could have tipped the film into out-and-out parody but still works remarkably well. The makeup effects may come off as cut rate, but in every other respect this is European horror at its classiest.

The cast is a Euro-horror fan's dream come true. Helmut Berger is marvelous as the devious Dr. Flamand. After rising to fame as Luchino Visconti's star discovery/paramour in such films as *The Damned* (1969) and *Ludwig* (1972), he started dabbling in more salacious fare like Massimo Dallamano's updated *Dorian Gray* (1970) and Tinto Brass' *Salon Kitty* (1976). By the time he came to top-line this film, his career was on the wane, but his demons had not yet taken their toll on his appearance. He enters into the spirit of the film with sadistic glee and helps to propel the narrative. Former porno queen Brigitte Lahaie was in the midst of rehabilitating her screen image and undoubtedly saw her participation in a classy horror project such as this as a step in the right direction. According to Franco, she had some concerns that he would trick her into doing some nudity, but he respected her wishes to be taken seriously as a "straight" actress and gave her ample room to prove herself. Lahaie had already made a powerful impression in such Jean Rollin horror films as *The Grapes of Death* (1978) and *Night of the Hunted* (1980), but she was new to Franco's universe and handles herself with aplomb. Her dynamic screen presence lends an erotic charge to some implied scenes of kinky sex, but she is able to do this without resorting to nudity or performing anything openly explicit; it's all in her eyes and her attitude. Lahaie could have become a major "fetish actress" in Franco's universe, but she came to the fold too late and would only work with the director one more time, on the disappointing (and truly "faceless") war

Gérard Zalcberg plays Dr. Flamand's crazed henchman Gordon, who looks at a trophy from his latest kill.

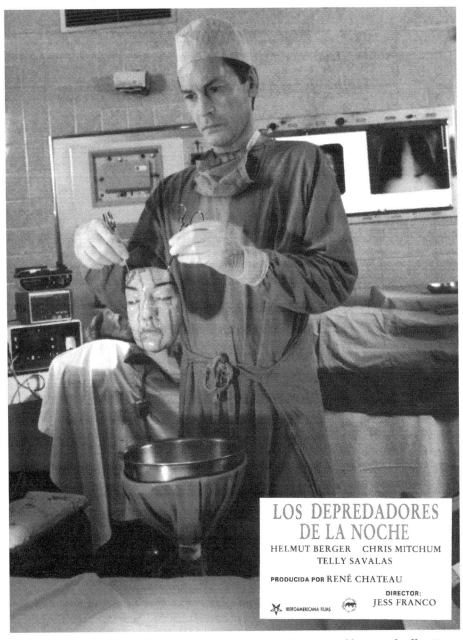

LOS DEPREDADORES
DE LA NOCHE

HELMUT BERGER   CHRIS MITCHUM
TELLY SAVALAS

PRODUCIDA POR RENÉ CHATEAU

DIRECTOR:
JESS FRANCO

IBEROAMERICANA FILMS

Helmut Berger as the mad surgeon Dr. Flamand, in the surgical horror thriller *Faceless*. The sequence shown above is similar to one in the French classic, *Eyes Without a Face*.

film *Dark Mission: Evil Flowers* (1988). Telly Savalas appears in a few scenes as the concerned father; it's obvious that he was just along for a paycheck, but his classy presence adds to the film's prestige value. Caroline Munro is effective as the cocaine-addicted model whose abduction sets the plot into motion; she, too, had been warned of Franco's "devious" methods, but she speaks enthusiastically of working with him in the interview material included on the Shriek Show DVD release. Lina Romay and Howard Vernon make welcome cameo appearances, appropriately as Mrs. and Dr. Orloff, but the

film is stolen by the great Anton Diffring as Flamand's mentor. Diffring's casting pays lip service to his most iconic genre role as the demented surgeon in Sidney Hayers' wonderfully lurid *Circus of Horrors* (1960). Diffring was frail and ailing by the time he made the film, but he gives a performance of wit and surprising warmth; there's a marvelous moment when he confesses, "Deep down inside, I'm a real sentimentalist," which is equal parts amusing yet oddly moving. The veteran actor would die only two years later, and his subsequent work was limited, making this something of a final bow for one of

the screen's premier purveyors of silky villainy. Christopher Mitchum, son of the legendary Robert Mitchum, is merely adequate as the private eye, but he does bring a touch of self-deprecating humor to some of his scenes.

Faceless is Franco at his most purely entertaining. It doesn't aspire to reinvent the wheel, nor does it need to do so. It revisits familiar ground with an eye toward bidding adieu to old tropes, reminding one of Mario Bava's Gothic throwbacks *Baron Blood* (1972). The film seemed to promise a classy new chapter in Franco's career, but sadly it was not meant to be. He would follow up with some very impersonal projects, including the aforementioned *Dark Mission: Evil Flowers*, and their failure seemed to rob him of his passion for filmmaking for a period of time. He would rebound in the mid-1990s, however, just around the time that a new generation of cineastes began to rediscover his work. From there, he would begin to experiment in the medium of shooting films on video …

And there I have elected to leave my cinematic history lesson … not because Franco didn't continue working right up until the end. He most certainly did. Others have a greater tolerance for the later films than I do, so it is perhaps fitting that I leave it to them to fill in the blanks and elucidate the final stages of his career. The important thing about these later films, above anything else, is simply this: No matter how poor they were, no matter how amateur they may come across, they nevertheless enabled him to keep working. For Franco, the process of creation was life itself … and on that level, the producers who threw him a few bucks to crank out these shot-on-video confections deserve a tip of the hat. Beyond that, there is much to look over and savor in his earlier work, even if one doesn't have the stomach to endure the final chapter of his career. This article only scratches the very surface of Franco's mammoth filmography, but hopefully the titles here will serve as a good guide for those who are finally willing to take the plunge and explore his unusual cinematic universe. Some of you will be glad you did; others will likely curse the day that they bought their first Franco movie. Franco probably wouldn't have had it any other way.

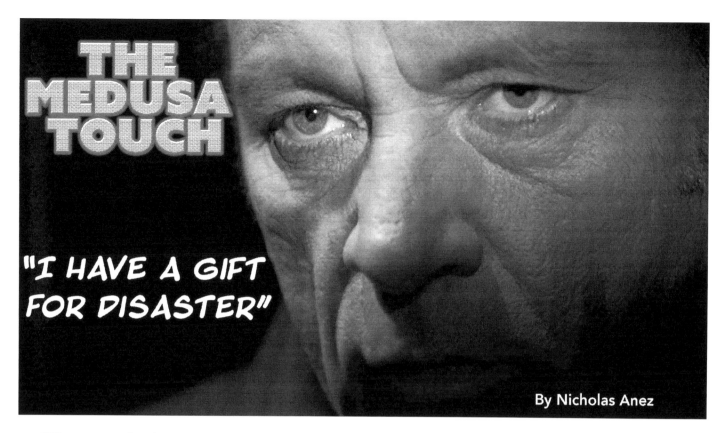

THE MEDUSA TOUCH

"I HAVE A GIFT FOR DISASTER"

By Nicholas Anez

"The moment they kneel to pray, I will bring the whole edifice down on their unworthy heads!"

These words reveal the hatred that John Morlar feels for the establishment, for the government, for the church and, essentially, for humanity. Does this threat indicate the delusional threats of a lunatic? Or does it foretell death and destruction on a massive scale?

John Morlar is the central character in the 1978 motion picture, *The Medusa Touch*, starring Richard Burton, Lino Ventura and Lee Remick. It is about a man who believes that he possesses telekinetic powers. The movie fits into many categories. It begins as a crime film with traces of neo-noir; it develops into a suspenseful psychological thriller; then it finally enters the realm of supernatural horror before climactically evolving into a disaster film of epic proportions. Though it was commercially successful in England and France, the movie didn't make much of an impact at the American box-office, due in part to negative reviews. There have been numerous other films about telekinesis, such as *The Power* (1968), *Carrie* (1976), *The Fury* (1978) and *Firestarter* (1984), to name a few. But this is by far the most intelligent, the most haunting and the most horrific of all of the films on the subject.

The Medusa Touch is based upon a 1973 novel of the same name by Peter Van Greenaway. John Briley, whose previous genre work was *Children of the Damned* (1963), wrote the screenplay and it follows the novel fairly closely, with some exceptions. Most noticeably, he changes the sex of the psychiatrist from male to female and converts the novel's British detective, Inspector Cherry (the protagonist of several novels by Van Greenaway), into a French inspector assigned to Scotland Yard as part of an exchange program. The film omits many biographical details of Morlar's life that are included in the novel, such as his military service. The film only hints at the political subtext regarding the reasons for the government's animosity toward Morlar, which the novel develops more extensively. And Briley does not identify the mysterious "L" that Morlar refers to in his journal, though the novel specifies his identity.

Jack Gold is the director and also co-produced the film with Academy Award-winning editor (for *Lawrence of Arabia*) Anne V. Coates. Gold directed 11 theatrical films and, upon the release of his first movie, *The Bofors Gun* (1968), critics praised him as one of England's distinctive new talents. His résumé includes the underrated science fiction film, *Who?* (1975), which was also unjustly dis-

missed by critics due in part to its genre. He worked more extensively on the small screen, receiving praise for such television movies as *The Naked Civil Servant* (1975) and *Escape from Sobidor* (1987). Similarly, Briley's renown is due to other more prestigious works, particularly *Gandhi* (1982), for which he won an Academy Award. Nevertheless, *The Medusa Touch* is a highpoint in the careers of both director and screenwriter. And Richard Burton's performance in this film is the equal of any of his acclaimed roles throughout his career. Contrary to some critical judgment, Burton's best years were not behind him during this period, although his participation in the abysmal *Exorcist II: The Heretic* (1977) supports this belief. He provided fine performances in *Equus* (1977) and *Absolution* (1978), while his third release in 1978 was the hugely popular (except in the U.S.) *The Wild Geese*.

The Medusa Touch begins with the attempted murder of author John Morlar by an unseen assailant, who bludgeons his brains into mush as he watches a news report on television of a doomed American lunar landing. By all accounts, he should be dead. And this is what Inspector Brunel and his assistance Sergeant Duff assume merely by the sight of the victim's extensive brain matter seeping out of his shattered skull. But as they search for

John Morlar (Richard Burton) agonizingly begs for help from his psychiatrist, Dr. Zonfeld (Lee Remick).

clues throughout the victim's London flat, much to their amazement, Morlar suddenly starts breathing. An ambulance rushes him to a hospital where Dr. Johnson and his staff quickly attach life-support systems in what they feel is a hopeless attempt to save his life.

Brunel then begins his investigation to apprehend the assailant, whom he presumes will soon be a murderer. Morlar's journal provides clues to the victim's state of mind, especially his feelings toward the establishment. Brunel doesn't understand references in the journal to "the West Front" but the name of Zonfeld leads him to Morlar's psychiatrist. Dr. Zonfeld informs Brunel that Morlar believed that he had the telekinetic power to cause death and disaster by merely *willing* events to happen. Brunel considers this to be preposterous, which was Zonfeld's initial impression. As Brunel pursues his investigation, the doctor and various people who knew Morlar provide facts about the victim's life as well as clues regarding possible suspects. It does seem that a number of people who have harmed Morlar in some way met with untimely deaths.

However, these relatively small-scale tragedies are in the past. As Brunel rides through London, there are signs of a more recent and massive catastrophe involving a crashed Jumbo Jet airliner and a demolished skyscraper. And there are also the reports of the impending trag-

edy aboard the lunar space mission. Brunel initially sees no connection between these disasters and his investigation, but his skepticism gradually crumbles as the comatose patient exhibits increasingly intense brain wave activity. Brunel's investigation eventually leads to the inescapable

conclusion that Morlar is plotting another disaster regarding an historic London cathedral. However, this catastrophe is only a warm-up to Morlar's intention to unleash nuclear devastation upon London and the world. Even more horrifying is the fact that Morlar is plotting to inflict such horrors from a smashed brain that refuses to let his body die.

A superficial summary can not convey the multifaceted intricacies of John Briley's script, the depth of the characterizations, the sharp dialogue or the philosophical and theological questions that the story raises. The script is a precise blueprint of intertwined themes. Each flashback provides new information about Morlar's relationships with other persons, whose deaths he may or may not have caused. In turn, the scenes in the present reveal the increasing possibility of his connection to the recent tragedies, along with implications of future catastrophes. The story develops from the perspective of the detective, a device that allows the viewer to see and experience only what he does and thus gradually come to believe the disturbing reality of the situation as he does. The result is a surprisingly plausible film, despite its implausible subject.

Inspector Brunel (Lino Ventura) and Sergeant Duff (Michael Byrne) examine Morlar's body, assuming that he is dead.

Jack Gold's direction complements this realistic approach. He avoids sensationalism and creates the appropriate atmosphere to make the farfetched events look credible. For each of the initial deaths, Gold and Briley avoid assigning responsibility to the young Morlar and suggest an alternate explanation for the fatalities. Gold stages the scenes of the investigation in the manner of other police films, while the relationship between the inspector and his subordinate convey similar familiarity. Though the investigation assumes priority, the director often displays reminders of the larger tragedies that have occurred in the surrounding environment, covertly linking the events. The meticulously detailed scenes of devastation in the streets add to the sense of authenticity, which will make the cause of the tragedy (when it is revealed) seem equally believable. As the story progresses, reports of fatalities from the plane crash and the lunar mission, along with potential hazards at the nuclear plant, become increasingly prominent.

The detailed exposition of the character of John Morlar is chillingly credible, despite the unnatural circumstances that infuse his entire life. There is something very believable about Morlar and this is what makes the film so much more frightening than other films on the subject that appear more fantastic than real. Furthermore, the focus of this film is not on some trivial matter, such as who is taking whom to a high school prom, but about whether or not the human race deserves to survive. Beneath the surface of a horror story, the film raises questions about the nature of humanity. It provokes serious discussion about human beings and supreme beings, both good and evil. During the course of the story, it is suggested that Morlar may be either God's avenging angel or Satan's disciple of death. This sounds like some heavy stuff, but there is nothing pretentious about this film. It is on the surface an entertaining movie but, simmering under the main storyline, there are serious ideas to contemplate.

The Medusa Touch introduces Morlar as an adult in a pre-credits sequence just prior to the murder attempt. In the film's first scene, the camera focuses on Edvard Munch's 1893 Expressionistic painting *The Scream*, which is on the wall of Morlar's flat. It depicts a distorted person who

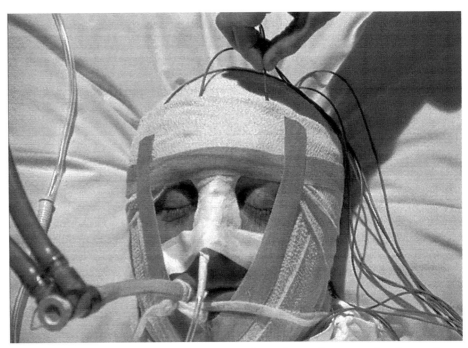

Though his brain has been severely damaged, Morlar is about to unleash a nuclear cataclysm.

is experiencing emotional suffering with mouth and eyes wide open in a screech of horror. Munch reported as inspiration for his painting the sight of blood red clouds caused by the setting sun accompanied by "an infinite scream piercing through nature." Critics have stated that the painting reflected the chaotic emotional state of the artist who had a lifelong fear of insanity. References will be made later in the film to Morlar's brain silently screaming through his EEG. Morlar will also express his terror to his psychiatrist over going insane.

From this painting, the camera moves slowly and settles upon Morlar who is intently watching—and concentrating upon—the unfolding tragedy in space. He doesn't appear to be surprised at the sight of his visitor and makes a typically sarcastic remark as he discerns the visitor's deadly intent. He doesn't even try to evade the figurine of Napoleon as it crashes into his skull over and over again.

The titles of the film then appear over Caravaggio's 1597 painting of Medusa, her hideous face caressed by serpents instead of hair. Anyone gazing upon Medusa's face, according to mythology, will turn to stone and die. During the course of the film, Morlar will furiously stare at certain persons, who will die soon afterward. Brunel later explains to his subordinate, "Medusa is a monster who

was created to do battle with the gods." As he grows older, Morlar will increasingly express his contempt for God and for those who believe in a deity. He will believe that, by destroying believers, he is doing battle with God.

When Dr. Zonfeld describes to Brunel her experiences with Morlar, she explains her patient's beliefs as purely delusional. Her tone indicates disbelief as she relates Morlar's initial experience as a five-year-old child to the detective. In this flashback, young John cringes in terror as a malicious nanny fills his impressionable mind with fears of hellfire and damnation. The frightened boy silently and desperately pleads for help, not from God but from Lucifer. This is the first indication that he may be a child of Satan. Then again, he may only turn to the devil because of the images that the nanny placed in his mind. All that is certain is that a disturbed adult is frightening the daylights out of a vulnerable child. She won't be able to do that again.

In another flashback that Zonfeld relates, John is 10 years old. At this time, he seems to be a normal boy, running and playing like any child of his age, hurrying to do his mother's bidding in an attempt to please her. But his parents, the two persons to whom he is closest, appear to consider him somewhat odd and he is obviously hurt upon overhearing their unkind

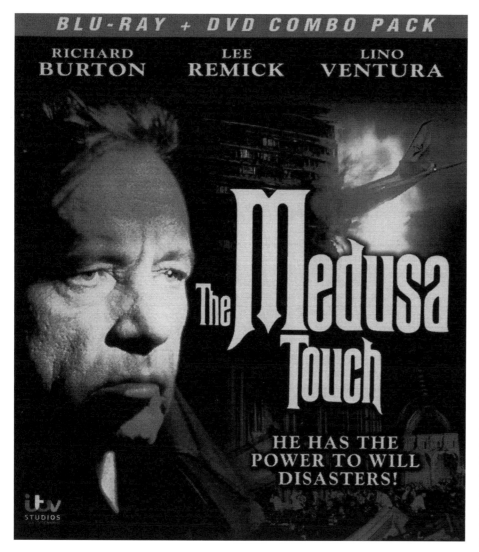

words about him. Nevertheless, as he sits behind the wheel of his father's car, there are no signs to indicate that he wants to kill them. While he may have accidentally released the brakes, it is also quite possible that his father did not secure the brakes of the automobile.

Initially, Zonfeld appears to minimize the significance of these events to Brunel. But the detective discerns that the psychiatrist seems to be concealing information. In the next flashback, John is now a 14-year-old student in a boarding school, obviously wise beyond his years as he ignores a pompous schoolmaster. When John verbally embarrasses the teacher in front of the class, the teacher unjustly punishes him. (In the novel, the teacher is a pedophile but this criminality is not evident in the film; however, when John reports to the teacher at nighttime, another boy is in the background, suggesting degeneracy.) This punishment will initiate a series of events that will end in an early

demise for the teacher and for several students. Authorities determine the cause of the deaths to be accidental, which is quite possible in view of John's distressed emotional state caused by the teacher's cruelty.

Brunel also meets with a barrister, a former partner of the adult Morlar when he was practicing law. He relates a significant event that prompted Morlar to leave the profession. As a defense attorney, Morlar defended a young man, Loveless, who committed a minor act of defiance against the Imperial War Museum. From his spirited defense, it is apparent that Morlar has developed passionate anti-government and anti-war sentiments. He is extremely emotional about his beliefs but unwisely expresses them to Judge McKinley, who takes his revenge upon the defendant. This will be the last case that the judge will ever hear. And appropriately one of the last things that the judge will see is Morlar's ominous stare, filled with anger.

This deadly gaze, similar to that of Medusa, tends to support the theory that the devil to whom the young Morlar prayed may have rewarded him with special powers. Two more flashbacks hint at the possibility of Satanic influence. In a desperate effort to find an explanation for his powers, Morlar visits a fortune teller whose frightened response indicates that he detects an inherent evil within Morlar. And Mrs. Pennington, Morlar's former neighbor, makes the mistake of shouting too loud and pays the ultimate price, leaving her husband devastated. This same husband bitterly informs Brunel that he believed that Morlar was demonically possessed.

However, Morlar's justified resentment of the government's militaristic policies is humane and negates the theory that he may be demonic. If he were Satanic, he would applaud war. Instead, he vehemently expresses his anger against his government for sending thousands of young men to die in unnecessary wars and profiting from wholesale death and destruction. He condemns the establishment for its misuse of the atom to create a weapon of mass destruction. He will also criticize the American government for spending a fortune to send a space ship to the moon, while millions of people are starving. And it is significant that, at one point, Morlar emphatically denies his own possession, scornfully dismissing such a possibility as simplistic and superstitious.

Loveless does not again appear in the film—except possibly as a tramp. But there is that aforementioned "L" in Morlar's journal. In the novel, L is Lorimar, one of Morlar's former clients who provides him with information about the government's illicit activities. In the film, the Assistant Commissioner of Scotland Yard hints at this sub-plot when he informs Brunel that so-called interested parties want the case solved as quickly as possible. The novel depicts Loveless's imprisonment and eventual suicide. The film eliminates Loveless's death and L's identity remains unknown. Incidentally, the only other character in the film whose name begins with L is the recipient of the young John's prayer: Lucifer.

Brunel meets with Morlar's publisher who suggests that the reason for the government's hostility toward Morlar was the author's controversial novels (one of which is ominously titled *The Incinerator*), which may have contained politically sensitive information. But the intriguing part of this flashback occurs when Morlar, after looking out the window, suddenly leaves the publisher's office to talk to a tramp who is sitting on a bench in a park. Morlar's concern for this nameless tramp, who is only seen from a distance, is apparent since he talks to him for several hours. If this tramp is Loveless, the fact that the government reduced his former client to poverty is the kind of injustice that would fuel Morlar's hatred toward the establishment.

Another incident in Morlar's past that Dr. Zonfeld relates to Brunel appears to have signified a turning point in his life. As Morlar returns home from work, he finds his wife, Patricia, in the company of her lover, Parrish. When Patricia tells John that she is leaving him and that he will never see her again, she doesn't realize how truthful her words are. This sequence demonstrates Morlar's embittered personality as he expresses both indifference and contempt toward his wife. But it also reveals his grief over the death of his child and his anguish over the child's deformed condition, about which Patricia makes a particularly nasty remark. The fact that Morlar was unable to sire a normal child suggests that perhaps his own birth may have been abnormal and that this is the source of his powers.

This incident definitely causes a change within Morlar. Prior to this event, Morlar did not think he had caused the deaths of the people who had harmed him. He only believed that he somehow sensed that those persons would die. But, regarding his wife's death, he tells Zonfeld that he didn't just *know* that she was going to die. He now believes that he *made* her die, but he does not know how. In Morlar's mind, this knowledge initiates severe anguish over the fact that he may have subconsciously caused the deaths of his parents along with several schoolchildren. However, since he did not consciously instigate these deaths, he believes that some mysterious element is in place. He hopes that Zonfeld will give him the answer to this dilemma.

Morlar elicits sympathy when he agonizingly begs for help from the psychiatrist. After many sessions, Zonfeld still believes that he is mentally ill. She

Morlar unwisely expresses his anti-establishment beliefs in court, as his client Loveless (James Hazeldine) watches helplessly.

dismisses any kind of supernatural influence and believes that medication may be necessary to calm her patient's increased anxiety and depression. Her refusal to believe him pushes him over the edge and he succumbs to the seduction of his power. It is unfortunate for both of them that she realizes only too late that she has been mistaken. When she witnesses his demonstration of his powers, she shockingly sees that he is not delusional and, for the first time, causes the deaths of people who are innocent of ever harming him. The horror of this appalling event convinces her that she must stop him from committing further acts of carnage. Sadly, she will fail. And when Brunel arrives at the same conclusion, he will also fail.

The Medusa Touch is quite provocative, particularly regarding the numerous religious references. During different stages of his life, Morlar's attitude toward religion fluctuates. From his diatribes, it is apparent that the human capacity for evil is one reason for his nihilistic beliefs. At one point he tells Zonfeld that he doesn't believe in either God or the devil. Yet, at another point, he bitterly states that he is "doing God's dirty work." He curses practitioners of organized religion for their hypocrisy and sarcastically sneers at the fact that "God and gentle Jesus are now the in-thing." Reacting to the many disasters all over the world, he states that "we are all the devil's children." And it is sig-

nificant that a prominent cathedral filled with worshippers, whether their heads are unworthy or not, will eventually become the target of his destructive powers.

The film also succeeds as suspenseful and exciting entertainment. The script and direction proceed at a tempo which reflects the progress of the plot. The film begins at a methodical pace as Brunel pieces together information from various sources that gradually chip away at his skepticism. As he begins to believe the reality of Morlar's powers, the pace of the film steadily increases. The tempo reaches fever pitch as he races against time to prevent a horrendous tragedy. In the final terrifying sequence of the film, Brunel and the doctor realize that the catastrophe unfolding before them, as terrible as it is, will actually seem insignificant compared to the nuclear cataclysm that neither they nor anyone else will be able to prevent.

Concerning the source of Morlar's powers, the film leaves this question unanswered, which is a wise decision by the filmmakers. Whether he was possessed by a demon or born with a defective gene remains unknown. In fact, the film suggests some other reason not known by science or theology, something beyond human knowledge. And this is what makes Morlar so frightening and yet so pathetic, for he may be as much a victim as a villain.

Richard Burton has relatively few scenes but yet he dominates the film, not

The effects crew prepares to have its Jumbo Jet model crash into the skyscraper.

only because people talk about Morlar when he is not on screen but also because the actor projects such intensity into his character. He faultlessly projects Morlar's misanthropy through his bitter tone and sour expression, aided at times by gritted teeth and bulging eyes. And yet he also imbues his character with pathos and suffering. He conveys the mental anguish of a man who is experiencing internal torment and is becoming increasingly unstable. The impact of Burton's precise elocution and perfect diction is also an enormous asset. He recites his dialogue, particularly his passionate tirades against bureaucratic injustice, with every ounce of conviction. In the pivotal sequence with his wife, he hurls his acerbic insults toward her in such a pitiless manner that it almost evokes sympathy for her. And when he says, "I have a gift for disaster," it commands attention. It is a masterful portrayal that convincingly conveys all degrees of Morlar's descent from desperation in his pleas for help, despondency over his condition, fatalistic acceptance of his powers and, finally, a fanatical determination to use those powers to create massive bloodshed and destruction.

Lino Ventura was born in Italy but established his film career in France. Since the movie is an English-French co-production, his participation must have been part of the deal. Regardless, he is a tremendous asset to the film and very convincingly conveys his character's evolution from skeptic to believer. Initially, he is not particularly expressive as he begins his investigation of what he assumes to be just another homicide case. The subtle differences in the manner in which he looks at Zonfeld as he slowly develops suspicion of her are particularly informative in view of later developments. As his pursuit of the truth steadily yields distressing information, he exhibits increased emotion along with a more vigorous speech and manner. The sequence in which he finally understands the meaning of "the West Front" is particularly effective. He also adds dry humor to his interactions with Duff, especially when he contemplates puzzling aspects of the investigation while giving the sergeant culinary instructions. Ventura makes Brunel a very likeable protagonist and evokes empathy when he frantically attempts to terminate Morlar's increasingly powerful brain waves.

Lee Remick, as Dr. Zonfeld, has a difficult role to play but she believably makes her character sympathetic and, ultimately, tragic. Upon her introduction, she must convey the impression that she is pretending to be surprised of her patient's plight and, immediately afterward, disheartened to hear that he is still alive. She also has to imply in her demeanor not only that she is concealing information from Brunel, but also that this is a terrible burden for her to endure. Her fate is a truly sad one because the incident that Morlar forced her to witness changes her from a healer to a destroyer. Consequently, she sees no solution for her actions or her guilt, other than a drastic one. Remick's performance is a multi-faceted one and the fact that her role often requires her to serve as an apparently objective relator of past events, while concealing her own involvement, makes her achievement even more impressive.

Eminent British actors in supporting roles contribute enormously to the film's impact with Harry Andrews as the Assistant Commissioner, Gordon Jackson as Dr. Johnson and Michael Byrne as Duff, among others. Michael Hordern, Marie-Christine Barrault, Alan Badel, Derek Jacobi, Jeremy Brett and Robert Lang are among the many fine performers who appear in the flashback sequences and enhance the film's plausibility.

John Morlar is a tragic character who was cursed with a power that he never wanted. During the course of his life, he progresses from a sensitive child to a defender of justice, from a callous cynic to a vengeful executioner. He eventually embraces the paranormal powers that he formerly cursed and utilizes them to punish the human race for which he has so much contempt, the same human race that he formerly tried to protect from the corrupt establishment. In effect, he becomes exactly what he so passionately criticized and fought against all of his adult life. He appoints himself God and, like the establishment that he despises, becomes a mass murderer of innocent people.

The Medusa Touch is a classic horror film that builds slowly and effectively to a spectacular and horrifying climax. There are many brilliant scenes of suspense and horror, but the moment when Morlar's eyes suddenly open beneath the bandages is one of the most memorable.

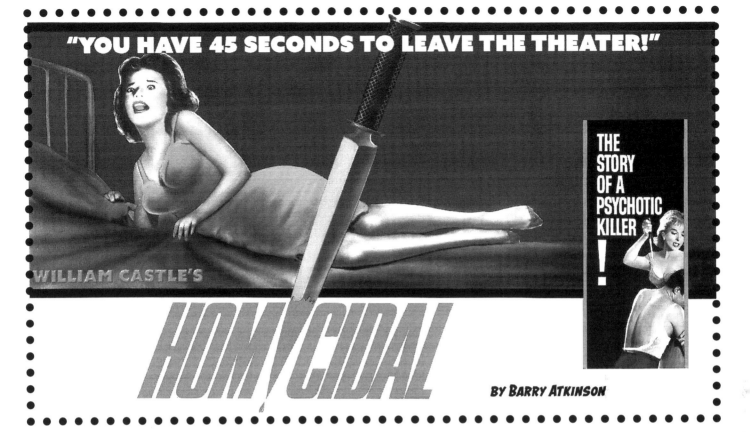

"YOU HAVE 45 SECONDS TO LEAVE THE THEATER!"

WILLIAM CASTLE'S

HOMICIDAL

THE STORY OF A PSYCHOTIC KILLER !

BY BARRY ATKINSON

In the wake of Alfred Hitchcock's groundbreaking and phenomenally successful *Psycho*, filmmakers served up to horror fans a rash of psychological thrillers focusing on madness, insanity, mental instability, twisted psyche and split personality, most of those produced in Britain emanating from Hammer Film Productions (*A Taste of Fear*; *Hysteria*; *Paranoiac*; *Fanatic*; *The Nanny*). Hitchcock's *Marnie*, Michael Powell's *Peeping Tom*, Roman Polanski's *Repulsion*, Samuel Fuller's *Shock Corridor*, Blake Edwards' *Experiment in Terror* plus an influx of shock/horror features from the Continent and even a couple from William Castle himself (*Strait-Jacket*; *The Night Walker*) added to the never-ending list, satisfying the appetites of those fans with a penchant for something a bit darker and salacious on their horror menus. But how many have stood the test of time and had the following accolade bestowed upon them: "It even surpasses *Psycho* in structure, suspense and nervous drive." These words from *Time* magazine's film critic were leveled at Castle's Columbia outing *Homicidal*, the King of the Horror Movie Gimmick's 5th horror feature and one which many fans rate as his best. Released in 1961, *Homicidal* (X-rated in Britain) went

the rounds on England's infamous (and much-missed) Sunday one-day circuit in the mid-1960s, but it has rarely been seen in the United Kingdom since. (I caught it in May 1965 on a double bill with *Creature with the Atom Brain*.) A recent two-disc set containing five Castle movies has allowed me to catch and reappraise this pared-to-the bone, masterful cross-dressing shocker, one that rivets from start to finish, not only for Castle's blatant tongue-in-cheek scene stealing from the Hitchcock classic, but for Jean Arless' central role as the psychotic knife-wielding blonde nurse, Emily, a very dark secret festering in her warped mind. Hers is the kind of charismatic performance that can lift a grade-B horror thriller several notches up the scale: big round expressive eyes staring out of a flawless, doll-like face, switching from sexy feminine guile to savage animalistic fury in a flash. Arless commands attention over 87 minutes, a once-in-a-lifetime "minor" star turn, creating one of horror cinema's creepiest and deadliest of all femme fatales. Okay, she might be hammy and guilty of over-exaggeration in some instances, but boring she isn't, putting her all into the part of sick, demented Emily, resulting in a larger-than-life horror character that sticks in the memory.

Jean Arless holds a sharp object while flipping through a magazine.

A pressbook newspaper ad details the rules of finding the "Coward's Corner" during the "Fright Break" for *Homicidal*.

First, a word about Arless herself, a woman almost as enigmatic as Emily in *Homicidal*; in fact, she's actress Joan Marshall (born Joan Marie Schrepfermann, 1931), credited as Jean Arless on this one occasion only and for reasons best known to herself (the ambiguity of her first name and character's sexual orientation is most likely the reason she is billed as "Jean" and not "Joan"). Perhaps it was this inner quirkiness and oddness of character, not to mention those androgynous looks, that made her attractive to Castle in the first place, and made him choose her for the lead. Rumor has it that she was either married three times and had two children, or five times producing five children. She was also said to have carried on an affair

with Richard Chamberlain after meeting him on the set of *Dr. Kildare* in 1966, although how far this alleged liaison went is open to conjecture, due to the actor's self-confessed homosexual leanings. Marshall spent most of her career in television, dying from cancer at the age of 61 in 1992 on the island of Jamaica, where her ashes are buried. *Homicidal* was Marshall/Arless' crowning achievement (and, it could be said, Castle's as well); let's examine the movie and its obvious *Psycho* influences in depth, in order to obtain a better understanding of why many veteran horror buffs now hold *Homicidal* in such high regard.

Castle rattles through his customary opening cameo in double-quick time

(thank goodness!), the film's title sewn on an embroidered tapestry, a homely touch to the not-so-homely events that are to follow. We kick off briefly in 1948. A young girl plays quietly with her doll when into her room walks a weird-looking kid (resembling Alfred E. Neuman of *MAD Magazine* fame) who, much to her distress, steals her toy and cuddles it. Forward to the present day, Ventura, California; A slim, attractive young blonde (Arless was 29 at the time of shooting) walks confidently down the sidewalk, elbow-length white gloves offsetting to perfection a smart black outfit. Pausing at a jeweler's window to view a tray of wedding rings, she strolls into the Ventura Hotel's lobby, registers under the name of Miss Miriam Webster and orders a double room for the day—September 5. Bellboy Richard Rust is only too pleased to help the ice-cool dame carry her luggage upstairs, and even more pleased when she offers him $2,000 to get married that night, *but* (to Rust's dismay) on the strict condition that the marriage is to be annulled straight after the ceremony, a clear-cut case of "you can look at the goods, but you can't touch." Note the moment when Arless steps out of the shower in a titillating bathrobe, Rust's eyes on stalks—*Psycho* influence *number one*! In these early buildup stages, Castle keeps the pace and his camera steady (and a lot of the time focusing on the actress' fined-boned immobile features), Hugo Friedhofer's music a menacing drone in the background, content to let the audience take in Arless' frosty role-playing and wonder just what on earth her game is. They'll soon find out!

Arless, now dressed in a white wedding suit (and she'll remain in white for the rest of the movie), has the bemused Rust drive her to Justice of the Peace James Westerfield's place, close to midnight, where grumpy Westerfield (as Alfred S. Adrims, looking and speaking like John McIntire in *Psycho*: influence *number two*!) performs the ceremony, his disapproving wife playing the organ. "Now I get to kiss the little lady," leers the JP after Arless has said, "I do," and offered his congratulations, a big mistake. Her eyes wide open in revulsion (Castle zooms in on those eyes), her face a rigid mask of evil, Arless grabs a surgical knife from her bag and plunges the nine-inch blade into Westerfield's stomach at least six times,

Emily (Jean Arless) confronts the handicapped housekeeper Helga (Eugenie Leontovich) with crazed eyes.

a few seconds of uncontrolled ferocity guaranteed to jolt audiences out of their seats. As chaos reigns and blood flows, Arless hurriedly leaves the room, jumps into Rust's car and drives away.

Next we have a very unmistakable *third* *Psycho* influence: Arless in the automobile, a huge facial close up, being pursued by a police vehicle, siren wailing. The cops move closer and closer, Arless presses the gas pedal, her anxiety (and ours) mounting—then the police pass her by, homing in on a parked vehicle and its occupant. Yes, the Master of Suspense did all this with Janet Leigh as she drove off toward the Bates Motel and her death, punters sharing her every fear. So, if you're going to replicate what Leigh was experiencing, why not replicate it from the best? Arless pulls in, clambers into her own vehicle, Castle including more close-ups of her startled features, police bulletins on the car radio tell of the murder, as she tosses the worthless ring out of the window and drives up to a large, ornate house. Unruffled and calm, as though nothing has happened, this strange, highly dangerous woman has completed stage one of her twisted plan, whatever that might be.

Hitchcock perfected the "slow walk up the staircase" shot in *Psycho*; here (influence *number four*), Castle performs an identical sequence, Arless ascending the

stairs toward the camera, entering her bathroom and washing the blood from the blade—curiously, in view of what we will learn later on, the arm that holds the knife is a man's arm, not a woman's (a red-herring tossed in by the director to confuse an already confused audience, no doubt). Arless then confronts the family's old housekeeper Helga, played by Eugenie Leontovich; she's wheelchair-bound and mute after suffering a stroke, and Arless looks after her, a nurse of the type you *wouldn't* want around if you were housebound! "Adrims died tonight—screaminggggg!" Arless spits into Leontovich's creased face; the housekeeper can only rap desperately on the wheelchair arm with a gavel as she descends in a stair lift and forced to drink milk, Arless threatening to leave her. "Who would feed you? Put you to bed? You would dry up and die!" she yells at her terrified companion. Yep, this is one mysterious female with a boatload of mental problems, and they're only gonna get worse!

Patricia Breslin enters the fray as Miriam, the half-sister of Warren. He's returned from Denmark and is working in San Diego after the death of his surviving parent; they're both heirs to the family estate. Arless, so the fabricated story goes, was taken in as a child and classed as part of the family. Breslin owns a flower shop

and is busy romancing store owner Glenn Corbett (wasn't John Gavin a store owner in *Psycho*? Influence *number five*!). Arless drives into Solvang to fetch Leontovich's pill prescription after Dr. Alan Bunce has revealed that it was the housekeeper who delivered Warren, his father an abusive misogynist who wanted a male heir to inherit the family estate and fortune, not a female. Unseen, Arless enters Breslin's shop, smashes wedding figurines, wrecks a bridal wreath and, in a paroxysm of rage, rips the head off a model of a groom. Then, spotting a photo of Warren, she hurls the frame to the floor, breaking the glass. When Corbett discovers the damage, he's slugged over the head by Arless and woken by Warren, who has just come back from San Diego preparing to grab his $10,000,000 inheritance, when he reaches the age of 21 in two days' time.

It's a complex, murky brew that writer Robb White conjures up, not helped by the disturbing fact that Warren and Emily are never actually seen together; at one point, Arless enters Breslin's bedroom clutching a doll to her chest (remember that opening scene in 1948?); intrigued, Breslin watches her leave, go into her own room, strip down to black underwear and talk to Warren ("Warren darling, I'm back."), who answers in his distinctive, *deeper* voice (*Psycho* influence *number six*, as we shall later discover!), much to Breslin's puzzlement and disgust. Arless then denies ever being in Breslin's room. "You better see a doctor dear. You're imagining things," she coos to Breslin before viciously turning on her: "*I'll* take Warren his breakfast. If you stay in this house one more minute, I'm going to kill you." The blonde viper then announces that she and Warren were, in fact, married in Denmark some time ago but kept it secret. Police officer Gilbert Green, on the trail of Westerfield's killer (he's the Martin Balsam character from *Psycho*; influence *number seven*), questions Breslin over her name (given by Arless at the hotel), but bellboy Rust says Breslin doesn't fit the description of the lady he was wedded to for all of 60 seconds. The plot thickens by the minute! However, Arless is coming under suspicion, particularly as a sketch of her appears in the local papers under the headline "HOMICIDAL KILLER AT LARGE" and Leontovich's pill bottle is found on the florist's floor. "How can you

tell if a person is homicidal?" asks Corbett to Bunce. "Anybody could kill that didn't have an outlet for their hate," is the response, and Arless hates just about everyone in this picture, her old housekeeper rapping frantically on her wheelchair to no avail; she would love to spill the beans on this flaxen-haired monster and tell all concerned who she *really* is … but can't. Cinematographer Burnett Guffey composes many scenes in half-shadow to drum up an atmosphere of urban Gothic madness (*Homicidal* is a very dark film *per se*); when drifting through the roomy house, Arless' porcelain features and white attire resemble Edith Scob wandering through *her* house in high-necked white dress and mask in Georges Franju's *Eyes Without a Face* (was Castle also guided by the scary images of Scob in Franju's surgical masterpiece?), a disquieting effect heightening the general air of uneasiness when the nurse is around, an unreal, Barbie doll-type figure harboring terrible secrets known only to herself.

That long shiny blade, sharpened by a professional, is ready for the next kill. "It's a surgical knife. Doctors use it," the sadistic murderess says innocently to the handyman. "What do you use it for?" he asks. "Various things," she smiles, knowingly. Back inside the house, Arless, sick and tired of Leontovich's constant gavel-banging which has now, understandably, taken on a frantic edge, torments

the housekeeper to the point of frenzy, her face contorted in anger; she goes to stab the defenseless cripple but Bunce's unexpected arrival stops her dead in her tracks. When Bunce eventually leaves, wondering why Leontovich is so desperate to communicate with him (she's aware that, for her, death of a grisly kind awaits), Arless forces the old lady up the stairway (another Hitchcock-type reverse-zoom shot) and lunges at her neck with

the knife. Meanwhile, dogged Green has finally identified Arless as the killer, Rust recognizing the woman who slaughtered Westerfield from her photo, and he telephones Breslin at the flower shop with the grim news, Warren listening in a chilly silence. Breslin puts the phone down and Warren, distinctly agitated, informs her that he's off to the house pronto ("Do you think Emily's a cold-blooded murderess? Miriam! Answer me!"), fearing for Leontovich's life, ordering Breslin to wait in the car as they pull up outside.

To the sound of a rapidly beating heart, Castle then throws in his trademark gimmick, a 45-second Fright Break. In effect, audience members could exit the auditorium if too shaken to muster up enough courage to sit through the harrowing reveal. Apparently, about one per cent of patrons *did* leave the theater (or did they?), afterwards demanding a full refund on their ticket price, which basically wasn't forthcoming (and which Castle found less than amusing!). "Ten seconds more and we go into the house! You're a brave audience!" booms Castle and it's straight back to *Homicidal*'s tense, horrific (for 1961) climax. Breslin slowly approaches the darkened house (à la Vera Miles approaching the Bates Motel; influence *number eight*) and cautiously enters to see the alarming sight of Leontovich's wheelchair slowly descending via the lift,

Curiously, Helga towers above Emily as the ladies are locked in a stare-down contest that will ultimately end with one of the combatants dead.

the old lady's posture stiffly upright, her face expressionless; in silhouette, her head suddenly slumps forwards, parting company with the torso, rolling down the steps onto the floor. Breslin gapes in speechless horror, Arless appearing behind her, blade poised high in the air, eyes gleaming, ready to strike. "Warren! Warren!" screams Breslin, hoping for help. "I'm right here Miriam," gloats Arless, taking off her blonde wig and placing prosthetic teeth over her own, Breslin staring in disbelief. "Of course, I've always been Warren." Cutting her/his arm with the blade and drawing blood, Warren states that he'll claim to the police: "Emily attacked me. She tried to kill me. Emily was hopelessly insane. She escaped. She's gone—for good!" Grinning maliciously, she/he goes to sink the knife into Breslin, who's frozen to the spot in terror, when Bunce bursts in through the door; turning, the transgender killer walks quickly over to murder the doctor (aping Anthony Perkins' cross-dresser in *Psycho*'s final sequence; influence *number nine*) and is shot in the back by Breslin, slumping dead in the doorway.

Influence *number 10* is the psychiatric explanation, the truth behind the Warren/Emily split personality, similar to Simon Oakland's summing up of Anthony Perkins' Norman Bates in *Psycho*. Warren's

Jean Arless as she appears playing Warren

Karl (Glenn Corbett) and Miriam (Patricia Breslin) look concerned.

father would only leave his entire wealth to a son on his 21st birthday. When he died and if there wasn't a son Breslin, his eldest daughter, would inherit the fortune. A girl was delivered by Leontovich, the mother paying the housekeeper and Westerfield to falsify the records in the alternate identity scam, the birth certificate naming the girl as Warren, a boy; if the father found out, the female child would have been harmed or even killed. Warren, his mind unbalanced from masquerading as both girl and boy, had created Emily in Denmark in order to eliminate Westerfield, Leontovich (the two who knew about the deception) and Breslin, so that she/he could gain the inheritance. Breslin is now a very rich woman, much to Corbett's delight; he now gets the girl *and* the estate thrown in for good measure.

Considering the task of playing dual female/male roles, Castle had Arless cut her hair short and dyed brown, wear brown contact lenses, a blonde wig and fit large false teeth over her own; fitted appliances also altered the shape of her nose and mouth, Warren's voice dubbed throughout to make it lower in tone. Before the curtains close over the end credits, Arless appears as both Emily and Warren, bowing to the audience in appreciation. Denmark was frequently mentioned in the narrative as if it was the only country in the world at that time that legally performed operations on those of a transgender nature. *Time* may have raved about the film, but the *New York*

Times dismissed the production as a "dismal imitation of *Psycho*," another reviewer stating that Arless' performance was "embarrassing." Wrong on both counts: *Homicidal*, like *Psycho*, represents the early beginnings of what was to become the slasher genre that flourished throughout the 1970s/1980s, a seminal horror thriller that remains compelling over 50 years down the line. And why does Castle's slant on Hitchcock's trailblazer remain so watchable? The answer is Jean Arless. Arless is to *Homicidal* what Anthony Perkins was to *Psycho*. After decades spent in watching countless horror pictures featuring assorted deranged maniacs from all over the world, I cannot think of a single female in any one of them that matches her performance in this brilliant little picture (Tippi Hedren, another ice-cold blonde, is the exception in *Marnie*). And as a gauge to how mesmerizing Arless is, my wife (*not* a horror fanatic like her husband!) actually put down her puzzle book and watched the actress go through her predatory paces, totally absorbed in what this particular transgender, sadistic blonde psycho dressed all in white was up to, as you will be, too. I rest my case. In my book, fright merchant William Castle's *Homicidal* is an underrated, low-budget, B-horror movie classic, highlighting the director's often overlooked skills behind the lens; like *Psycho* it has become, over the years, an influence with horror filmmakers itself, albeit on a more modest scale. Accept no substitute!

MIDNIGHT MARQUEE BOOK REVIEW

BY GARY J. SVEHLA

Riccardo Freda: The Life and Works of a Born Filmmaker by Roberto Curti; McFarland www.mcfarlandpub. com; Order 800-253-2187; 367 pages (7 by 10 inches); Softcover $45.00

Riccardo Freda is credited with inventing the Italian horror movie (although he directed movies of differing genres, including historic dramas, pepla, adventure films and swashbucklers), making *I Vampiri* on a bet with two producers, Ermanno Donati and Luigi Carpentieri, that he could write the script in one day and film the production in only two weeks. But a third producer, Goffredo Lombardo, bankrolled his share of the project, a very low-budget production. Freda stated that he sometimes made movies simply as an exercise to prove that various projects could be made on time and on budget, more as a mental exercise than an artistic expression.

As author Curti makes clear, Freda shied away from making horror films similar to others being made at the time in the United States (*Return of Dracula*, *I Was a Teenage Werewolf* and *Blood of Dracula*) and Mexico (*The Vampire* and *The Vampires Coffin*). Freda was a fan of the offbeat horror film classics of the past, with Murnau's *Faust* and Carl Dreyer's *Vampyr* being two of his favorites. Instead of imitating the Gothic Universal template with creepy Bela Lugosi descending a decaying castle's steps, Freda's vampire in *I Vampiri* resembled Countess Báthory of Countess Dracula fame. In his movie, the Duchess du Grand hides her face behind a dark veil and transforms (in an eerie Jekyll/ Hyde nod) into the beautiful alter ego Giséle (played by the lovely Gianna Maria Canale) by using the blood of female sacrificial virgins. Unlike stereotypical mythical vampires that bite the necks of their victims with animalistic fangs, here the Duchess has an army of criminals who use chloroform to render victims unconscious, where they are transported to sterile medical labs where their blood can be drained out of their bodies. As Freda

is quoted by Curti, "Horror and reality nowadays march side by side." Syringes in *I Vampiri* become images of horror, the supernatural being rejected and replaced by the subgenre of medical horror that would become a popular Euro-horror staple in such movies as *Seddok* and *Eyes Without a Face*.

Roberto Curti draws a parallel between *I Vampiri* and Poe's short story *The Fall of the House of Usher*, where the decaying castle interiors parallel the vampire as played by Canale. Just as the castle is literally decaying and crumbling before our eyes, so is the youth and vibrance conveyed by the sensual Canale, as she reverts to the weak and also decaying Duchess who becomes old and brittle before our eyes, needing a new influx of fresh virgin blood.

Curti does a wonderful job of comparing the original Italian print to the bastardized (and partially re-filmed and reedited) American version of the movie, citing how the Americanized version added some nudity and a more sexual overtone. But Freda's vision of vampirism was unique and modern and created a new Gothic vision for the horror genre, one that would proliferate for decades to come.

Unfortunately *I Vampiri* died at the box-office, based in part upon the erroneous assumption that Italians could not make good horror movies, so a few years later, Riccardo Freda billed himself as American-sounding director Robert Hampton (misspelled Hamton in the film's credits) in hopes of attracting a wider audience for his first science fiction film, *Caltiki il mostro immortale*. At the time Hammer Film Productions had a hit on their hands with *The Quatermass Xperiment* (which focused on an astronaut returning to Earth infected by an alien presence, who slowly morphs into a blob-like creature). Also, the American independent production *The Blob* made that type of faceless monster a virtual sensation across the cinematic world. Science fiction magazines were appearing on the racks in Italy and became popular rapidly. So even though Freda did not like science fiction at all, he wanted to use *Caltiki* as a launching board for his cinematographer/special effects director Mario Bava to become a director on his own. Freda worked on the film until the final two days of shooting and then abruptly left the set, supposedly over a dispute of money with the film's producer. According to director Luigi Cozzi and Mario Bava, Freda gave simply too much credit to Bava, Bava claiming that he did the photography and special effects including miniature sequences and flame-thrower scenes. Both Cozzi and Bava give full credit to Freda as the director of the movie, even though revisionist history makes *Caltiki* seem to be a Mario Bava-directed production. Bava biographer Tim Lucas and *Caltiki* scriptwriter Massimo De Rita support the claim that Bava directed over 50 percent of the movie and deserves at least an equal credit with Freda. At this point in time the truth will never be known.

Curti goes into detail explaining the magnificent job that Bava performed creating the impressive special effects, on a budget. And this does not only include the glob-monster Caltiki but also all the glass mattes depicting the Mayan landscape with fantastic depth of field photography,

Riccardo Freda
The Life and Works of a Born Filmmaker

Roberto Curti

incorporating shots of an erupting volcano. And of course, even though done on the cheap, the climax and finale featuring Caltiki slinking through the house, trying to absorb mother and kid, is classic monster B-moviemaking at its best.

Freda directed a few other horror movies amid a career of contrasting genres, including *L'orribile segreto del Dr. Hichcock* (*The Horrible Dr. Hichcock*) and *Lo spettro* (*The Ghost*). Surprisingly, the rise of the Italian horror film was met with enthusiasm and sales in America, while apathy ruled in the homeland of Italy. Yet Freda forged ahead with *L'orribile segreto del Dr. Hichcock*, based upon a script written by veteran horror writer Ernesto Gastaldi, with a story influenced by both the work of author Edgar Allan Poe and cinema auteur Alfred Hitchcock, one that dealt with the taboo subject of necrophilia. Curti reveals the on-set working style of Freda in this lengthy chapter. First, realizing the potential for American success, the entire cast and crew donned Americanized names in hopes of appealing to this huge foreign market. Riccardo Freda once again became Robert Hampton, but it seemed the crew had a little fun in making the transformation from Italian to American. For instance, set designer Franco Fumagalli became Frank Smokecocks,

The candle of his lust burnt brightest in the shadow of the grave!

THE HORRIBLE DR. HICHCOCK

TECHNICOLOR

BARBARA STEELE · ROBERT FLEMYNG

a literal translation of his Italian surname. Unfortunately, star Barbara Steele, who took a 10 day leave from the set of Fellini's *8 ½*, delivered what Curti describes as her most conventional performance in any Italian horror picture, her role accented by becoming "the designated victim, all wide-eyed stupor, faints and cries of terror."

Director Freda claimed (as he usually did) that the movie was shot in two weeks, while film scholars Alan Upchurch and Tim Lucas claimed the movie was shot in 14 days (thus making it almost a three week shoot, as there was no shooting on weekends). In order to meet the deadline, Freda called Gastaldi to the set and told the screenwriter that he needed to omit 10 pages from the script and would Gastaldi agree. Gastaldi told Freda to do whatever he wanted, but the omitted pages explained characters motivation. According to Gastaldi, "The film became incomprehensible, but people loved it."

Freda, according to Curti, never did more than three takes on a scene, which obviously did not leave much time to focus on performances. According to Marcello Avallone, "He just didn't give a shit about actors." To offer proof to the statement comes the following anecdote about Barbara Steele sometimes arriving late to the set. During a heated argument with Steele, the producer Ermanno Donati slapped Steele and she left the set in tears. Freda was not the least bit flustered

and announced to Marcello Avallone that Steele's scene would be filmed … and that Avallone would be playing Steele! At the time Avallone was very thin, so they dressed him in Steele's costume and he did the entire sequence in long shot. "So, this is how much Riccardo cared about actors." Cast members Silvano Tranquilli and Harriet White confirmed the director's "autocratic attitude" and, as Tranquilli stated, "was easily irritated and was explosive at the slightest provocation." White referred to Freda as "an ugly little man."

When *The Horrible Dr. Hichcock* was released in the United States, the film was initially severely trimmed and featured a different edit, clocking in at a mere 76 minutes. Many direct cuts now appeared as dissolves. Thus Freda's meticulous direction was compromised, resulting in the U.S. cut "spoiling his pace and atmosphere." Also some unnecessary lines of dialogue were added to the dubbed American version and the translation of Ernesto Gastaldi's script was "badly written, awkward and unfaithful."

Finally Freda's *Lo spettro* (released as *The Ghost* in the U.S.) appeared as the result of Freda's frustration with continuing to make adventure films as a hired hand, his name not appearing on the credits and the directorial credit going to various American directors, whose work Freda considered

inferior. At least while working in the horror genre he could allow his love for "the darker realm" and love for authors such as Poe and Stevenson to take center stage. For this production Freda co-wrote the screenplay with writer Robert Davidson (aka Oreste Biancoli) so he would have a little more control over the story and thus the overall look of the film. Once again the main character is named "Hitchcock" (not Hichcock), but a different actor plays him and the time and setting have been changed, so this is in no way a sequel to *The Horrible Dr. Hichcock*. But most likely producers thought they could cash in by using the "Hitchcock" name.

Of course the main star is Barbara Steele, who commits a more subtle and complex performance than her boilerplate character from the last film. Curti does a good job of defining such subtlety and complexity in his analysis. "Scene after scene, she goes from one extreme to the next: affectionate love and savage hatred, methodical scheming and irrational terror, utmost cruelty and willful self-destruction." The author carefully defines the film's effective lighting and color palette and how both create a "distinct dramatic flair." Curti notes how characters are "usually lit from below, their bodies protect towering, menacing shadows that look very much like the expression of their pitch black inner self, and their fea-

HORROR... SHARP AS A RAZOR'S EDGE!

Written in Blood!

THE BLACK SIGN OF DEATH IS ON THIS HOUSE!

MAGNA Pictures PRESENTS

The GHOST

TECHNICOLOR

tures are distorted, as in the apparition of Hitchcock's ghost …"

This is my type of biography. Just as much space and energy goes into recounting the details of Riccardo Freda's life and development as an artist as goes into detailed analysis of each individual film and what makes it work (or what fails to make it work). I have focused on his horror output, since our magazine is focused on the horror film genre. But it must be mentioned that the complete spectrum of all his cinematic endeavors are covered. For any fan of Italian cinema, Roberto Curti's book comes highly recommended.

After such insightful and marvelously interesting backgrounds are laid out, the bulk of the text is devoted to "The Films," presented alphabetically, within each chronological year, the format beginning with complete cast and credits listing, a brief synopsis and the bulk of the space devoted to insightful analysis and detailed production background. As is *de rigor* these days, each film discussion ends with notes and documentation of sources.

Italian Gothic Horror Films, 1957-1969 by Roberto Curti; McFarland www.mcfarlandpub.com; Order 800-253-2187; 220 pages (7 by 10 inches); Softcover $35.00

Featuring a *Foreword* by Italian screenwriter Ernesto Gastaldi, who remembers his career as one of the originators of Italian Gothic horror cinema, beginning as writer and assistant director of *The Vampire and the Ballerina*, moving on to werewolves with *Werewolf in a Girls' Dormitory* and then writing *The Horrible Dr. Hichcock* and *The Whip and the Body* (directed by Mario Bava). Other Gothics followed, including *Terror in the Crypt*, and soon the giallo genre opened up with Gastaldi writing the screenplay for *Libido*.

In his *Preface*, Roberto Curti defines the "Italian Gothic horror" genre as existing from 1957, the year Riccardo Freda's *I Vampiri* was released, through 1966, but he decided to expand his analysis through 1969, including a few Gothic Spaghetti Westerns and tracing the genre through the loosening of morals and relaxing of censorship, which occurred after Italian political and social turmoil in 1968. Curti includes a detailed and well-defined definition of the genre, which revolves around 10 points, presented most interestingly.

Curti contends that the vioence in Mario Bava's *Black Sunday* outdoes Hammer horror, as a nail is about to be driven through the eye of this undead victim.

Before he presents an analysis of all the Italian Gothics, he submits an *Introduction: Gothic, Italian Style*, where he attempts to place the Italian Gothic period into a historical frame, which traces the genre's roots all the way back to silent cinema and references pivotal influences through films released during the 1930s and 1940s. Even Gothic literature is cited as a major precursor. Gothic influences of the peplum genre are cited. However, Curti cites 1958's Hammer classic *Horror of Dracula* as the mover and shaker of the Italian Gothic movement. Curti feels the Italian Gothic genre marked a discovery of sexuality in Italian cinema, which furthered the dualistic conception of women, demonstrating their new complexity. He feels the loosening of censorship led to the predominance of eroticism on screen, a very essential aspect of Italian Gothic cinema.

Let us take a look at how Curti approaches two important examples of Italian Gothic cinema, beginning with Mario Bava's classic *Black Sunday* (*La maschera del demonio*). Twelve pages (including three photos/posters) are devoted to the discussion of this landmark Italian Gothic. Curti opens his discussion by focusing on the iconic opening sequence where an iron mask (with spikes) is hammered onto the

face of witch Barbara Steele, Bava showing the impact and aftermath of such violence that the author feels marked a quantum leap in the representation of violence in movies. Curti compares such a raw and arousing sequence to similar cinematic violence in movies made roughly around the same time (the gruesome monster portrayed in *Curse of Frankenstein*; the horrible disintegration of the vampire king in *Horror of Dracula*; Sir Hugo being torn apart by the hound from Hell at the start of *Hound of the Baskervilles*; the suggestive—but generally not shown—slaughter of the naked Janet Leigh in *Psycho*; and various violent atrocities shown in *Horrors of the Black Museum*, *Circus of Horrors* and *Peeping Tom*). Curti illustrates the violence in the Bava film and shows how "Italian horror exceeded by far Hammer's timid use of gore." His example is that "the stake was driven off-screen into the vampire's heart in Fisher's film, and the director allowed the audience just a quick shot of the aftermath, with the wood already lodged in the chest …" In contrast *Black Sunday* shows "the viewers were confronted with the sight of a long nail that penetrates the undead's eye. All this happens in close-up, without cuts." However, Curti does admit that Bava was definitely

An ugly vampire and beautiful victims abound in *The Vampire and the Ballerina*.

influenced by the Hammer classic with parallel sequences: the carriage ride, the crucifix that burns the vampire's forehead and similar characters such as the savant priest who helps the hero defeat the witch.

Curti reminds us that, just like *Horror of Dracula*, the image of the vampire is highly sexually charged but in this instance illustrating the power and dominance of the woman. "Asa's power is also based on the idea of control, due to the woman's irresistible sexual lure." Therefore, Kruvajan's vampirization has openly erotic undertones. "The camera focuses on Asa's motionless yet pulsating body, her heaving breasts and hands crawling on the edges of the sarcophagus and twitching. It is a language of the body which refers to sexuality, and which no man can escape."

Interestingly, Curti is able to show how individuals define spatial coordinates in Bava's universe, moving from one place to another. "Castle Vajda, the inn, the cemetery and the crypt where Asa's body is found are part of a microcosm where inner distances are constantly changing, stretching or contracting depending on who is traveling along." Thus the journey one character makes from point A

to B might be longer, shorter than the exact same journey another character takes. Curti reminds us of the great care that Bava took when filming the movement of a character journeying from one point to another and how he made such traveling sequences so dramatic. "… examples of this tactic are … the long tracking shot backwards that precedes the innkeeper's daughter's path from the inn to the stable. In the latter shot, the camera is placed almost at ground level, so as to frame the little girl from bottom to top, thus emphasizing her loneliness in the surrounding environment and exacerbating the passage from a familiar dimension to a menacing one, through the gradual disappearance of the inn behind her."

It must be noted that sometimes, not often, Curti's *Black Sunday* analysis becomes slightly pretentious and overblown, as if he were lecturing on a university campus.

But such academic excess is kept to a minimum and Curti's insights are never less than interesting. What impresses me the most is that even when Curti is writing about such oft-written films as *Black Sunday*, he always finds something new to focus on and not resort to the same old analysis. Curti has the insight to find something fresh and new in every film on which he writes.

Secondly, let us examine Curti's coverage of *The Vampire and the Ballerina*, one of the more underrated examples of Italian Gothic, but obviously a film with which Curti is not enamored. Five pages (including one poster reproduction) are devoted to the discussion of this less than classic Italian Gothic, but the film remains a favorite of baby boomers who remember seeing it on TV decades ago. Curtis augments his discussion of the film with anecdotes from screenwriter Ernesto Gastaldi's published autobiography, Gastaldi's reflections adding wit and humor.

Based upon the worldwide success of *Horror of Dracula*, the Italian Gothic film industry used the Hammer classic as its template for success. Screenwriter Ernesto Gastaldi was told that the screenplay for *The Vampire and the Ballerina* had to have a

bit of eroticism, a bit of sentiment, a hint of vulgarity and a happy ending … and deal with vampirism. The original script, written by Giampaolo Callegaris, was rejected, and Gastaldi and Renato Polselli and Giuseppe Pellegrini did the rewrite. Even with low-budget Italian genre movies, politics reigned supreme when it came to casting. Walter Brandi was cast as the vampire, and the vampire's friend was a big man from Tuscany (Gino Turini), who got the part because he put up some of the production money. French actress Hélène Rémy was cast as the vampire's victim, because the film was to be a French co-production. Tina Gloriani was signed to play the heroine because she was the director's current lover, and the "hottie vampire's lover" was played by Maria Luisa Rolando, "a big-busted protégé of the general manager."

Interesting, the skeletons that decorate the vampire's crypt were supposedly real skeletons, but director Renato Polselli and production manager Umberto Borsato had to work out a deal with a cemetery undertaker, who wanted to sell a skeleton for 300,000 lire. "This is a rich man's skeleton," Polselli argued, telling his production manager the bones cost too much. "Look, he's even got golden teeth!" It seems the production company held out for a poorer man's skeleton.

Curti defines the movie as "a mixed bag," simply because none of the creative minds knew how to develop an effective vampire film. Unlike *I Vampiri*, which managed to marry the 19th century concept of Gothic and modern sensibility (placing an ultra-modern laboratory inside the cellar of a decaying Gothic castle), *The Vampire and the Ballerina* came up short when it attempted the same result. Curti notes how Polselli once again follows the template established by *Horror of Dracula* by reimagining specific scenes from the Hammer classic and spending ample time explaining the vampire mythos in detail, for those unfamiliar. However, Curti notes problems resulting from the film developing "its own internal logic and coherence," which both "innovates within the genre's trappings" and creates "mind-boggling reversal of clichés." For example, the male vampire "drives a stake through the heart of the woman he just vampirized, because, as he claims, I am and must be the master of

my own world." Losing the subtle sexuality established by Hammer, Hélène Rémy displays obvious sexual pleasure after she has been bitten in the neck and "caresses her own breast."

It is amazing to be reminded just how many Italian Gothic horror movies appeared in the United States during this time period (many redubbed and reedited productions released directly to the drive-in theater circuit or kiddy Saturday afternoon matinees at smaller neighborhood theaters). Roberto Curti's book does a marvelous job of reminding us of the pleasures created by such genre endeavors and his insight gives the reader detailed analysis of which productions rose above, which ones stood as mediocre testaments to greater productions and which ones sank under their own creative weight. Since far too little has been written about Italian Gothic cinema, this book is one to own and return to … often.

Italian Gothic Horror Films, 1970-1979 by Roberto Curti, McFarland www.mcfarlandpub.com; Order 800-253-2187; 256 pages (7 by 10 inches); Softcover $39.95

Even though Roberto Curti defined the era of the Italian Gothic horror film as existing between the years 1957 to 1969 in his first volume, here we trace the evolution of Italian Gothic cinema as it morphed during the 1970s. In his *Introduction* to this second volume Curti explains: "The history of the Italian Gothic horror cinema in the 1970s is one of dissipation and contamination. The main characteristics that made the films produced in the early 1960s a tight and rigidly circumscribed subgenre were diluted, hybridized and contaminated by outside influences, resulting in much looser boundaries and in a variety of approaches to the Gothic canon. As a consequence the genre's identity became much more volatile and multi-faceted …" Curti goes on to explain that the main factor for such change was sex. Where earlier Gothic horror was defined by suggestive eroticism and mild nudity, such subtlety was soon to be thrown out the window. Movies made after 1968 saw the relaxation of censorship, which

gave way to total female nudity and simulated sex on the big screen. Another influence affecting Italian Gothic cinema was the appearance and popularity of "adults-only comics that flooded newsstands" and pushed the limits of "nudity, perversion and violence." Another factor in the mutation of Italian Gothic cinema was the rise of the giallo, "resulting in a number of crossovers that borrowed the black-gloved killers and creative murder scenes from Dario Argento's films and transplanted them into typical Gothic scenarios, and even played on the alleged supernatural nature of the murderer. As a result, the line between giallo and Gothic is often blurred."

For me the era of the late 1950s and the entirety of the 1960s resulted in Italy's greatest Gothic horror films ever produced, and while the decade of the 1970s still contains a few pivotal horror movies, the list of great ones is far reduced. However, because of the increased amount of movies produced, yet with far fewer released in the U.S.A. theatrically (and far more movies released directly to home video and television), this second volume in Curti's Italian Gothic series means we have far more films to discover.

Curti's coverage of two of the more familiar titles (not necessarily the best) illustrates his style of analysis. First comes

ONLY THE MONSTER SHE MADE COULD SATISFY HER STRANGE DESIRES!

Lady FRANKENSTEIN

Starring JOSEPH COTTEN · SARAH BAY · Mickey Hargitay · Paul Muller
Produced by Harry Cushing · Directed by Mel Wells · METROCOLOR A New World Pictures Release

The catch-line and iconic movie poster art helped to make *Lady Frankenstein* a cult favorite for Roger Corman's New World Pictures.

Lady Frankenstein (covered in roughly five pages with two illustrations). Once again the formatting of cast, credits and synopsis is repeated from the earlier volume. American actor/director (*The Undead* and *Little Shop of Horrors*) Mel Welles was living in Italy, working as a voice actor, dubbing foreign films into English, when he was approached by an American expatriate Harry Cooke Cushing about directing a movie he was producing, starring Italian beauty Rosalba Neri, with whom he was supposedly in love/lust. Since Neri, besides being a beautiful starlet, was very comfortable appearing nude in movies, this aspect made her one of the country's most sought after "erotic bombshells." The good-looking Cushing, who pursued

and was continually rejected by Neri, had money to burn and lived a fantasy life (never required to work a day in his life) thinking that if he produced a movie starring his object of passion Neri, that she would suddenly respond to his advances. Welles was happy as a pig in shit: "So here, in my lap, he dropped the script and money to do it. What a windfall." Unfortunately, after running around prepping the production for months, Welles discovered that Cushing did not actually own the script he was peddling. Former peplum actor Brad Harris owned the rights to the script. So Welles and friend Edward Di Lorenzo (who was a television writer who wrote scripts for *The Wild, Wild West, Space: 1999* and *Miami Vice*) knocked out a brand new script in three weeks, supposedly based upon the comic book story *For the Love of Frankenstein*, which appeared in *Vampirella* #4 (April 1969). Thus *Lady Frankenstein*, a movie conceived and filmed in Italy, was actually the product of American money and ingenuity. The cast included Joseph Cotton, Mickey Hargitay and Paul Muller, besides the main attraction, Rosalba Neri, who takes over as the mad scientist after Joseph Cotton's violent end. By casting a sexually charged female in an otherwise male role allowed Mel Welles to claim he was making a feminist movie, with Neri uttering such dialogue of empowerment as, "I may be a woman, but I'm primarily a doctor!" In the movie Neri's older assistant Charles (Paul Muller) is so gob-smacked by her that he willingly allows her to use his brain to transplant (paralleling the actual relationship between Harry Cooke Cushing and Rosalba Neri in real life).

Rosalba Neri admitted that she traveled around with director Mel Welles, his wife and children, but never thought of him as a great director. She felt that talented cinematographer Riccardo Pallottini, who worked alone, solving all the creative problems, was totally deserving of all the credit for any creative highpoints the movie achieved. However, Mel Welles was insistent about having realistic special effects, especially for one sequence where Neri was supposed to place probes into a large beaker with the brain in it, causing a sparking effect. After reminding his effects crew for days about the required mechanics, he was told the night before the shoot that the crew was not ready, and besides, they needed $300 additional to create what they needed. In disgust Welles went out to the local tobacco store and bought half a dozen pinwheel firecrackers and concocted the shot, which cost him $1.80 and worked just fine.

Roger Corman's New World Productions released the film in the U.S., selling the movie based on a great tagline ("Only the Monster she made could satisfy her strange desires") and an even better full color movie poster. However, "Corman cut over 10 minutes, shortening or eliminating no less than 20 scenes" to get to the action that much faster and thus eliminate talky exposition. Of course the film became a cult favorite in the United States.

Curti's coverage of Dario Argento's *Suspiria* is quite insightful (covered in almost seven pages with one illustration), although a tad too pretentious for its own good at times. Dario Argento and Daria Nicolodi (the love of his life, even though they never married) were anticipating the birth of daughter-to-be Asia and wanted to create a dark fairy-tale to tell her when she was grown up. Argento reflected on Walt Disney's *Snow White and the Seven Dwarfs* that haunted him as a child. At the same time Nicolodi remembered a sinister story her grandmother told her about the time, as a child, that she was enrolled at a musical academy (to improve her piano playing) located between Switzerland and Germany. Daria Nicolodi maintains that she wrote the script for *Suspiria* based upon the transcription of her grandmother's tale, but that Dario Argento was eventually given co-writer credit. It was Nicolodi's idea to even use the Thomas De Quincey occult book *Suspiria de Profundis*, located in the library of their home, as the basis for the movie's title. When filming began in mid-1976, many sequences from the script had to be altered or dropped, such as a complex introduction sequence when the character Suzy arrives at the entrance of the academy and meets all the other major characters, which Argento intended to stage "like a Busby Berkeley choreography." More unfortunate, Daria Nicolodi, who had been promised the starring role of Suzy, was replaced by American actress Jessica Harper for purposes of distribution to American markets, and this caused a major fracture between Argento and Nicolodi and "resulted in a temporary separation."

Suzy (Jessica Harper) is attacked by swooping terror in Dario Argento's *Suspiria*.

Argento was clever in the manner in which the production was created, having the musical group Goblin pre-record the music for the movie before filming begun, so that the thunderous score could be played on set to create a horrific mood for the cast and crew. The Technicolor photography was enhanced when Argento decided to use old Kodak low sensitivity film, which required the sets to be flooded with light. For close ups the cinematographer "filtered the light through velvet panels that lit the actors' faces with dense color stains." This film was then processed in a specific manner so as to emphasize blue, red, green and gold. Since *Suspiria* marked Argento's first supernatural horror movie after working exclusively as a giallo director, he wanted to leave his visual mark by establishing something brand new for the genre. "With *Suspiria*, Argento clothed Italian Gothic in a new style, bringing it to an unexpected commercial and artistic rebirth, and developed an irrational dimension where everything … contributes to the construction of … a self-sufficient universe."

Author Curti establishes that *Suspiria* creates a contrast between two sets of in-dividuals. First we have the new student, a classic ballet dancer, "a soul voted to artistic expression," Suzy. "She is a perfect damsel in distress, virginal and out of time, and with the same morbid sensibility as an Edgar Allan Poe heroine." In contrast, we have the academy's teachers. "The teachers … are elderly and severe spinsters, embodiments of the harassing aunt in *Jane Eyre*, and the climax revolves around the encounter with an octogenarian authority figure."

Director Argento "remained faithful to his original idea of making a movie peopled with little girls" (at first he intended them to be between eight to 10 years old), but he had to change their chronological age even though he still made them act as children. As Argento stated: "The girls speak naively, they are scary, they make faces and don't know sex." To further enhance the concept of young adult females as children, Argento had the set designer create oversized objects such as "huge doors with higher handles." Another student Sara piles up her luggage as a child might; instead of putting the larger suitcase on the bottom, she places the larger piece on top of smaller piec-

THE WEREWOLF FILMOGRAPHY
300+ Movies
BRYAN SENN

es, thus creating an unbalanced pile, as might a child. As noted, Suzy's killing of the elder witch allows her to become an adult. Curti reveals that Argento created a female-centric hive where "the male presence is secondary if not superfluous. The males are … either asexual …, foolish and monstrous servants … or eunuchs."

Suspiria became the fifth highest grossing film in Italy that year and did very well overseas around the world. This created the dual cinematic universe for future Argento productions: giallo or supernatural horror, often alternating film genres.

This second volume of Italian *Gothic Horror Films, 1970-1979* might not feature the most recognizable Italian Gothics as Roberto Curti's first volume did, but that might not be a bad thing. Certainly the non-Italian reader will most likely learn

more about the genre from reading a book featuring more films awaiting his or her discovery. But for any fan who purchased the earlier volume, it only makes sense to possess the second (and potentially a third and beyond?). Curti's analysis is intelligent and he includes marvelous anecdotes, quotes from other sources and detailed production details. With so much that has already been written about American Gothic horror, isn't it about time that Euro-horror be explored as carefully?

The Werewolf Filmography by Bryan Senn; McFarland www.mcfarlandpub.com; Order 800-253-2187; 408 pages (8.5 by 11 inches); Hardcover $49.95

Isn't it amazing that over 300 werewolf movies have been made to date, but

perhaps what is not amazing is that many of the modern ones are not worth the film or hard drives they were created upon. But we must thank author Bryan Senn for compiling the definitive A-Z guide with so much wit and insight. Each title analysis demonstrates that Senn watched (recently before writing) and thought deeply about the film; some entries are longer or shorter than others, but every title is worthy of all the space devoted or lack of space not devoted. The book is broken down into the following chapters: *Introduction*; *The Films*; *Pseudowolves*; *Other Were-Beasts*; *Appendix A: Film Chronology*; *Appendix B: Film Series* and *Subsets*; *Bibliography*; and *Index*.

In Senn's *Introduction* he reveals his surprise at the sheer number of werewolf movies produced, citing the incredible fact that more than *half* of all werewolf films have been released since the turn of the Millennium. As Senn admits, "Quality werewolf films are definitely in the minority, with the subgenre loaded with subpar specimens." Yet Senn wisely feels that the cultural importance of metaphoric movies that "present the germ of an intriguing idea about our savage selves" warrants the creation of such a comprehensive tome. Senn feels that the recent resurgent in werewolf movies can be attributed to one of the great themes in horror cinema: randomness, or being in the wrong place at the wrong time and bad things happening to good people. The werewolf movie can be seen through many different lenses: the psychological, the sociological, the anthropological and the ecological. Filmmaker James Isaac, speaking of his 2006 film *Sleepwalkers*, asserts: "The werewolf mythos encapsulates the notion of nature vs. nurture, the conflict between our inner, animalistic selves and the behavioral restraint thrust upon us by the society we have constructed." Interestingly, Senn brings up the fact that the werewolf film might be the best example to explore a significant horror cinema trope: fear of the "Other" or those who are different from us. But Senn feels that ultimately the appeal of werewolf cinema comes in the form of our attraction to and fear of the predator. For nearly two million years man has been the prey in fear of other animals, which might come out of the darkness and stalk them, viewing them as "meat." Only recently, through development of intellect and sociability, has man risen to the top of the food chain, evolving from *Homo praeda* ("Man the fearful") to *Homo necans* ("Man the killer") … thus creating a "merger" of both. We sometimes think that a child's fear of the dark is irrational, but based upon our evolutionary past, the fear of predators attacking from the darkness was a very real feeling. And the world of werewolves plays right into this fear. The evolution of storytelling has been the essential way in which we manage such fear, turning dangerous animals into "monsters, gods, benefactors and even role models." Senn continues to develop such analysis even further, and such insight into the mythology of the werewolf is quite probing. Furthermore, Senn goes into a historical examination of lycanthropy and the earliest appearance of the term "werewolf." This allows Senn to closely examine the evolution of the concept of lycanthropy and how it came to be and how it evolved. In this well-developed *Introduction*, Senn offers a brief overview of werewolf cinema and traces its development. This then leads into a discussion of the werewolf as potentially a psychological disease and perhaps not only an actual physical transformation. Finally, Senn lays out the parameters for what is included and not included in the volume, citing the concept that some sort of transformation establishes the most important aspect for inclusion. But, for Senn, many others exist.

Once again a chronological discussion of individual movies becomes the heart and soul of the book, some obviously discussed in more detail than others. But just so the potential reader gets an idea of Senn's analytical style, let us examine how Senn sees a few specific examples of lycancinema.

Obviously, Universal's *The Wolf Man* is a pivotal example and here the film is covered in almost three pages with one illustration (remember, this book is size 8.5 by 11 inches and the font size is quite small; baby boomers beware). Senn devotes about four to six lines to document the major names in both cast and credits (as by this point in time we can approach the IMDb and other online sources to get complete cast and credits list). A brief synopsis is worked into Senn's review (here one 16-line paragraph does the job).

Quite properly Senn declares, "This is the one," establishing this 1941 classic

(more so than the six year earlier *Werewolf of London*) as the instigator of the werewolf movie genre and the film that inspired other studios to produce similar cinematic examples. Senn creates a hierarchy of creative talent most responsible for *The Wolf Man*'s success: screenwriter Curt Siodmak, make-up artist Jack P. Pierce and actor Lon Chaney, Jr. "stand at the head, heart and soul of *The Wolf Man*." The next tier includes director George Waggner, set designer Jack Otterson, actors Claude Rains and Maria Ouspenskaya and John P. Fulton's marvelous lap-dissolve transformations.

Senn states that Curt Siodmak's approach was a more psychological approach to the concept of lycanthropy, "keeping his protagonist's transformations subjective by showing them only through Larry's eyes." Senn notes that in Siodmak's original draft of the script, the actual werewolf was not seen for most of the picture, something that did not make Universal's monster-centric staff very happy (and forced a change of showing the werewolf more often). As Senn notes, Siodmak had the opportunity 10 years later of re-crafting this more-subtle approach of human to animal transformation in the inferior *Bride of the Gorilla* (which he wrote and directed). In developing a scenario, Siodmak believed " … for me it had to contain a theme, a point of view,

opening an avenue of thought, which might induce the public to think." And Senn notes that Siodmak unconsciously constructed a Greek tragedy where "the gods tell man his fate, and he cannot escape it." Whenever the moon rises, Larry Talbot (Lon Chaney, Jr.) knows that he must kill, and he is powerless to resist the will of fate. Also at the heart of the script is the conflict between science and superstition, where Sir John (Rains) and the local doctor explain lycanthropy "as a variety of schizophrenia." When Talbot seeks solace from a stern father, Sir John tells him, "I do believe that most anything can happen to a man—in his *own mind*." According to Senn, the film's final impact and lasting power comes from "the tragic consequences of rationality succumbing to (and literally beating to death) the Unknown." Senn reminds us just to look at Rains' "horrified, confused and achingly pitiable reaction to having killed his own son [and that this] … hammers home the horror of rationality's failure."

Jack Pierce's iconic werewolf make-up for *The Wolf Man*—which he evolved from his original makeup for Henry Hull from the earlier *Werewolf of London*, less wolf based and more human oriented—became the template for cinematic werewolves for the next four decades.

Senn details inconsistencies in what Talbot is wearing just before his first were-

Bill (Christopher Stone) turns into a werewolf and lets the beast out, by having sex with a woman, Marsha, not his wife.

wolf transformation and his first appearance in full make-up in the fog-shrouded woods. Apparently the production's continuity person was snoozing and the editor did not notice the change in wardrobe.

Senn ends his coverage of *The Wolf Man* by including the sources for all the quotes used in his coverage of this iconic werewolf movie. And the use of such quotes does enliven the overall discussion.

For our second film, I wanted to move from the Universal classics of old and include a more modern werewolf movie, to contrast. So I selected Joe's Dante's *The Howling* (appearing slightly over three pages with one illustration). Senn immediately establishes the fact that the Rob Bottin werewolf make-up for his "Big Bad Wolves" made the now formerly quaint man in yak hair (that *The Wolf Man* made the template for decades) obsolete. Senn considers *The Howling* to be "one of the most well-constructed werewolf movies of all time," due to "its multi-layered script" by John Sayles, its technical adeptness (mainly because of Rob Bottin's "groundbreaking effects work") and overall entertainment value (due to the "deft and slyly humorous direction by Joe Dante"). What appears to impress Senn the most is the fact that the film stands as one of the most "insightful" werewolf movies ever made,

"with ideas and issues writhing beneath its skin like a lycanthrope waiting to burst forth from its human shell."

Senn establishes that sexuality (as well as violence) plays a very important role in *The Howling*, "just as it does in nature." Such a concept is personified "in the figure of the wild, untamed Marsha … sexuality sits side-by-side with lycanthropy." Married Bill, once he transforms into a werewolf, rushes to the moonlit forest to have sex with Marsha, who also has changed into her wolf self. "Giving in to one's primal urges … results in the emergence of his inner beast." Senn states that sex, as much as violence, is linked to lycanthropy. "Our animal natures are not merely comprised of bestial violence but equally of unbridled sexuality." Senn rightfully claims that sexuality, as much as lycanthropy, breaks up the relationship between Bill and Karen and forces him into the arms of she-wolf Marsha.

Director Dante, a film fanatic as Senn notes, fills the movie with referential in-jokes, such as placing a copy of Alan Ginsberg's *Howl!* or a can of *Wolf Chili* in the background, having Disney's *Three Little Pigs* cartoon play on television and naming characters after earlier werewolf movie directors. Dante even cuts to pivotal sequences from older werewolf movies

to comment upon or accent an idea established in the current movie. Such "winks" enhance the overall film experience for those buffs in the know, and for people who aren't as savvy, these references never distract from the enjoyment.

To add credibility to the analysis, Senn embellishes his text with substantial quotes from director Joe Dante and screenwriter John Sayles, comments that create a sense of how the creative duo added a new slant to werewolf movies. We learn that Dante first hired Rick Baker to design the werewolf and execute the make-up effects, but that director John Landis reminded Baker of a past promise to do only Landis' werewolf movie. So Landis recommended his 21-year-old assistant Rob Bottin, who immediately accepted the job. As it worked out, Bottin, according to fellow make-up artist Steve Johnson, consulted with Baker for creative ideas and suggestions and Bottin "ripped off Rick's ideas," and *The Howling* was released first, thus making Bottin appear to be the innovator and Baker the copy-cat.

Bryan Senn's book of lycanthropy on screen is an insightful and well-researched analysis of the werewolf movie, with the introduction establishing the historical and psychological (and even mythologic) basic for the genre, and when it comes to the movies themselves, Senn always finds something intelligent and interesting to add to the mix. His use of quotes from other sources only adds additional spice. For a large-size hardback book with 400 pages, the asking price of $50 is more than fair. This is a book well worth having on your library shelf.

Universal Terrors: 1950-1955: Eight Classic Horror and Sci-Fi Films by Tom Weaver with David Schecter, Robert J. Kiss and Steve Kronenberg; McFarland www.mcfarlandpub.com; Order 800-253-2187; 440 pages (8.5 by 11 inches); Softcover $49.95

In Tom Weaver's concise and quite witty introduction, he explains that this book is a sequel to his earlier *Universal Horrors: The Studio's Classic Films: 1931-1946*, arriving 26 years after the release of the first book. Weaver admits that McFarland sent him a contract in 1997, with the manuscript expected by 1999, but it was not delivered until 2017. Weaver explains all the frustration in creating the parameters for this 1950s follow-up. In the original volume the Brunas Brothers and Weaver wanted to include every Universal movie (from 1931-1946) that contained even a hint of horror. Since a few of the Basil Rathbone Sherlock Holmes movies contained elements of horror, they reviewed the entire series. Weaver admits that, "soon we also found ourselves writing about movies that weren't horror by any stretch of the imagination but were *advertised* as horror." But since coverage was only at 5 or 6 pages per movie in the original volume, Weaver felt such borderline inclusions were no big deal. Weaver decided to stop the first Universal book at 1946, so *Abbott and Costello Meet Frankenstein* (a horror comedy) was omitted, which stirred up controversy back in the day. But with this first (of two) sequel, only eight films are covered in 440 pages, the thought of including shorter film coverage alongside epic film coverage just did not sit well with the Weaver team. In other words, the brief thought of including the 1950s's Abbott and Costello film series was dropped. While *Meet the Invisible Man* and *Meet the Mummy* exist as bonafide horror and monster movies of the era, such inclusions would have led to potentially adding *Abbott and Costello Go to Mars*, "which has no horror or monsters." So other films like *It Grows on Trees, Ma and Pa Kettle Back on the Farm, You Never Can Tell* (a fantasy film), *Harvey, Bonzo Goes to College* or the entire Francis the Talking Mule series had to be dropped in favor of actual horror, sci-fi and monster movies. However, Weaver promises that all these borderline movies will be covered in an appendix in the second and final edition (which will cover the years 1956-1960). So the following films made the cut for the first volume (covering the years 1950-1955): *The Strange Door, The Black Castle, It Came from Outer Space, Creature from the Black Lagoon, This Island Earth, Revenge of the Creature, Cult of the Cobra* and *Tarantula*. But as Weaver and his team demonstrate, the coverage of each film is close to being definitive as far as interviews, production information, analysis of movie and musical score and historic information goes. One final note, the chapters covering *Creature from the Black Lagoon* and *Revenge of the Creature* are "vastly abridged" edits from Weaver and Company's 2014 opus *The Creature*

Tom Weaver with **David Schecter, Robert J. Kiss** and **Steve Kronenberg**

Chronicles (which McFarland insisted be included here since these are two of the most important "Universal Terrors" that were released between 1950-1955).

To offer an idea of the book's flavor, I wanted to examine the chapter on *Tarantula*, one of my favorites from the era and a defining example of the giant mutated horror film sub-genre. The chapter begins with a complete "Credit and Cast" listing. Next comes a "Production History" by Tom Weaver. Tom mentions that this movie was Universal's reaction to the success of *Them!* from a year earlier, Universal jumping aboard the Giant Bug boom. What makes the movie so special is the use of actual tarantulas photographed giant size, which communicates to the audience that they are not watching a special effects stop motion critter (i.e. *The Black Scorpion*

or witnessing a giant puppet monster (i.e. *Them!*). And besides the giant tarantula, we get three human monsters, one even appearing before the credits. So audiences of the era were getting more than their money's worth.

Universal's marquee 1950s science fiction/monster director Jack Arnold started production on *Tarantula* in June 1955, but earlier in February he directed the third episode of Ivan Tor's sci-fi television series *Science Fiction Theatre*, "Food for Thought," an episode that predicted *Tarantula* in so many ways. Otto Kruger, who stars in the TV episode, gives a speech very similar to the one delivered by Leo G. Carroll in *Tarantula*, voicing the woes of world over-population and a lack of food and the need for a new synthetic food nutrient to feed the masses. Robert

SCIENCE'S DEADLIEST ACCIDENT

TARANTULA!

STARRING JOHN AGAR · MARA CORDAY
LEO G. CARROLL with NESTOR PAIVA · ROSS ELLIOTT

A UNIVERSAL-INTERNATIONAL PICTURE — DIRECTED BY JACK ARNOLD · SCREENPLAY BY ROBERT M. FRESCO and MARTIN BERKELEY PRODUCED BY WILLIAM ALLAND

M. Fresco, then only 24 years old, wrote the screenplay for "Food for Thought" and Jack Arnold told the kid he saw a feature film potential from the half-hour episode, but Arnold added, " … you gotta put a monster in it." Weaver always likes to spark a fire, as he does when he notes that Fresco submitted a seven-page story with the giant spider in it, the product of Fresco's imagination. But Weaver states that Jack Arnold tried to take credit for the giant spider premise by noting in the book *Directed by Jack Arnold* that the concept was his and initiated when his driveway, during a certain time of the year, was covered with tarantulas … and that's how he came up with the idea. Except, Weaver adds, when Arnold appeared on German TV in 1983 he credited his idea of using giant tarantulas to a documentary he made in 1948, *The Chicken of Tomorrow*, that dealt with creating larger chickens to create larger breasts to feed more people in an over-populated world. And finally in an interview with Bill Kelley in *Cinefantastique* he claimed the idea came from how botanists were growing larger vegetables, which could be applied to creating larger animals. From reading articles and books we all know that Weaver has never been a big fan of Jack Arnold, even though the person who actually thought of using giant spiders in the movie has little to do with the movie's worth or artistry (but I admit it was clever of Weaver to use dif-

ferent interviews with Arnold to show conflicts of misinformation, but isn't this just as much an indictment of the interview format [is Jack Arnold alone guilty of changing his stories in multiple interviews?] and does it prove that Arnold deliberately lied or simply created different anecdotes when under pressure by an interviewer?). Okay, Tom, give credit to Fresco for conceiving the specific giant monster threat but also give credit to Arnold for creating a classic giant spider/tarantula movie! Weaver even reminds us that in the movie credit it states, "Story by Jack Arnold and Robert M. Fresco," even though, according to Fresco, Arnold never wrote a word. Fresco says, in order to land the job of writing his first script for a feature film, "he had to give Arnold an undeserved co-credit *and* a hunk of money." Fresco accepted the deal as "the price of admission," and Fresco's agent even agreed to the deal. And was this the first time in Hollywood history that a virgin to Hollywood had to "pay" for his admission to the club? Fresco's agent seemed to understand how the game was played. And Fresco admits he had lots of fun writing the script for *Tarantula*.

But then Fresco finally met producer William Alland and all the good vibes faded. Arnold dropped Fresco off at Alland's office and disappeared, leaving the young screenwriter alone with the wily Alland. "I find myself in this oversized office with

this man who starts telling me how terrible the story is. How unhappy he is that he has to be involved with it … It was a pure 'I'm gonna fuck with his head' kind of meeting … Alland was saying, 'I'm the boss and you better believe it.' I didn't realize he wanted me to walk out so he could put [screenwriter Martin] Berkeley on the script." But when Fresco remained faithful to his contract and delivered his finished script and left, that is exactly what Alland did, bring Berkeley on board since "he and Alland are buddies," according to Fresco Once again, whether Weaver favors William Alland's comments over Jack Arnold's, or in this case Robert M. Fresco's views over Arnold's, it is apparent that Weaver always likes to "color" the facts he lays out, favoring one subjective view over the other in a make-believe objective sea. It must be remembered that Arnold is long dead and cannot give his side of cinematic history; William Alland recently departed the planet as well.

Weaver notes how *Tarantula* is a combination of the old and new, illustrating with photos the "acromegalic" Ralph Morgan from 1944's *The Monster Maker* looking quite similar to one of the "acromegalic" human mutants from *Tarantula*. Also Tom notes that the tarantula, a victim from the desert laboratory, along with other mutated animals and humans, is the latest victim of the Atomic Age and thus combines the monster mentality of the old with the technologically new.

Next comes a two-plus page "Synopsis" of the movie, followed by detailed, insightful "Cast Biographies." Weaver brings his personal style to such bios, always filling them with depth and including plenty of anecdotes. And when it comes to star John Agar, he shows him to be an ambiguous and struggling actor, warts and all (but basically pretty well-balanced).

Next comes a detailed "Production" history, coming in at about 13 pages. We get a pretty good detailed sketch of exactly what was filmed on Day One and Day Two of the production (with other days to follow), and we get to hear Mara Corday's reflection of working with director Jack Arnold: "He was a prankster, and I happen to like a very fun set … I like to tell jokes and kid around … He would tell dirty jokes, and then all of a sudden he'd break into a little dance. He used to be a chorus boy in New York … He was not the type of director who gives you a lot, but then, in this kind of film, what's there to do? There's not much plot." Corday goes on to say how she did not like her wardrobe ("really conservative") and felt in the final sequences, when the giant tarantula attacks the Deemer residence in the middle of the night, that she should have been wearing a sexy negligee instead of the plain pajamas she had to wear. "So there was no sex appeal there!" In the fifties a rising young starlet recognized the need of sex appeal to rise through the ranks.

Weaver notes specifically what occurred on specific days of the production, when the desert sequences were filmed, etc. So this production section does a good job of breaking down how the movie was filmed and how the stars responded. Robert Fresco was still angry with Jack Arnold for ignoring his advice that one line of dialogue was horrible (as the writer he knew what would work and what would not) and should not have been shot and included. "That was one of the reasons Jack [never made it]. Jack didn't take chances. He wouldn't stand up to Bill Alland and say, 'That's a terrible line. The writer said it's a terrible line. I agree with him, let's cut it.' He was a good director … but he didn't have the balls." After the film's release Weaver includes follow-up information and box-office numbers reported by *Variety* and other trade magazines.

Then a section is devoted to "Other Script-To-Screen Changes," offering many interesting changes that occurred either before or during production. And then Weaver offers a "Marginalia" section where he submits brief reflections that stand apart from other specific sections of the production history. For instance, Fresco admitting that *Them!* was an influence on *Tarantula* but Arnold admitting the idea for the movie was his alone and *Them!* had no influence. Weaver adds, "From Arnold it isn't surprising since he thought the sun came up every morning just to hear him crow," making the claim that Arnold definitely had to remember that the major inspiration for *Tarantula* was "No Food for Thought." However, Weaver is beside himself when producer Alland says, "*Tarantula* came from an idea of my own." In stark disbelief Weaver reminds his reader that Alland was "a

Mara Corday, during the final tarantula-invading climax, thought that she should be wearing a sexy negligee instead of plain pajamas.

'credit where credit was due' kind of guy, never a credit-poacher." Weaver then assumes, since Alland got a story credit on *The Deadly Mantis* (written "very soon" after *Tarantula*), that the producer "may have mixed up the two Big Bug movies in his head" and thus Weaver assumes Alland "misremembered" the facts, while he states that Arnold lied. Weaver ends his rant by saying: "*We* report; *you* decide." But when the "report" arrives with such clear bias of intent, the coloring of facts must be factored in.

Robert J. Kiss offers "The Release" which is an outstanding add-on that documents when the film opened, how many theaters showed the film and in what cities, whether it was shown solo or double-billed, and if double-billed what film it was paired with, how many 35mm prints were shipped across the U.S., what the press book and ballyhoo publicity material consisted of, etc. In other words, this section shows what happened to the film after its release, how the film hit the theater circuit across the U.S. and how the film was promoted. Kiss even offers "Beyond the First Run" where he documents how the film continued to be shown in theaters from 1956 to 1957 (unlike today's blockbuster movies, back in the 1950s and 1960s, films were released first-run to exclusive down-town theaters, then they moved second run to smaller neighborhood theaters and many films still had legs for additional theatrical releases a year or two or three later). Kiss follows the trajectory of the theatrical release until the film is eventually sold to television (in the case of *Tarantula*, in 1965).

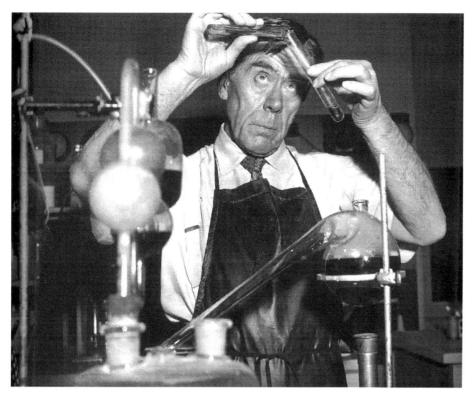

Leo G. Carroll "carries the show" and gives *Tarantula* its element of mad science, making the film a full-tilt work of horror rather than just an Atom Age yarn.

Next a brief "Critics' Corner" follows, where excerpts from published critical reviews are reproduced, giving the Universal horror fan an idea of how the film was perceived upon its initial or subsequent releases, often touching upon revisionist perceptions that appeared in the press decades after its initial release.

Next David Schecter offers an insightful 9-page analysis of the "Musical Score" for *Tarantula*, including reproductions of pages of sheet music and what musical cues were paired with specific sequences in the movie. The musical department at Universal-International received credit for composing the musical scores at the time (actually one composer usually composed the majority of the score but was never given a solo credit), so it is difficult to know who actually composed the musical score for *Tarantula*. Schecter states the consensus among buffs in the know was that Henry Mancini composed the score for *Tarantula* (based in large part upon the credit given on the fan favorite *Themes from Horror Movies* record by Dick Jacobs), but Schecter states that assumption would be wrong. Mancini wrote only 38 seconds of original music for the movie, even though music Mancini wrote for other movies was recycled here. It was Herman Stein who wrote the majority of the original music

used for *Tarantula*. It turns out the mostly tracked score "contains an astonishing 90 cues, 52 by Stein and 38 by Mancini, but there were really more pieces than that." In Schecter's fascinating musical contribution, he documents whose musical cue is used where and tries to describe the effect the music had on the audience. He demonstrates that the score was definitely a patchwork quilt of fascinating musical snippets that somehow produced satisfying results. "*Tarantula*'s soundtrack was extremely well put together from previously existing sources."

Finally Steve Kronenberg writes the "Analysis" of *Tarantula*, explaining why the movie was so much more than a knock-off of the formerly successful *Them!* Kronenberg details how the pre-credits human mutant monster adds a touch of old-school horror to a film that was advertised as a "Big Bug science fiction opus." In other words, it is difficult to pigeonhole *Tarantula* since the movie offers a blending of monster and science fiction pleasure. Leo G. Carroll "carries the show" and "Carroll gives *Tarantula* its element of mad science, making the film a full-tilt work of horror rather than just an Atom Age 'monster-on-the-loose' yarn." Kronenberg feels the rest of the cast "pales alongside Carroll's subtle, layered and

menacing performance." He feels, besides Carroll, that the other real stars of the production were the technicians, especially cinematographer George Robinson and the effects crew, and Kronenberg describes how creepy and effective the major sequences with the giant tarantula are, marrying effects, moody photography and an insightful musical score to produce an above average monster/sci-fi picture. In a concise four pages, critic Kronenberg demonstrates how so many assets merge to produce a B-movie that continues to impress and please legions of fans, even to this day.

And this is how each of the eight movies in this book is probed beneath the microscope of critical insight. The Weaver team literally leaves no stone unturned.

But with so much excellent research and enthusiasm evident (the joy of writing on such critically ignored little gems shines through), it is a shame that at times Weaver's biases (his dislike of Jack Arnold, for example) rip through with grat-

Director Jack Arnold

ing negativity. As Weaver reminds us, "*we report; you decide*"; of course personal opinions are always to be allowed, but let's be sure that we can differentiate information that is presented as factual from cleverly manipulated opinion, especially when the quotes appear to be presented and edited in such a way as to *prove* what is actually an agenda-driven *assumption* (even those celebrities who were there on the set reflect and interpret with memories distorted by time and ego).

However, Weaver brilliantly utilizes his creative team to offer multiple voices in his coverage of each movie, ultimately creating (perhaps) the final word by focusing on cast and credit listings, production history, synopsis, cast biographies, the production, script-to-production changes, marginalia, the release, the musical score and critical analysis. After reading each chapter we have to literally put the book down, jump up and applaud the information and insight offered. For all fans of 1950s horror, science fiction and monster movies, this is an essential book to purchase. So much information is covered (with great illustrations), with so much fun in evidence.

Where Monsters Walked: California Locations of Science Fiction, Fantasy and Horror Films, 1925-1965 by Gail Orwig and Raymond Orwig; McFarland www.mcfarlandpub.com; Order 800-253-2187; 379 pages (7 by 10 inches); Softcover $49.95

Back in the FANEX days, Sue and I were always happy to meet enthusiastic like-minded fans, such as married couple Gail and Ray Orwig, truly wonderful folks who traveled all the way from the West Coast to the East Coast to partake in the communal experience of celebrating the movies and celebrities who made them. The Orwigs returned multiple times to our various shows and we became good friends. When FANEX ended the Orwigs continued to be librarians and teachers by day and dedicated Monster Kids both day and night, eventually publishing *The Big Eye* journal, a celebration of everything horror with a focus on the fan scene in California.

Imagine my surprise as I was finishing up the book reviews for this latest issue of *Midnight Marquee* when a last minute book arrived on my front porch, one

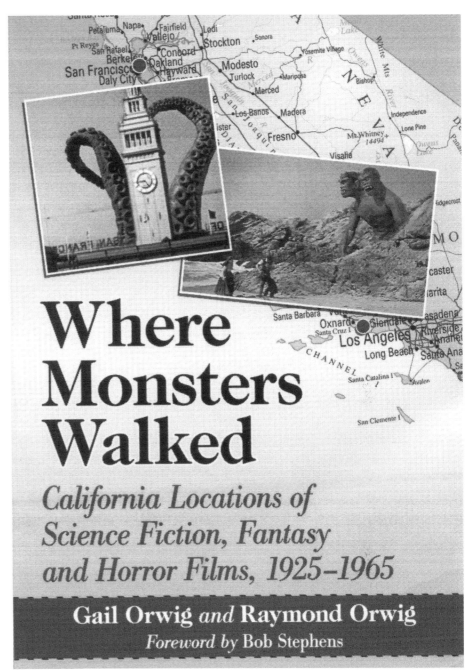

Where Monsters Walked

California Locations of Science Fiction, Fantasy and Horror Films, 1925–1965

Gail Orwig *and* Raymond Orwig

Foreword by Bob Stephens

written by the Orwigs. Over the course of 15 years, Gail and Ray ventured all over California locating the exact locations where specific scenes from various horror movies were filmed (their quest dedicated to the glory years 1925-1965 only). Of course many photos of the location as it now appears were taken, but these shots had to be so specific that fans could say, hey, that is where they filmed the town square sequence of loading the pods into trucks in *Invasion of the Body Snatchers*! And of course Ray and Gail had to find the exact movie still from the 1956 Don Siegel production that shows how that town square looked back in the day. Also, as a guide for other Monster Kids, the Orwigs

had to offer specific directions so people who wanted to find that town square could find it on their own, and perhaps repeat the fan experience of recognizing the location and taking their own photos, perhaps with themselves posing in the picture.

The Orwigs laid out the rules for how the book works. The "then" shots are on the left and the "now" shots are on the right, unless the shots are too wide and in that case "then" is on top and "now" is on the bottom. A few locations were found to be not accessible, such as Three Arch Bay, which is now a gated community (and back in the day was a location used for *Doctor X*). Many locations are labeled

Gail and Ray Orwig help fans find this cave in California; the top shot is from *Invasion of the Body Snatchers* (1956), and the bottom is from *Return of Dracula* (1958).

as "No Longer There" because the house used in a 1940s Bela Lugosi PRC movie was torn down decades ago. Sometimes Gail and Ray use old postcards to show how the location looked after the movie was shot and how real life differs from cinematic reality, but often postcards were used to show the location is "No Longer There," just so fans wouldn't waste their time chasing after the past. Sometimes the Orwigs label a location as "Unable to Find" and they wish that anyone who might have found the location notify them so they can add the location to the file. Finally, Gail and Ray list their own rules of etiquette that refer to when it is okay to take photos or not and when and how to ask permission. It's all very common sense oriented but we all know obsessed film fans sometimes forget their own common sense. Sometimes the authors add "Notes" to the movie coverage adding interesting little tidbits of information that movie fans would enjoy.

McFarland does a pretty good job of reproducing the scores of photos included, half of which are of the snap shot variety, not professional shots. However, McFarland missed the boat when they decided to do the book as a 7 by 10 inch book, since the side-by-side photographs would be larger with details much easier to see if they used their 8.5 by 10 inch format.

This is the type of book that fans can open to any page and pick out any movie and compare the "then" and "now." Movies are organized alphabetically and the format is a simple one. Under the movie title comes the director and the major cast members. Then a brief synopsis follows, basically a short paragraph. Then we have a description of "Locations," including driving directions, where to park and where to walk or climb or turn. Finally we arrive at the various "then" and "now" photos, most of the time offering many different sets of photos showing related

yet different locations, which often are located fairly close to one another.

For instance, in the coverage for *The Curse of the Cat People*, we are shown the Reed house (a movie still) where the spooky encounters occurred. We are told the house is "No Longer There," but we still learn that the very same house was seen in William Castle's *13 Ghosts*.

Many interesting photos appear in the coverage of *Day the World Ended*, including shots of the canyon and cliffs seen in the rustic outdoor sequences. Often we are reminded that these same cliffs were used in *Invasion of the Body Snatchers* and *Return of Dracula*. So, at least for me, I can now remember various sequences from *Return of Dracula* and say the same locations were used for *Day the World Ended*. In other words the universe of one movie intercepts with that of another, and suddenly the classic *Invasion of the Body Snatchers* offers a world also seen in the low-budget B-classic *Day the World Ended*. Only by staring at the specific photos chosen, pausing and reflecting, can we overlap one universe with another.

In the coverage of *Earth vs. the Spider* we have very effective side-by-side photos of the giant spider crossing the road with the exact dusty road as it appears today, shot almost from the same position and angle. We see people enter the mouth of the cave at Bronson Canyon, shot from inside looking at the arched opening. And to the right we see the same arched opening shot from almost the same angle. It is truly amazing to see how movie sets and production design change but that nature remains virtually the same, even though separated over decades of time. We are also told that the gym used in *Earth vs. the Spider* was the same one used in *I Was a Teenager Werewolf* and is actually The Hollywood Recreation Center at 1122 Cole Avenue in Los Angeles.

The coverage on William Castle's *Homicidal* demonstrates that not all the locations shown in this book happen to occur in the hills, caves and canyons of California, as the Orwigs offer two separate split photos to replicate the opening shot of the movie driving down East Main Street in Ventura. The movie photo contains buildings on both side of the street, but Gail and Ray were afraid of getting crushed by speeding cars if they dared photograph while standing in the middle of the street. But once butted together, the two modern photos capture perfectly what was seen in *Homicidal*.

For coverage of William Castle's *House on Haunted Hill*, we have photos of the iconic Frank Lloyd Wright designed house, built in 1924 (it is now known as the Ennis House or the Ennis-Brown House and it is located down the street from Forrest J Ackerman's most famous Ackermansion). We have photos of the movie cast arriving at the front gate of the haunted house alongside modern-day photos showing the same areas but as the house appears today. We are told that the house's living room was used in the movie *The Rocketeer* and that the guest bedroom was used as Harrison Ford's apartment in the original *Blade Runner*.

Where Monsters Walked even goes back to Universal's 1932 production of *The Mummy*, starring Boris Karloff. You did not actually believe that Universal sent a production crew to Egypt, did you? Those archaeological digs were filmed in front of the Acropolis at Red Rock Canyon and Hagen Canyon, which is now part of the Red Rock Canyon State Park. The book includes three pages of photos contrasting shots from the movie to similar shots today of the same locations.

For *The She-Creature*, known for its seaside landscape with the large, extended pier, we are reminded the actual location was Paradise Cove, just north of Malibu, just off Pacific Coast Highway. Even more interesting was finding out that this movie featured the debut of Spike the Dog, who played King. Trainer Frank Weatherwax, brother of Lassie trainer Rudd Weatherwax, owned the rescue dog, a mastador (a mix of Labrador retriever and mastiff). One year later Spike played the title character in Walt Disney's *Old Yeller* and become one of the most well known dog heroes of all time.

Readers can spend hours contrasting the past and present and learning interesting incidental facts pertaining to the history of each movie depicted. And in 369 pages, a massive amount of movies filmed in California are covered and illustrated. This book is not intended as intellectual fodder, nor can its virtues be argued in a point-counterpoint debate. No, this is the type of book that requires flipping through the pages, looking here and there and comparing photos and reading the

A Hollywood Tragedy
LAIRD CREGAR
GREGORY WILLIAM MANK

text for sidebar facts, many of which I never knew. *Where Monsters Walked* is terrific fun and will leave most Monster Kids spellbound for many, many hours.

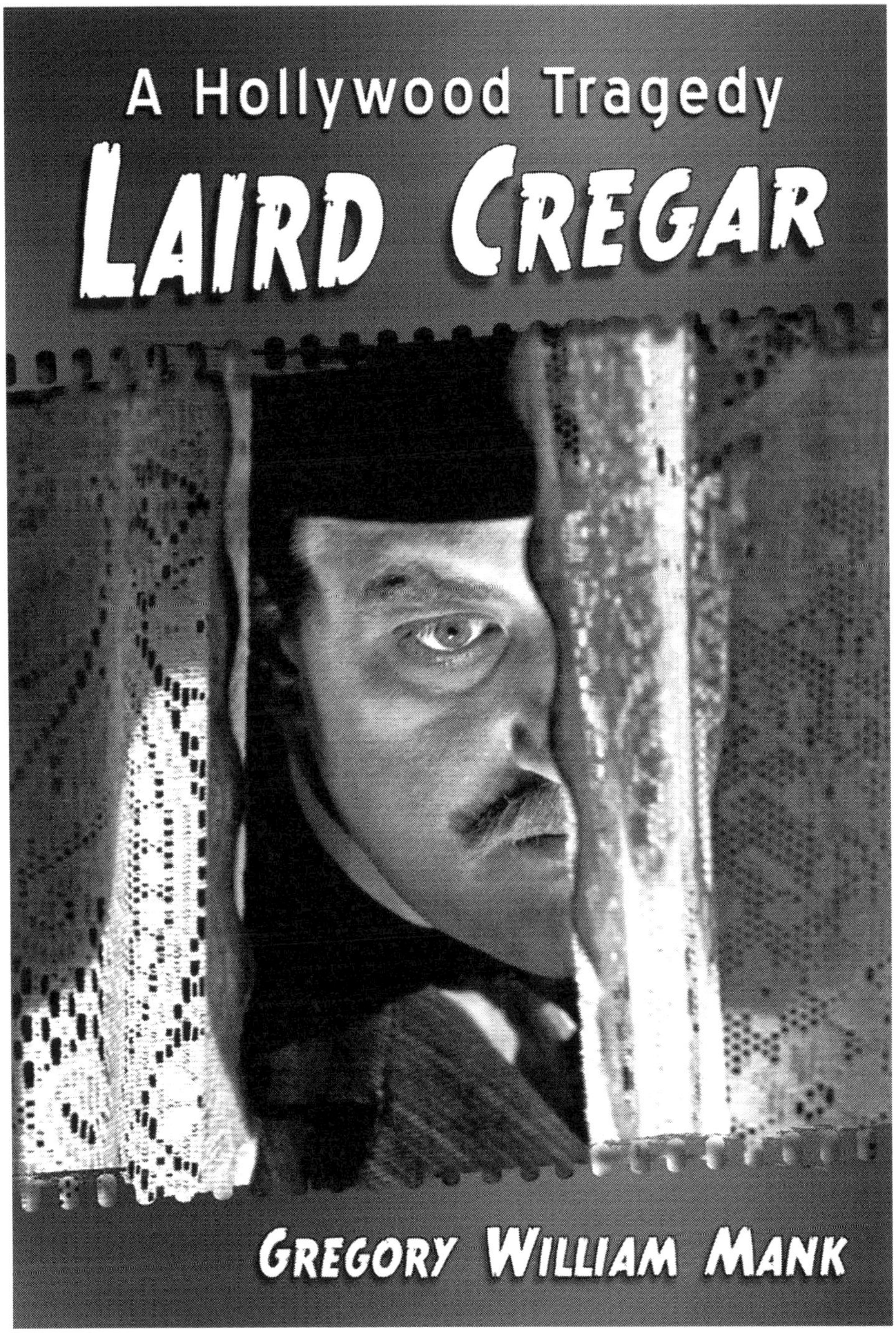

Laird Cregar: A Hollywood Tragedy by Gregory William Mank; McFarland www.mcfarlandpub.com; Order 800-253-2187; 329 pages (7 by 10 inches); Hardcover $49.95

While holding this latest horror film biography from Greg Mank in your hands, it seems everything is right with the world. With his hyper-dramatic style and flawless research, Mank has become

one of the finest classic film writers/historians working today, and he has been raising the bar of film scholarship for decades. Now Mank turns his attention to tragic cult star Laird Cregar, who died much too young at the age of 31.

Even though 70 years have passed since Laird Cregar's death, Greg Mank vowed to use as many primary sources in his "lifetime of gratitude" biography as possible. People such as Elizabeth Cregar Hayman, Laird Cregar's niece, who died in 2015, shared many insightful memories of her "Uncle Sam" for Mank. De-Witt Bodeen, who died in 1988, provided

Laird Cregar and Merle Oberon in *The Lodger*

or, "sadistic, self-righteous moviegoers" wrote of the specific ways in which they desired to murder him. "Cregar's Ripper … is a rock star," making his character scary and sexy and larger than life. Later in 1944 Cregar starred in *Hangover Square*, "one of the great horror films of the 1940s," but Cregar still "despises it." He at first refused to do the movie, and as punishment for his actions, was suspended by 20th Century Fox, caving in only after immense studio pressure. He also fought bitterly with the film's director John Braham. "I hate Hollywood," he raged, rebelling against being typecast as a "bat-shit crazy, sexually deranged ogre." Cregar tells his co-star George Sanders that in truth he wants to be "a beautiful man." The six-foot-three-inch actor, who approached 350 pounds at his most indulgent, was hoping to achieve his goal with plastic surgery and living on a 500 calorie per day diet. "It's a morbid obsession that is literally killing him."

Mank reminds us that in 1941, when Cregar portrayed the 300-pound "kink of a detective," becoming an absolute sensation in *I Wake Up Screaming*, basing his

Mank with many stories associated with Cregar over the years. And the list goes on and on.

Mank decided to open and close his biography with "uniquely personal stories" involving Laird Cregar, starting off (in *Author's Notes*) with the story of first seeing Cregar's *The Lodger* on Sunday afternoon television in 1958, watching only the stark final five minutes (which showed Cregar at his creepiest best) with his father. Mank's lifelong fascination with Cregar resulted from "a single, unforgettable shot. As the Ripper rampaged across a catwalk in a Victorian theater, the shadows cast by the lights below rippled up and down his face and body … Cregar's Jack the Ripper seemed a were-zebra." And this was just the start of a happy, lifelong obsession with the man and his work. In fact an article about Cregar that the 22-year-old Mank submitted to Leonard Maltin for his *Film Fan Monthly* was published and in turn read by film book author James Robert Parish, who hired the wet-behind-the-ears Mank as a research associate, making Mank an underpaid professional writer. And it was all because of Cregar.

In 1944 when *The Lodger* opened at Broadway's Roxy Theatre, Laird Cregar made a personal appearance and received a five-minute long ovation. Cregar had been receiving "fan" mail from obsessive

fans, mostly women, who wrote him hoping that he would become their personal Jack the Ripper and murder their parents,

Laird Cregar as he appeared in *Hangover Square*

depraved performance on "lovelorn eyes and a silky flat voice, keeping a macabre shrine to a dead blonde." His underplayed yet subtle performance positively stole the show from the so-called stars: Victor Mature, Carole Landis and Betty Grable. Back in 1941 Laird Cregar was enthusiastic about his future. Even with his great bulk, "Sammy" Cregar attended a well-publicized Beverly Hills party dressed as a Mack Sennett bathing beauty, wearing a blonde wig. When his theater friend was ill, Cregar happily filled in for him in a musical stage revue, dancing up a storm with chorus boys a third his size. Cregar also appeared at a Hollywood party whose theme mocked the 1942 Academy Awards, Cregar winning an "Oscar" (at the party) for "Best Female Impersonator of the Year," mocking Greer Garson's long-winded acceptance speech for *Mrs. Miniver*. A few years later the mood had decidedly changed. While playing Jack The Ripper in *The Lodger*, his close actor friend David Bacon was murdered, the killer doing the damage with a knife. And when Bacon's wife suffered a miscarriage as a result, Cregar nursed her back to health. Laird Cregar is "a very emotional man, hypersensitive, even for an actor. He laughs and cries easily." But while filming *The Lodger* and *Hangover Square*, Cregar "is the victim of a vile whisper campaign, spread by an adversary—maybe his own studio—portraying him as an out-of-control sexual degenerate (he is in fact 'closeting as a homosexual'), and calculated to destroy his career." All this and more breaks his heart. By December 9, 1944, 60 days before *Hangover Square* will open in New York, Cregar, only 31, suffers two heart attacks and dies.

Mank debates the two major trains of thought or agendas concerning Cregar. First, that he was "Saint Laird, martyr … professionally anguished by his typecasting as a villain," at war with both his studio 20th Century Fox and himself, trying to transform into the handsome, romantic lead he always dreamed of being, "the 340 pound character star [who] became a 235-pound corpse." But as Mank explains, others see it all differently: "a classic show biz Death by Vanity. Cregar's pitiful self-crucifixion unfolds as a Hollywood Passion Play, with a dogmatic moral …" This involves defying your studio, revealing your sexual deviance, trying to change your type and taking your $1500 weekly salary, fame and fortune for granted. And Mank agrees that there's middle ground in between both of these extremes, constantly fueling the big debate over whether Laird Cregar wanted to be a "beautiful man" to "attract a male or a female." George Sanders, who appeared with Cregar in three movies, "expressed it eloquently: Hollywood virtually 'assassinated' Laird Cregar." Or, Mank asks, "Did Cregar assassinate himself?"

What a fabulous set-up for this Hollywood biography.

The format of the book is as follows. We start with *Acknowledgments, Author's Notes* and *Introduction*, all these brief chapters setting up the context of the biography. The main heart of the book is broken into *Part I: If You Try to Find Me, I Will Kill Myself; Part II: The Lion of the Hour; Part III: Betsey; Part IV: We Want You Just As You Are, Mr. Cregar; Part V: A Beautiful Man;* and *Part VI: Denouement.* Here Mank offers us the full story of Laird Cregar, starting with his life as a child and progressing through his early adult years, his work in the theater and finally in films. Fully developed and insightful chapters are devoted to Cregar's movies and major theatrical productions. Finally, the book ends with *Filmography, Theater Credits; Radio Credits; Unrealized Film Projects; Chapter Notes; Bibliography;* and *Index.* Chapter 32, "A Final Tribute," ends the book with another personal reflection involving the first time Greg and his wife Barbara sought out Laird Cregar's tombstone/grave (on December 8, the actual date of Cregar's death) and the tremendous problems (the caretaker getting the lot number wrong and taking Greg and Barbara to the opposite end of the cemetery, the daylight fading, a sprinkler system that goes off and almost drowns the Manks, etc.) that resulted in a huge delay finding the gravesite. As it worked out, in the fading rays of the sun, Barbara found the grave and a ghastly internal voice prompted Greg to look at his watch. It was 4:52 p.m., the exact moment that the death certificate registered Cregar's time of death. The tombstone read, "I Am With You Always," and Mank states, "I like to think so."

As is to be expected, *Laird Cregar: A Hollywood Tragedy* is another excellent addition to Greg Mank's body of work, maintaining the high standards associated with his other books. While *Laird Cregar* does not possess the mythology and iconic status of a Boris Karloff or Bela Lugosi (the subject of earlier Mank biographies), his life and career has never had the light of scholarship and film criticism shine on it until now, and there is so much here to discover and enjoy. The photographs and poster illustrations are well chosen, and the portrait of young "Sammy" as a child with curly hair and a big smile stands out.

It goes without saying that *Laird Cregar: A Hollywood Tragedy* comes with the highest recommendation.

MIDNIGHT MARQUEE DVD/BLU-RAY REVIEW

BY GARY J. SVEHLA

Ratings:
5 (excellent); 4 (very good);
3 (good); 2 (fair); 1 (poor)

Caltiki, the Immortal Monster
3.0
Arrow Video

One year before Mario Bava made his official directorial debut with his classic *Black Sunday*, Bava had already partially directed two earlier films that were initiated by director Riccardo Freda, but these were actually films where Freda bowed out and Bava stepped in to complete (*I, Vampiri* in 1956 and *Caltiki* in 1959). *Caltiki, the Immortal Monster* is a genre montage of many different styles and remains one of Freda's/Bava's most outrageously creative works. The scenario deals with the vanishing Mayan civilization in Mexico hundreds of years earlier, this fantastical world made Mayan-less by the re-animation of Mayan female goddess Caltiki, initiated and fueled by the appearance of

a comet whose increased radiation makes the blob-type monster only more powerful. Now in current-day Mexico, an expedition returns to the scene of the great disappearance in hopes of solving the mystery, but most of the party is only motivated by acquiring lost Mayan treasure. And of course this is the very same time that the former comet from hundreds of years ago is now approaching Earth to once again bring Caltiki back to life and full strength (the plot sounds suspiciously similar to *The Brainiac* at this early point).

Mario Bava's major contribution to the film was as special effects creator and cinematographer, his photography casting deep supernatural shadows over his miniature Mexican landscape of statues, caverns and an ancient idol of the Mayan goddess. His creation of Caltiki is quite different from the silicone-created (and garishly red rubber) American Blob of one year earlier. Caltiki is most similar to the giant monsters in the tanks from *Quatermass II/Enemy from Space*. Photographed

in silvery tones of black and white, Caltiki appears to have a hairless rawhide body, almost leathery, and the monster's mayhem seems more frightening than the Pennsylvania Blob ever appeared. Like Hammer's *The Quatermass Xperiment/ The Creeping Unknown* (and even *The Blob*), we have a human being whose arm and hand become contaminated by the alien presence … and here in *Caltiki* the victim Max (Gerard Haerter) grows mentally unhinged until the re-animated monster at the movie's climax completely absorbs him.

What makes *Caltiki, the Immortal Monster* so delightfully involving is the different directions the movie takes, from start to finish. The movie begins with a safari camp in the Mexican jungle with a sexy half-dressed female dancing around the fire. We then add a little soap opera with contrasting couples (John and Ellen and Max and Linda) creating a little sexual tension. Max is married to Linda (Daniela Rocca) but he is attracted to more upscale

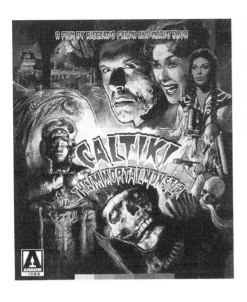

Ellen (Didi Sullivan), who is married to Professor John Fielding (John Merivale), one of his best friends. We then have the giant monster Caltiki, who rises from a spooky underground Mayan lake near the statue of the female goddess. Any human that comes in contact with the glittery blob finds that body part burned, as if by acid. The movie then becomes the story of John, Ellen and Linda dealing with Max, whose arm has been severely burned by the monster blob and whose mental state is constantly deteriorating. Bava's most startling moments involve the menacing Max suddenly appearing, bathed in mood-evoking light, to demonstrate just how much he has become infected and is morphing into something far less civilized. Here Freda and Bava balance blob monsters from the Mayan past with a depraved human fiend, a victim of that Mayan horror in today's world. Then the movie evolves into a monster-on-the-loose giant blob vs. humanity movie. The film maintains interest by nature of its divergent screenplay.

In the film's final quarter hour we have defenseless heroine Ellen and son alone in their stately home, being attacked by the rapidly dividing Caltiki, whose strength is increasing by the minute because of the comet whose presence streaks across the night sky. Bava's affects, while not totally believable or realistic, are always quite incredible and seem just perfect for the B-movie monster fanatic. We see the monster split into separate blob monsters as well as absorbing the washing machine in the basement, as high-angle shots frame the quivering fiend slithering up the living room staircase. The approaching fiend

forces Ellen and son outside, the terrified victims escaping through their oversized room windows onto the thin ledge outside their home that contacts one room with another, and they barely are able to escape. Pretty soon John arrives, just as the police and military do too, the military using their flame-throwers to incinerate the monster, now multiplying at an alarming rate. Bava's effects are always well photographed, his miniature set photography almost becoming quaint and old school in the most cozy of ways. *Caltiki, the Immortal Monster* is never aiming for prestige or longevity; the movie knows exactly what it is and remains faithful to the B-movie Saturday afternoon matinee aesthetic. This is exactly how I first saw the movie back in 1960 with my father, when I was only 10 years old, in a theater packed with kids. I loved the monster rally then and I can still appreciate its rewards today. Arrow has done a spectacular job in restoring the movie and removing over 60 years of wear and abuse … the film most likely never looked quite this good back in 1960. Spectacular extras include audio commentaries by Troy Howarth and Tim Lucas, numerous documentaries, as well as specific analyses of Riccardo Freda, the making of the film, an alternate opening for the U.S. version and multi-language versions including newly translated subtitles. In other words, for anyone a fan of Mario Bava, Riccardo Freda or Italian cinema, this collection is a must-have and remains one of the most important Blu-ray releases of 2017.

The Undying Monster
2.5
Kino Lorber

When recalling classic horror movies of the 1930s and 1940s, Universal Pictures come immediately to mind, perhaps followed by RKO (the Val Lewton factory), with Paramount and MGM trailing along. But 20th Century Fox!!!!??? When it comes to horror, Fox is hardly ever considered.

First of all, the Universal classic *The Wolf Man* did influence other films in its wake, most importantly Jacques Tourneur's *Cat People*, probably a horror classic equal. But 20th Century Fox followed in the tracks of the beast with their own nifty little B-production, *The Undying Mon-*

ster (even a four-line poem alluding to the beast is quoted throughout the movie, reminding us of a similar one from *The Wolf Man*). Too bad the quasi-mystery/horror production is a tad too tepid for its own good.

First of all, let's examine the strengths of *The Undying Monster*. First and foremost is the cinematography by master Lucien Ballard. His low and high angle shots filmed in the mansion and the surrounding moors create a delightful macabre flavor of suspense and dread. The film's opening sequence focuses upon young and vulnerable Kate O'Malley, as she flees for her life late at night, chased off the seaside road and into rocky terrain. Many sequences take the p.o.v. of the beast, as the cowering victim-to-be registers fear with her bulging eyes, running for her life. However, when Helga Hammond (Heather Angel) finds the nearly dead woman, she also finds her brother Oliver (John Howard), wounded and bleeding near by. Oliver claims he heard screams and tried to intervene, only to be attacked by some unseen presence. Except for the film's climax, *The Undying Monster* never gets any better than this sequence.

While the direction of German John Brahm is visually tension filled, the screenplay (most likely encouraged by the studio) supported an old dark house mystery scenario, keeping the horror under wraps until the final five minutes. The plot involves an ancient family curse that involves family members transforming into some type of monster. Such specifics about the family curse are not verbalized until the very end, when the term lycan-

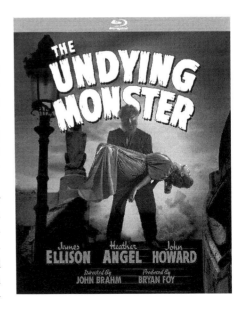

thropy is first used. Everyone seems close-mouthed, especially when police inspector Craig (Aubrey Maher) is present questioning everyone about the attack (and resulting death) of Kate. Even when fresh footprints are found in a hidden room in the cellar crypt, the family scientist Dr. Jeff Colbert (Universal's Bramwell Fletcher) pretends to lose his balance and steps right through the footprints, apologizing for his clumsiness. The masterful Halliwell Hobbes, playing Walton the butler, is always an ominous presence, hiding in the shadows or spying upon household members. However, too much of the 60-minute running time is wasted on creepy talky sequences at the Hammond mansion, while director Brahm and cinematography Ballard demonstrate how effective the film could be when told visually. Too much of the running time is bogged down in alluding to the Hammond family curse without explaining much about the specifics. Such attempts to generate suspense become tiresome and soon the film sinks into tedium with the audience wondering, just where is that monster from the film's beginning (a monster never shown, mind you)?

With literally minutes remaining, the werewolf, always photographed in medium or long shots, invades Helga's bedroom and carries the sleeping victim off into the night. Heading for the rocky bluffs surrounding the mansion after first running through the mansion and jumping down by the front door, the werewolf tries to hide in the boggy, rocky landscape as family members are in hot pursuit. Once again the photography of Lucien Ballard is allowed *carte blanche* with marvelous camera setups among the incredible studio-constructed art direction, created by Thomas Little and Walter M. Scott. Finally, after showing the werewolf traverse twisted tree stumps and fog-shrouded terrain, the audience sees the werewolf in one dramatic close-up, as he tries to scale a rock, as the camera hovers above and photographs his emerging face. It is at this moment that the werewolf is shot and killed, the wolf's identity revealed as the beast reverts to human form.

The werewolf make-up is adequate at best and is most effectively shown, as it was, in long shot, but *The Undying Monster* is a perfect example of too little too late. While most horror movies are guilty

of showing the monster too soon and too often, here the audience loses patience by the time the hardcore horror elements arrive. Even at the brief hour running time, B-filmmakers understand that maintaining pacing and keeping the monster front and center matters the most. Here the studio seemed to be too ashamed to highlight the horror quotient and instead disguises the movie as an old dark house mystery, but without much visual interest until the werewolf finally arrives in the final minutes to reawaken us.

World Without End
2.5
Warner Archive

When it comes to 1950s science fiction, some movies are constantly viewed and written about (*Forbidden Planet, Invaders from Mars, War of the Worlds, Them!, Invasion of the Body Snatchers*) and others are almost forgotten. *World Without End* was a movie I saw in the theater with my father around 1957 or 1958 and thoroughly enjoyed and fondly remember. The brilliant Technicolor photography and CinemaScope impressed me, not to mention the horrifying giant spider. *World Without End* has been released to home video in different formats over the years, but never in its CinemaScope aspect ratio and restored.

What makes *World Without End* so special is its screenplay written by director Edward Bernds, a scenario that offers ideas as well as juvenile thrills. As mentioned, the movie appeals to the little boy (and geeky girls!) in all of us. We have the droopy-eyed "Mutates," the genetic offspring of nuclear annihilation that are called "The Beast." We have the quickly concocted giant-sized spider, a monster that appears to have been pushed off the edge of the rock above where our explorers pass. We have the 1950s-style rocket ship (for me made famous by the *Rocky Jones* TV series; remember the Silver Needle?) that rattles and shakes, flying through a time dimension barrier that makes it appear that outer space is on fire. We have the sexy female aliens that wear short skirts and flash lots of bare leg. We have the amazing underground corridors that lead to scientific labs created by amazing futuristic technology. We even have rocket launchers that fire explosives

that light up the screen. Such is the stuff of Saturday matinee kiddy fare.

But *World Without End* also features fodder for thought. By midway through the movie we learn that our Mars bound rocket did not land on another planet, but instead catapulted into the future, landing on Earth around 2508. Of course this was a few hundred years after the nuclear war that destroyed mankind and its cities. Now Earth is populated with two distinct varieties of humans: the fearful underground human dwellers and the primitives (some are genetically mutated into monsters and others appear as normal human beings). The primitive humans are tribal savages whose chosen leader remains as leader until someone throws him off the side of a mountain. Brute force rules! On the other hand the underground dwellers, at least the men, are cowardly and avoid direct confrontation and opt to live a life of reclusiveness. The women, on the other hand, are less fearful and more aggressive and not entirely supportive of the male leadership (where most of the males are old and afraid, the females are young and at their sexual prime). When our visitors from Earth arrive, their courageous and macho attitudes collide with the peace-loving elders, who rule the planet. In fact our heroes are a blend of the wisdom of the cowardly underground dwellers and the savagery of the primitives. In other words, in Bernds' screenplay, neither extreme is desirable and it takes the Earth visitors from out of time to re-establish the balance.

Of course the film's story revisits clichéd sci-fi territory, with the underground elders not trusting the more aggressive humans from Earth's past (they carry weapons and aren't afraid to use them). Of course when Garnet (Nancy Gates) falls in love with John (Hugh Marlowe), the jealous elder Mories (Booth Colman) kills one of his own and frames the Earthlings for the crime, causing leader Timmek (Everett Glass) to banish the four to the land of the Beast and almost certain death. However, Mories is revealed to be the evil one and, at the film's end, the Earthlings, who can repair their damaged ship, realize that they will never be able to replicate the time barrier jump to return to the Earth of old. Resigned that their fate lies with the Earth survivors of 2508, our heroes work with the artisans and craftsmen of the future to expand their underground technology to the world above ground, but this occurs only after our hero John confronts and defeats the Beast's leader for leadership of the tribe. Then above ground will be as safe as below ground and technology can advance over the entire Earth once again. The only married (with children) member of the space crew accepts the fact that his wife and children have aged and died and so he becomes the teacher to the young students, becoming the surrogate parent to a new evolving world of children, who will repopulate the planet once again.

No other 1950s science fiction movie covers the same thematic ground as does *World Without End*. Instead of journeying to an alien planet, our space travelers come back to Earth. There's no need to wear oxygen-producing space suits and, for once, it is okay if the landscape appears to be Earth-like and not an alien-looking Venus or Mars. The civilization of the future requires strange new architecture and strange fashion choices (such as, why do the men underground wear head coverings but once outside, in the bright sun, wear no head covering at all?). However, the future of Earth can appear just as alien as the future of Mars. Five hundred years of elapsed history can make the commonplace appear ancient and the future appear alien-like.

A strong cast here includes the mature Hugh Marlowe (a tad too old to play the battling heroic role) and the youthful Rod Taylor, a few years away from

starring in *The Time Machine*. Even the unknown players do a fine job, and the direction of Edward Bernds always maintains quick pacing and an interesting plot. As filmed in Technicolor and CinemaScope, the film has a majestic, sweeping look that adds budget to an otherwise-B production. *World Without End* will never have the reputation of the better-known movies of the 1950s science fiction era, but it remains worthy nonetheless.

Devils of Darkness
2.0
Witchcraft
2.5
Fox

This Fox double-feature is for me of major interest since both of these witchcraft and satanic cult movies have gained a cult status over the impending decades but have also remained relatively obscure on home video.

First up is *Devils of Darkness* (1965), an Eastmancolor (sporting fairly drab color) British Hammer clone, directed by Lance Comfort. The movie, surprisingly, is slightly over two hours long, an epic length for a B-horror programmer. Of course the movie suffers with a meandering plot that is, geographically, all over the map. And then its most impactful sequences are over far too soon.

The plot, introduced by a pre-title sequence that opens 500 years in the past, involves Gypsy dancer Tania (Carole Gray), who seduces and wins the heart of her lover. But during the marriage ceremony, the shadow of the bat intrudes and the beautiful bride falls over dead. Once buried, the mysterious Count Sinistre (Hubert Noel) digs her casket back up, and as soon as the white lid is removed, Tania, eyes open, is awake and ready to follow her master to the end of time. No dramatic sense of a reanimation exists, just a reawakening. Basically it's just a pop-open-the-lid-and-follow-me, baby.

After the credits, we return to the same village, but now in modern times, where Sinistre and Tania are the secret leaders of the village cult. As the plot unfolds, we are led to believe that the village does not embrace Sinistre and the occult, but things quickly fall into place in *Wicker Man* style. Paul Baxter (a suave William Sylvester), our titular hero, is on vacation

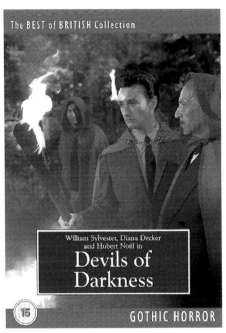

and he watches as his friends die off mysteriously, all having some type of mark on their necks. In the first of several odd sequences, a cave explorer plunges down a crevice and looks inside a large cavern to find two battered old wooden caskets. Just as a woman's hand emerges from one coffin, a figure attacks the unsuspecting explorer, killing him. Baxter, who is enjoying his vacation with antiques dealer Madeleine Braun (Diana Decker), wants to fly the bodies back to London so an autopsy can be performed (the doctor of the small village quickly closes the cases with minimal investigation). However, unknown to Baxter, Sinistre's cult resurrects the bodies of his friends, only to immediately torch them. And so the caskets are lost and never arrive in London.

Back home, Baxter and Madeleine renew contact and this allows director Lance Comfort to try to exploit swinging London of the time. Madeleine's antiques shop is a visual feast, but her party, occurring almost midway through the movie, is marvelously camp. Gaudy costumes clash with horrible décor and lighting. Baxter is set up with trendy-chic Karen Steele (Tracy Reed), an exotic artist model, who comes to the party pale enough to already be a member of Sinistre's vampire cult. Sinistre already has his sights on her and invites her up to his artist's apartment (actually the upper level of Madeleine's shop) to pose for him by provocatively lying on his bed, actually pretending to be dead as Sinistre paints her. Tracy Reed strikes a sexually intense pose whiles he paints her.

In this U.S. lobby card, Morgan Whitlock (Lon Chaney, Jr.) warns young Todd Lanier (David Weston), in this dramatic confrontation from *Witchcraft*.

But it quickly becomes clear that Sinistre wants to replace his current mate Tania with this new hottie … and Tania is not happy. Sinistre explains he is simply using Karen, who is becoming nice and cozy with Baxter, as a lure to get his talisman back from Baxter. But the Gypsy is not buying that answer!

Sinistre so foolishly drops his metallic talisman as he carries off one of Baxter's friends before killing her and disposing the body in the lake (interesting, Baxter is on the hunt for her and only one loud scream might have saved her). The talisman contains the vampire's power and he wants his golden bat sculpture back! Even when sending agents to wreck Baxter's apartment to recover the bat talisman, these fools never check the inside of Baxter's typewriter to see that it is hidden inside.

The movie's climax, promising to be a marvelous sequence with the oddly powerless Sinistre (did I mention that the fairly unimposing Hubert Noel sports a 1960s pop music style haircut that makes him look like a diminutive Robert Vaughn) dressed in bright red cape over a black suit and tie, turns out to also be a dud. Occurring in the basement of a local mansion, the cultists assemble to sacrifice Karen to the cult of the undead, but Baxter

and his police detective friend crash the party. Just when the suspense is building and we are lead to think the climax will be exciting and a thrill a minute, lightning strikes from outside, the altar is set ablaze and most of the cultists catch on fire and quickly run around burning to death. Count Sinistre runs outside with Karen, gets caught in the sun and quickly turns to ash and bone in one of the most anti-climatic endings of any horror movie of the 1960s or beyond. Don't get me wrong, *Devils of Darkness* features a few genuine first-rate sequences, but buried within the ridiculously trendy 1960s setting and low-budget pitfalls, the film falters and fails. Bottom line, Hammer knew this formula inside out and made it an art form. Lesser studios such as Planet Film Productions only learned the hard way that replicating the formula has never been as easy as it appeared.

Witchcraft, on the other hand, is the main feature of this double-bill. It is British as well and boasts Hammer alumni such as director Don Sharp (*Kiss of the Vampire*; *Rasputin—the Mad Monk*), camera operator Len Harris and Diane Clare (*Plague of the Zombies*), yet the film once again fails to properly duplicate the Hammer formula, although the stark black-and-white cinematography of Arthur Lavis features

a moody mansion with underground caverns and witches' coven ceremony chamber. In one gripping sequence Lanier family matriarch Malvina Lanier (Marie Ney) slowly pulls herself out of her wheel chair and inches her way down the stairs, under close watch of revived spiritual entity Vanessa Whitlock (Yvette Rees). Slowly and silently Vanessa sneaks up behind the unaware grandmother, until finally she pushes the woman rolling and tumbling down the stairs. The sequence is creepy, horrific (with Vannessa's witch presence drawing heavily upon Mario Bava's look for Barbara Steele from *Black Sunday*) and suspenseful.

Less successful are the possession murder sequences that confuse and confound and seldom mesmerize. Twice in the movie, motivated by a curse planted by the Whitlock family via a devil doll hidden on the fender of the car, two drivers are kept in a trance as their car veers through a landfill to drive over a steep cliff. In the first sequence Helen Lanier (Viola Keats) is killed, in the second Bill Lanier (Jack Hedley) is snapped out of his trance by a presence in the back seat. The cinematography switches between the driver's point-of-view (the car is driving slowly down a suburban street lined with houses with pavement and gutters) and close ups of the muddy trash-littered dump in long shot. The juxtaposing of such sequences is jarring and at first seems a mistake, as if the scenes of the landfill and suburban streets are one and the same. It almost takes that second victim and second murder attempt to properly sort out the logic here.

The basic plot shares a great deal with *Devils of Darkness*, as the quaint world of the past clashes with the commercial one of the present. Two old and established families, the Whitlocks and the Laniers, are at war with one another. The Laniers, land developers, are awaiting the Whitlocks to transfer bodies from their generations-old family cemetery, but Morgan Whitlock (Lon Chaney, Jr.) refuses to be rushed. The Whitlocks follow the old religion (being the major part of a modern witches' coven), while the Laniers follow the modern ways. In the best Romeo and Juliet model, young Todd Lanier (David Weston) loves cute and perky Amy Whitlock (Diane Clare), yet even their innocent love cannot bring the families

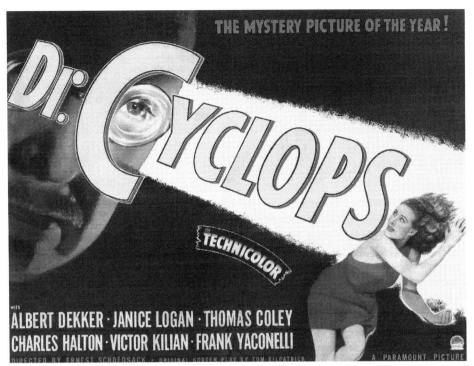

together. Lon Chaney, Jr.'s performance as Morgan Whitlock is little more than a walk-on cameo, and instead of playing a human being, he plays an attitude, a loud, angry one. However, he does look menacing and threatening when required and demands our attention in his limited time on screen.

The film's best sequences include the resurrection of Vanessa after bulldozers destroy several of the above ground burial crypts. Unlike the bombast of a Bava, Don Sharp simply shows the black hole in the crypt and allows us to hear the wind blow and a haunted voice down below. Soon, the shrouded presence of Vanessa stands alongside her broken crypt and simply overlooks the home, as it looks in the modern day. Her witchy role remains effectively mute throughout. Finally, the climax of *Witchcraft* delivers upon the promise of satanic ritual rites that *Devil of Darkness* presented and curtailed much too soon. Here, in a similar sequence, we see the 13-member coven (not all members are Whitlocks) assemble underground with the shocking revelation that Amy is a fully cooperating member, and thus her death is assured. There will be no happy ending. However, as Todd and Bill attempt to rescue the already drugged and captured Tracy Lanier (Jill Dixon) as the coven prepares for its ultimate sacrifice, only the purging fires can save the day. During the explosive climax the entire house goes up in smoke and flame, be-

coming a black-and-white counterpart to Roger Corman's colorful inferno at the end of *House of Usher*.

To me Don Sharp has always been a clunky, second-tier director (just look at *Kiss of the Vampire* vs. Terence Fisher's always superior vampire cinema) and here his direction is journeyman at best. While the production contains several quite moody sequences that are well staged and photographed, too much of the movie involves tiresome filler and dialogue. To me *Witchcraft* is very slight in the 1960s canon of horror, and while its rarity makes it a treat, its over-exposure will only reveal the flaws.

**The Classic Sci-Fi Ultimate
Collection Volume 2
Dr. Cyclops** (3.0)
Cult of the Cobra (2.5)
The Land Unknown (3.0)
The Deadly Mantis (2.5)
The Leech Woman (2.5)
Universal

When it comes to this second Universal 1950s sci-fi box set, the buyer must admit all the better movies were on the first Collection: *Tarantula*; *The Monolith Monsters*, etc. Here the collector gets those beloved second-tier productions beautifully re-mastered. Ultimately, we have a great product here.

Dr. Cyclops is the anomaly, a Universal monster/adventure epic released in 1940

in beautiful Technicolor photography. Directed by Ernest B. Schoedsack, the man who directed *King Kong*, *Dr. Cyclops* plays as more an adventure film with a mad scientist and miniature human victims than an all-out horror or even science fiction movie. However, I feel *Dr. Cyclops* shares roots with a classic Universal horror movie, *The Invisible Ray* (1936). Instead of having the reclusive madman Janos (Boris Karloff), we have the equally myopic Dr. Thorkel (Albert Dekker), whose soda bottle lenses become his downfall. Both scientists find the source of their power and scientific discovery at the bottom of a tunnel drilled into the Earth. The radiation discovered could be a source of great good or great evil and each scientist uses his discovery for evil.

Both Janos and Dr. Thorkel share basic character traits. Thorkel invites a team of great scientific minds to the jungles of Peru, they think, to join his team. And since Thorkel works alone, this is a major breakthrough. However, once the scientists arrive and are praised to high heaven by Thorkel, he invites the scientists to look through his microscope and confirm his findings (his deteriorating eyesight does not allow him to see clearly through the microscope); he then unceremoniously invites them to leave for home tomorrow morning, his arrogance only needing these second set of eyes for one brief moment. No longer needed, the scientific team is almost kicked out of camp. Janos, also reclusive and a man who does not work well with other people, according to his blind mother, finds his own discovery taken from him by the scientific team that assumes too much power. So in both films we get a ying and yang or balancing act between maverick, loner scientist and a more socially approved team.

But the fun of *Dr. Cyclops* is watching the maverick team of scientists reduced to doll size and survive against the god-like captivity that Thorkel imposes upon his hapless victims. Of course the goal of the little people is to take Thorkel's glasses and render the god blind, a raving Cyclops, so to speak, and then use their intelligence to take him down. These sequences showing the cleverness of man vs. his environment create the adventure that the film is best known for. It is in these action sequences that director Schoedsack shines. And the Technicolor photography, restored to its

CULT OF THE COBRA

OUT OF THE MYSTIC EAST **TERROR** STRIKES AT THE HEART OF A CITY!

STARRING

FAITH DOMERGUE
RICHARD LONG
MARSHALL THOMPSON
KATHLEEN HUGHES

WILLIAM REYNOLDS · JACK KELLY · MYRNA HANSEN · DAVID JANSSEN

brilliance, has never looked better. Having watched 16mm prints and even screened a 35mm print on one occasion, the DVD with its color pop and crispness has never looked this good before. Not a classic film, but *Dr. Cyclops* is a film that stands by itself as one of the most quirky science fiction entries of the golden age. The film's allusions to mythology (even Thorkel's name, when shortened to Thor, illustrates his god-like status) add another level of meaning that only makes the film richer.

Cult of the Cobra is a Universal film released in 1955 that demonstrates a superior concept that does not quite live up to its execution. The story is a wonderful one, involving a group of buddy soldiers at the end of World War II who want one final fling before flying home to the States. They are able to buy their way into watching the sacred and secret ritual of Lamians, cultists who believe that people can transform into snakes and back again. The soldiers, fueled by curiosity, simply want to watch. But they are warned not to take any photographs, and one of the team stupidly interrupts the ceremony when he takes photos using a flash. As the temple is set ablaze, cult leader Edward Pratt announces that each of the soldiers will die a tragic death for their blaspheming intrusion.

Of course, back in the United States, the men meet the strange Lisa Moya (Faith Domergue), and one by one, the men all die tragically, never suspecting until much later that Lisa is a Lamian, who is carrying out the revenge promised.

What makes *Cult of the Cobra* interesting is the fact that the film illustrates the Universal-International star-making machinery that is mentioned so prevalently throughout biographies of John Agar and why he never became a star. In the Universal star factory handsome young men were groomed to become stars, and most had to star in low-budget B-films to work their way up to more prestigious movies. Of course those stars that never caught the audiences' eyes remained in B-picture hell. Let's look at the cast here, the buddy soldiers. We have Richard Long as Paul, Marshall Thompson as Tom, William Reynolds as Pete, Jack Kelly as Carl and David Janssen as Rico. While similar talents such as Rock Hudson and Tony Curtis rose to A-productions, these talents remained in the B-film arena or went on to television success. For instance, Richard Long appeared in Allied Artists *House on Haunted Hill* a few years later and co-starred in 1959-1960 on TV's *Bourbon Street Beat*. Marshall Thompson remained in B-productions, starring in *Fiend Without a Face* and *First Man Into Space*, before heading the cast in TV's *Daktari*. William Reynolds went directly to television and starred in two series, *The Gallant Men* and

The F.B.I. He never became a household name, but his constant TV work makes him a recognizable character actor. Jack Kelley co-starred in the A-production *Forbidden Planet*, but it was chiefly in TV's *Maverick* that Kelley made his mark. And David Janssen hit TV pay dirt as the star of the classic series, *The Fugitive*.

Amazingly, so many budding talents who attempted to break into the limelight all appear in *Cult of the Cobra*, and while not all have that star quality, they are effective and memorable professionals. And seeing them create an ensemble cast in this manner, for me, is the heart of the movie.

On the same track, when Howard Hughes took over RKO Studios in the late 1940s, he tried to transform his handpicked girlfriends into movie stars, and Faith Domergue was one of Hughes' women. While she has sizzle appeal and an odd beauty (not classic Hollywood in any sense), Domergue was not bound to remain in the majors without the intervention of star-maker Hughes, who quickly moved on to other women. So by 1955 Domergue had traveled downward through the Universal B-machine (she starred in *This Island Earth*, also in 1955, perhaps her best known genre movie) and by the time of *Cult of the Cobra* was required to do little actual acting. Instead, her performance required her to appear hypnotic, almost as if she were in a trance, and attempt to look and act as though she were a snake in human form. But after such promise at the star-making hands of Howard Hughes, *Cult of the Cobra* must have been a major come down for Faith Domergue.

With *The Land Unknown*, U-I spent a little more money for one of their B-programmers, because the film was photographed in black-and-white Cinema-Scope, which added a mysterious vastness to the proceedings. Producer William Alland teamed with director Virgil Vogel (who a year earlier directed *The Mole People*) to create one of the better dinosaur adventure features of the period. The plot surmises that the South Pole stands atop a potentially active volcano and that this small area literally froze time in a prehistoric period when dinosaurs walked the Earth. Some sexual innuendoes bubble over early on, surprising for a kiddy matinee feature of this time, focused on female

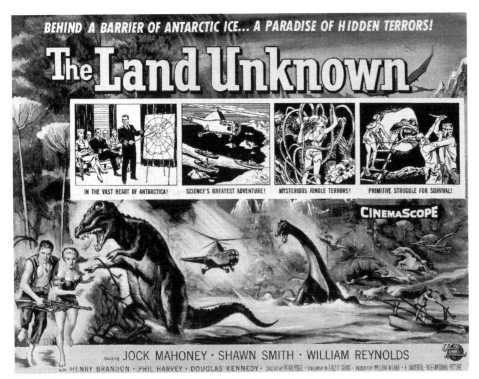

newspaper reporter Maggie Hathaway (Shawn Smith), who flirts aggressively with her male team. Maggie purrs, "I always love to meet men, captain." So when meeting helicopter pilot Lt. Jack Carmen, Maggie expresses concern that he will be piloting the first woman across Antarctica. With a gleam in his eye Carmen (William Reynolds) states, "I'd fly you up to the moon!" With a glean in her eye, she asks, "In a helicopter?!!!!" The captain assures Maggie that Carmen will "cool off as soon as he hits sub-zero weather." But Maggie seems most interested in the aloof and scientific Commander Hal Roberts (Jock Mahoney), who speaks of woman being comprised of water and salt and can only think in the most technical of manners.

What makes *The Land Unknown* so much fun is the interesting cast of chiseled and cute stereotypes that we care for, combined with the thrill of finding a tropical prehistoric monster-rama beneath the coldest spot on Earth. As the helicopter goes exploring and tries to avoid stormy weather, it descends about 3,000 feet below sea level avoiding clouds and the fog. And after crash landing in this widescreen land of monsters, the audience gawks at the impressive matte paintings and set design that make this prehistoric landscape look so creepy and inviting. Without benefit of a Ray Harryhausen to create state-of-the-art dinosaurs, Clifford Stine's

effects team more than rises to the challenge. We have models of flying dinosaurs swooping down upon the copter. We have a wonderful model of an undersea beast that emerges out of the lake and can only be repelled with fiery torches. We have the required iguanas disguised as prehistoric beasts that like nothing better than fighting one another. And surprisingly, the T-Rex-like beast, played by a man in a dinosaur suit with dwarfish arms, becomes the starring attraction with mechanically

blinking eyes and a mouth that opens and shuts, showing off its monstrous teeth. For a film that demonstrates how giant monsters can be created without the benefit of stop-motion animation, *The Land Unknown* does a credible job and keeps the thrills coming. Unlike many 1950s giant monster thrillers, *The Land Unknown* is filled with well-paced action/monster sequences.

The second treat is the appearance of Henry Brandon (Chief Scar in *The Searchers* and Barnaby in *Babes in Toyland*) as the lone, eccentric survivor of an earlier flight to the same crater. Brandon, a military man gone bonkers, is sympathetic enough until he takes every opportunity to molest Maggie and states that he will only give them the broken shaft to repair their helicopter if the men agree to leave the woman with him. Of course by the film's end the Brandon character (Dr. Hunter) becomes sympathetic and heroic and does the right thing, and even though he does not wish to be rescued and taken back to civilization, when he is rescued from drowning and taken into the rescue copter, he has a smile on his face.

The Land Unknown is one of those forgotten little gems that shine upon re-discovery and reevaluation. It is never better than it is, a low-budget "dinosaurs surviving in a forgotten pocket of our modern civilization" programmer. The script is written for youngsters and is meant to

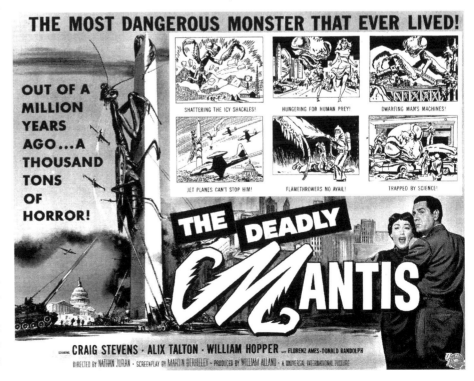

IN THE SAVAGE
HEART OF
THE JUNGLE
SHE FOUND
THE FORBIDDEN
SECRET OF
ETERNAL YOUTH!

She DRAINED MEN of their loves and lives!

THE LEECH WOMAN

Starring
COLEEN GRAY · GRANT WILLIAMS · GLORIA TALBOTT · PHILLIP TERRY
Directed by EDWARD DEIN · Screenplay by DAVID DUNCAN · Produced by JOSEPH GERSHENSON
A UNIVERSAL-INTERNATIONAL PICTURE

appeal to childhood imagination. But in spite of limited budget, sets and effects, *The Land Unknown* manages to create its own stylized fantasy vision and does so effectively.

Also released in 1957 was *The Deadly Mantis*, a film inferior to the lesser-known *The Land Unknown*. First of all, while Nathan Juran proudly used his real director's name on *The Deadly Mantis*, in shame he used the name Nathan "Hertz" on another film he directed in 1957, *The Brain from Planet Arous*. While the latter film was independently released and made on a shoestring, it is the superior film and the

film that Juran should be proudest of making. Yes, *The Brain from Planet Arous* features brain balloons and voices that emanate from frisky hounds, but the film's imagination and John Agar's grinding-teeth performance are classic and cherished by fans, even to this day.

The Deadly Mantis has the reputation of being produced by a major Hollywood studio and featuring a solid cast including TV stars Craig Stevens and William Hooper. William Alland became the major U-I producer of science fiction and horror, and even by 1957 his name was recognized by horror movie fans. Howev-

er, the film's only major asset is the wonderful monster replication of the praying mantis created by Clifford Stine's effects crew, which once again proves that a viable alternative to stop-motion animation existed during the 1950s. The mantis, slightly silly when flying in the sky with its tiny wings working overtime, looks horrifically magnificent when stalking the Arctic military base.

Perhaps both the script (heavy on stock footage/military bases and hardware, and furthering the major 1950s flaw of not introducing the beastie until the second half of the movie) and the director (too much mediocre hokum, not enough suspense, monster sequences that are not well paced, a lack of rhythmic drive, etc.) undermine the production. We already noted clever dialogue and well-paced monster sequences in *The Land Unknown*, but in *The Deadly Mantis* the two stars are not particularly interesting and the leading lady, Alix Talton, can almost be described as matronly. No sexual sizzle (and youngsters can sense on screen chemistry) what so ever!

Even the climax of *The Deadly Mantis* is botched. The monster is riding the jet stream south and gets as far as Baltimore and Washington, but then suddenly the monster is headed toward Philadelphia and New York! The final sequence awkwardly cuts to the monster already in the Manhattan Tunnel, leading to New York City, but the script offers no explanation how the beast decided to go inside the tunnel. The movie suggests narrative explanations might have been cut, perhaps in the interest of time. But bam, there we are, right outside the tunnel, and the cut to that final sequence seems haphazard and sloppy. However, the film's best sequence, the mantis appears dead, so the Alix Talton character is allowed to take photos. Shockingly, as the reporter struts in front of the mantis' claws, the beast appears to come to life and creates the film's best shock sequence, as all hell breaks loose … we pray in anticipation. However, a quick explanation ruins the fun because the audience is told the beast is dead and this was simply an involuntary movement.

Isn't it strange that *The Deadly Mantis*, featuring one of the most impressive giant insects in science fiction cinema, is almost forgotten as a film and never generated much of a buzz over the 60-plus years since its initial theatrical release. Simply stated, *The Deadly Mantis* was always mediocre, sloppily directed, with a pedestrian script that failed to take advantage of all the potential thrills and chills. The movie is never awful, but it never once rises above bland.

Last on the box set is perhaps the most disappointing movie of all, *The Leech Woman*, a film best known for being on the bottom end of the double-bill with Hammer's classic *Brides of Dracula*. This David Duncan-scripted, William Dein-directed programmer is highly original in plot but so lame in execution. Even though the film is only 77-minutes long, it seems like it goes on for two hours plus.

Featuring a cast comprised of horror film vets (Coleen Gray, Grant Williams and Gloria Talbott), none of the featured performers stands out and none of the performances even approach anything memorable. Only Estelle Hemsley as Malla submits a creepy performance, playing a woman 152 years old. Of course she is augmented with age make-up that is sometimes more effective in some sequences than others, but her wrinkled and intense face, with her piercing eyes, make her a presence that commands every moment she is on screen. Her withered neck and her claw-like arms only attest to a characterization that surpasses even Coleen Gray, who performs much of the time under similar age make-up (none of it very convincing). And Gloria Talbott and Grant Williams seem to be sleepwalking through their roles.

The Leech Woman's flaw, very similar to *Attack of the 50 Ft. Woman*, is that the plot is focused on domestic melodrama, the disintegration of a marriage, and June Talbot's (Coleen Gray) descent into alcoholism. Too much of the movie highlights such domestic woes, and for a juvenile horror programmer, such subplots become the kiss of death. And only in juvenile programmer land could a handsome lawyer such as Neil Foster (Williams), engaged to lovely Sally Howard (Talbott), immediately kick her out of bed because of his attraction to the Coleen Gray character, once she has become rejuvenated and made youthful in Africa. While Sally waits in the car outside honking her horn, the seductive sexpot seduces Neil in the bedroom and Sally becomes past tense, even when she pulls a pistol on her rival

and demands she leave Neil alone. Within a day or two, not knowing anything about the supposed young niece, Neil begs June to marry him. Such shenanigans are ridiculous, even to children in the audience.

The horror paraphernalia involving the sacrificial ring, which is used to pierce the lower brain of the victims, makes it easier to withdraw a hormone that induces the reversal of the aging process (for about 24 hours). Such sequences are chill inducing, but little else maintains the audience interest. Sadly, the final feature here, and the only one given its own single disc, is the most disappointing feature.

However, even though this box set includes the more bottom-of-the-barrel Universal Bs, even the least interesting ones are worth a look at roughly around 80 minutes apiece. For me even science fiction melodrama can be interesting when it features familiar genre actors and inhabits a world of 1950s domestic charm, where the military is always mankind's savior. And even the lower end Universal thrillers, with their superior production values, often become much more interesting than their lower-budgeted competition.

The Colossus of New York
3.0
Olive Films

The problem with most science fiction movies of the 1950s is that they are generally over-exposed via home video (in multiple reissues) and streaming. But when an anomaly such as Paramount's *The Colossus of New York* comes to home video for the first (and second time in Blu-ray) time ever, there is cause to celebrate. Or is there? This William Alland production, made after he left Universal and came to Paramount to produce *Colossus of New York* and *The Space Children* (both in 1958), demonstrates that the producer's star was in decline. Neither of these two Paramount productions comes close to rivaling Alland's best Universal work, and both of the Paramount movies are preachy and overtly religious in the worse sense. *The Colossus of New York* is by

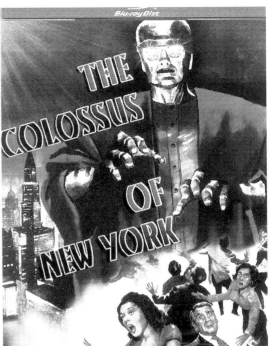

far the superior production, and because of its quirks and eccentricities, it becomes a rather novel entry in the 1950s science fiction oeuvre.

Basically the movie is equal parts cliché and a modernization of the Frankenstein mythos. The wonderful Ross Martin creates a brief yet memorable supporting performance, since his character (as humanitarian Jerry Spensser) is tragically killed after returning from Europe to receive the Peace Prize, mowed down by a speeding truck while fetching his son Billy's (Charles Herbert) toy plane. His father, William (Otto Kruger), a renowned brain surgeon, keeps his son's brain alive while he perfects a gigantic metal robot to re-animate his son's genius. William likens his son to the world-changing achievements of the great minds in history and he won't let his son's memory fade.

Basically the unique robot played by Ed Wolff is a special effects marvel, with glowing white eyes and an overwhelming physical presence. The movie is made even more eerie by its unusual Van Cleave piano score, something unheard of for the science fiction movie genre. The movie is peppered rather annoyingly with strange and quite loud electronic blips, blops and static that create the sense that this robot is electricity personified. That and the piano score make *The Colossus of New York* an odd duck among its peers.

Besides the cliché of the dedicated humanitarian dying too young and tragi-

The re-animated Jerry Spensser, now living as "the Giant," visits his wife Mala Powers, in *The Colossus of New York*.

few drops of oil leak from his eyes making it appear he was crying in death.

Waylaid by rather bland acting (Ross Martin's brief appearance is the highlight performance of the entire film), a rather slow-moving and melodramatic plot, an annoying piano score filled with electronic bleeps and a rather preachy message, *The Colossus of New York* fails to rise above the mediocre. In spite of such flaws, the movie does have a quirky originality that heightens its interest. The Colossus itself is a rather innovative and interesting mechanical man and its updating of the man-playing-God Frankenstein mythos is another frame of interest. Eugene Lourie, who directed the superior *The Giant Behemoth* one year later, brought a sense of malaise to this production and his direction sinks to the bottom of New York harbor, just as the Colossus also does. For renowned producer William Alland, *The Colossus of New York* only demonstrates that the creative support that Universal afforded him resulted in many landmark movies there, something lacking during his short time at Paramount.

The Bad Seed
3.0
Warner Bros.

Having finally caught up to 1956's *The Bad Seed*, I do not know what to quite make of it. Director Mervyn LeRoy, a classical Hollywood director who was directing motion pictures since the late 1920s, wasn't even near the end of his long career road when he made this movie. Still to come were *No Time for Sergeants*, *The F.B.I. Story* and *Gypsy*. However, his old school movie methods, combined with the source play (*The Bad Seed* was a sensation on Broadway when the movie was produced and six members of the theatrical cast were hired to do the movie) and opting to maintain the stage production look, *The Bad Seed* presents theatrical heightened reality where everyone seems to be going over the top, but delightfully so! In one highlighted sequence where emotionally distraught mother Christine Penmark (Nancy Kelly) screams at her daughter, and her daughter screams right back, I see parallels to *Mommy Dearest* with the Joan Crawford character yelling, "No wire hangers!!!" However, *The Bad Seed*

cally, we have the equally clichéd sub-plot of sibling rivalry existing between brothers Jerry and Henry (John Baragrey). Henry feels that Jerry got all the credit for some of *his* ideas. The jealousy also affects both brothers' relationship to Jerry's wife Anne (Mala Powers). It is apparent that Henry has the hots for Anne, and after Jerry's untimely demise, Henry makes it quite clear that he plans to protect and watch over both mother and son. Henry immediately plots to replace himself in the missing half of Anne's bed left cold and lonely because of her husband's death. And the plot adds another friend, Dr. Carrington (Robert Hutton), who only exists to preach morality and suggests that intelligence without a soul will always end up tragically. Of course Dr. William Spensser wants his son's intelligence to prosper inside the mechanical behemoth, but Carrington preaches that intelligence needs that guiding soul in order to do great things.

So the plot plays out with the re-animated Jerry speaking electronically from the robot's perspective, at first wanting to die and making the scientific team swear that his identity will not be revealed to anyone. Soon the metal man becomes

lonely and ventures to the wooded area near his gravesite, to try to communicate with his little boy Billy. Billy is not afraid of the robot because the child calls him the giant and the friendly robot reminds him of a character from fairy tales. However soon Anne catches on that the giant may indeed be her former husband. As the movie develops this soap opera plot, the personality of the robot/Jerry becomes far less warm and nurturing and more of a beast emerges. In fact the film's conclusion is perhaps one of the most shocking endings of any genre film of the era. The Spensser family and supporters of Jerry's work are called to the United Nations for a tribute to Jerry and his lifetime of achievement. However, the now evil robot, walking beneath the murky waters of New York's waterways, emerges at the U.N. by breaking through plate glass, causing screams and gasps. And the robot starts to shoot death rays at the assembled supporters almost immediately, killing innocent people at random. Such sequences were pretty shocking for the time. It takes the last humanity of the Colossus to urge his son to pull his shutdown lever, causing the robot to fall over a railing and crash onto the floor below. In a nice touch, a

ment custodian Leroy, and while his performance is marvelous at most levels, it involves Jones chewing up the scenery. He is on to the evil doings of little Rhoda from the get-go, even though Monica says he has the mind of a child (which may explain why he can read Rhoda's every act and knows her motivation). On stage the performance would be stellar, but as captured on film his performance's volume seems to be turned up to 11. And while the movie attempts to stay a pot boiling melodrama, the text becomes philosophical and preachy in the middle. We have crime fiction writer Mr. Tasker (Gage Clarke) debate the concept of the origins of criminality with crime newspaper reporter Richard Bravo (Paul Fix). One argues environment alone being the cause of why a person becomes a criminal, the other argues genetics and the passing on of a "bad seed." It was much funnier when Ralph Bellamy and Don Ameche had the same argument in *Trading Places*, but here Christine's father Bravo tries too hard to deny the bad seed theory, simply because he reveals Christine was adopted and her mother was a serial killer. So of course that explains why Rhoda, who fails to win a school medal for handwriting, drowns the child who did win, stomping him to death with the metal cleats on her shoes. And could a more dramatic set piece for the murder exist than at the end of a dusty old wooden pier that jets out into the woodsy tree-laden shore.

And speaking of the lack of cinema in this quasi-theatrical movie, I must cite the film's beginning and ending as being pure cinema of the most exciting variety. In the film's opening credits shot, we are observing this same pier as a high angle shot looking down onto the trees and pier. The camera slowly lowers toward ground level, and when it reaches this lower plane, the camera veers to the left to show the cityscape lit up at night. And then the camera, after the credits end, cuts to a Beaver Cleaver-style middle class American home and introduces the lovely family. Then at the end, we follow the demented Rhoda as she rushes to the pier wearing her rain slick as a thunderstorm rages. In a perfectly ridiculous jump cut,

an explosive lightning bolt literally blows away the end of the pier, along with poor Miss Rhoda, who is literally struck down by the hand of God! While the photography, sound and visual effects are creepy and effective, the jump cut to the lightning bolt literally blowing away the end of the pier is, like the rest of the movie, a bit much.

And into this mishmash of moods strolls the wonderful Eileen Hackart as Hortense, the mother of the murdered schoolboy who just senses that Rhoda knows more than she is telling. Hortense, who arrives unexpectedly and always drunk, plays a character that seems to have drifted out of Tennessee Williams. While her performance is a wonder to behold (her character drifts from polite to violent rage and finger-pointing accusation), it seems the most overripe piece of fruit in an already past-its-prime bushel. But just when one's jaw drops to the floor and expectations are primed for more hyper-dramatics, guess what, more surprises occur. At the film's end, again to emphasize the theatricality of the movie, we have a curtain call when the cast is introduced to the audience. After mom Nancy Kelly and demon child Patty McCormack are introduced, the movie ends with the mother taking the child across her knee and giving her the spanking of her life. Of course the tone of this ending is one of humor, completely obliterating the tone of Rhoda's tragic death only moments before. *The Bad Seed* demonstrates that which works on stage does not always succeed as cinema, and vice versa. And with so many conflicting tones in evidence, it is a damn shame that the movie cannot make up its mind what it intends to be to its audience. Only an overripe but effective performance by Patty McCormack lingers after the movie ends.

20 Million Miles to Earth
(50th Anniversary Edition)
3.5
Warner Bros.

1957 was a busy year for director Nathan Juran. Under the pen-name of Nathan Hertz he directed *The Brain from Planet Arous*, and under his real name directed both *The Deadly Mantis* and *20 Million Miles to Earth*, one of the classics of

is not quite that far over the top. We do have many interesting sequences of the distracted mother, growing increasingly more irrational throughout the movie, shaking her daughter and demanding to know the truth, even when mom calls her a pathological liar. Rhoda (Patty McCormack) always reacts calmly to mom's hysteria with kisses and smiles, oblivious to any wrongdoing (since she does not possess any moral conscience or sense of guilt). As mother Nancy Kelly rolls her eyes, daughter Patty McCormack flashes her evil, toothy smile.

The tone of *The Bad Seed* sometimes has me perplexed. I keep reminding myself that director Mervyn LeRoy envisioned the movie as almost a filmed stage play, because early on child monster Rhoda hugs her "aunt" Monica and we (meaning the audience) can see the little girl grimace, as though kissing the kind landlady who constantly gives the child presents is a painful chore. But such an aside to the audience is theatrical and it loses the subtlety of cinema, where the camera lens can get right up close. Sometimes the tone of the movie appears to be kitsch, something that a decade later would be called camp. So much mugging and exaggerated expressions seem inappropriate for the large movie screen.

The script encourages such an exaggerated tone. Henry Jones portrays apart-

stop-motion animation, as created by the master Ray Harryhausen.

While *The Deadly Mantis* and *20 Million Miles to Earth* both starred William Hopper, the direction of *The Deadly Mantis* is choppy, lethargic and lacks pacing. However, *20 Million Miles to Earth* rectifies all those flaws. Simply stated Ray Harryhausen was more than merely the special effects man. Harryhausen concocted the original story idea, he storyboarded the plot that included concepts of both set design and art direction and he sculpted the Ymir, the beast from Venus. He animated (as well as created the set ups, the lighting and the composite layers of the sequence) the monster as well. In other

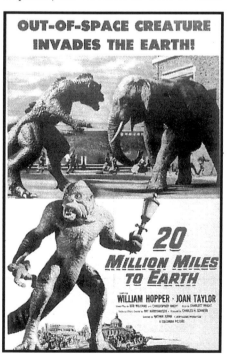

words, Harryhausen became the auteur of the film, B-programmer that it was. So in many ways Harryhausen, in theory if not contractually, became the film's director probably much more so than Nathan Juran was ever allowed to be.

Many fans argue whether *The Beast from 20,000 Fathoms* or *20 Million Miles to Earth* is the superior Harryhausen black-and-white production, and both are worthy of consideration. But to me *20 Million Miles to Earth* is the slightly superior movie featuring a more original vision (a humanoid alien crash landing in the waters off Sicily and then invading the wonderful ancient ruins of Rome), a better conceived alien, more animation sequences and better pacing (mostly because it contains more monster action). In many ways this is Harryhausen's tribute to *King Kong*, as Harryhausen's Beast from Venus contains more human attributes than any of his stop-motion creations before or since. The wonderful sequence when the alien is born, rubbing its face as it springs to life in an alien environment, is quite marvelous. Later when the Joan Taylor character surprises the beast by returning home and flipping on the lights, momentarily blinding the then tiny creature, is again a very sympathetic portrayal of a beast from space. During the climax and the destruction in Rome, the beast clings with one arm to the stonewall, before tumbling to its death, falling hundreds of feet below. Such a sequence is inspired directly by Kong clinging to the Empire State Building. At the very end, somber words are narrated as the dead, gigantic beast lies curled up in death, a crowd of people assembling to witness the spectacle. This too is taken directly out of *King Kong*. Never in Harryhausen's work has he created so much empathy for one of his monsters. And while the alien can be violent (the wonderful straight on shot of the alien charging toward William Hopper in the barn is quite terrifying), the audience always feels sympathy for its plight.

And *20 Million Miles to Earth* dazzles the imagination. Whether it be the stunning overhead shot of the rocket plunging into the sea near the fishermen, whether it is the awe-inspiring shot of the little boy who finds the canister and empties it, showing the egg housing the shadowy alien waiting to be born or whether it is the shot of the alien fighting and killing

the dog in the barn, all done in silhouette, the film features memorable imagery that lingers in the viewer's mind. As a major set piece, the destruction of the Roman Colossium, stone pillars blown away, walls smashed to smithereens, impresses. And the film's pacing is such that some type of monster shot is never far away.

Simply stated, *20 Million Miles to Earth* grows richer over time, and the pristine (dare I say perfect) print included here only enhances the viewing and audio experience. For me this is one of the top Harryhausen movies ever made and it is showcased here in the best possible way.

The Mist
3.5
Dimension

It's been a while since Hollywood released an original balls-out monster movie, and Frank Darabont's screenplay adaptation and direction of the Stephen King novella *The Mist* delivers the goods. Besides showcasing a world of flying demons, giant insects, acid-webbed spiders, tentacled beasties and giant Lovecraftian "Old Ones," the film delivers an intelligent script that focuses on the monsters inside all of us. And that's why *The Mist* shines, as it explores internal and external monsters with equal focus.

The story is basically textbook horror 101, but the script elevates the concept. What we have is a violent storm that damages property in a New England town, and when David Drayton (Thomas Jane) visits his new black neighbor Norton (Andre Braugher, playing a surly litigation-happy fellow) to exchange insurance information, Drayton tries to be the nice guy by driving Norton to town so the two of them can buy supplies for their damaged property. However, once arriving at the town's local grocery store, filled with a microcosm of diverse humanity, the mist moves in and completely blankets the entire town. One older man, bleeding from the nose, takes refuge there, ranting about something horrible outside. Soon a monster with tentacles attacks and kills a young bagger, but even after part of its still living tentacle is severed and lies flexing in the corner, many of the locals still do not believe what they see. One woman, a mother, asks one brave male to see her home, as her 8-year-old son is alone, and she refuses to barricade herself in the store. When no one helps her, she goes off alone, braving the mist and all the dangers lurking within.

Soon *The Mist* becomes two movies. One is akin to John Carpenter's *The Thing* where, in a claustrophobic setting, brave people face the monsters that attack them from outside. Here the handiwork of Howard Berger and Gregory Nicotero is on display, as they designed the creatures and the monster make-up. Besides the gigantic tentacles that creep into the loading dock area of the grocery store, we soon encounter the gigantic insects and flying demons that feed on them. Soon the creatures break through the plate glass and attack the humans inside. Using one loaded pistol, a garden rake and other store supplies, bugs and demons are splattered into submission, as human victims also mount up as well. Huge monstrosities, towering above the store and the car, lurk outside, such sequences resembling similar fog shrouded sequences from *The Deadly Mantis*. But perhaps the worst horrors are encountered when a crew of humans, led by Drayton, go to the nearby pharmacy to get pain-killing medicine and supplies. Inside the totally abandoned store, bathed in darkness, human victims are cocooned and become human hosts for monstrous babies and spiders that overrun the store. In a sequence very similar to *Alien*, the human hosts hang hopelessly, screaming in pain, as their torsos bulge with alien predators growing inside, waiting for the proper moment to burst free. The film is nicely paced with such monstrous sequences occurring regularly. However, unlike Rob Bottin's cutting-edge monster effects for *The Thing*, the monsters here, while effective, never quite achieve the believability or imagination of the creepy crawlers from Carpenter's classic. The CGI-created giant bugs and flying demons are the most effective.

But like the other movie, and perhaps the most effective aspect of the production, is the ensemble cast of characters that interact within the grocery store. We have class disputes (the local townies seem to dislike movie poster artist Draper because of his fame, success and college training, in an obviously very blue collar town). We have those people of common sense who believe and fear the beasties they see, while others (including neighbor Norton

who thinks the entire town is setting him up to be the butt of some extended practical joke) are in total denial. We have the young soldiers from the nearby military compound who speak of the dimensional link and horrors set loose by the scientists in charge. We have the certifiable town crazy, an evangelical Old Testament extremist who preaches of deeds against an avenging God and the sacrifices to such a God that must be carried out to save the rest of humanity. At first this charismatic yet disturbed woman, Mrs. Carmody (Marcia Gay Harden), seems harmless enough, if overly intense, but as time goes on more and more of the hostages align themselves with her philosophy and soon become a bloodthirsty mob ready to sacrifice anyone for the good of all. And in the mix comes Drayton's young boy Billy, who experiences more horror in one evening than most people encounter in their entire lives. But the film's strength lies in

large part in this microcosm of humanity, in the small interactions, in the self-sacrifices and mean-spirited greed, in the bravery, fear and reactions of people encountering what Carmody refers to as the End of Days.

Interesting, *The Mist* is a double-edge horror/monster movie. On the one hand the movie focuses on the attack of our world by monsters from another dimension (shades of *Equinox*), actual beasts that see humans as easy prey, perhaps as food, and as unwilling hosts for their spawning. Then, we have the internal psychological monsters that haunt our inner minds, becoming those demons that shape how we live and look at the external world. The final images of the movie bring both worlds together.

In an ending that might well be the most depressing finale to a horror movie since *The 7th Victim* or the original *Night of the Living Dead*, Drayton, son Billy, new friend Amanda (Laurie Holden), the town's quick witted school teacher (Frances Sternhagen) and the surviving victim with the nose bleed head out in Drayton's truck to see if they can get past the world of "mist." When the car runs out of gas, still encumbered in this monstrous fog-shrouded universe, Drayton sees that he has four bullets for the five people in the car (none for himself). In a mutual pact of acceptance, Drayton quickly kills the four people, then climbs outside his truck and screams for the monsters to quickly take him. The sound he hears, growing gradually in intensity, turns out to be a military caravan of rescued humans who are being ushered off to some safe haven. As one truck passes filled with people, Drayton eyes the mother who left the grocery store to go home to her 8-year-old child. She obviously has survived. As the trucks pass, the fog slowly lifts, as battalions of soldiers use flame-throwers to burn out the nests of the beasts. Now Drayton has to live the rest of his life knowing that his humanitarian mercy killings were for nothing, that rescue was only *seconds* away. As the movie ends, Drayton curls up into a ball outside his vehicle, screams uncontrollably, tears drowning his face, as this realization envelops him. For many people this depressing finale absolutely ruins the film.

As a side note, I find it very interesting in thinking about who lives and who dies. Obviously the small (almost) surviving group including Drayton appeared throughout the movie as the brave ones, the rational ones, and the people with whom we most identify. But when the car dies, their hopes die, and instead of continuing to face their fears, they opt for a quick death. The mother who foolishly went out into the mist on her own, ignoring everyone's pleas to stay put and safe, reminds us about her child having been left home alone. And foolishly or not, she leaves, and as we learn, survives, against all odds. But the remaining people in the grocery store, some of whom sided with Mrs. Carmody, become an ugly mob and are revealed to be terribly flawed and not overly intelligent. But a few of them, courageous and noble, survive. The people that we think are most like ourselves are the people who ultimately die, their deaths resulting from lack of faith and perhaps even a lack of courage. Is this Darabont's way of condemning suicide

for any reason? Or is it Darabont's way of stating people live and die in spite of the manner in which they conduct their lives? Who lives or dies is not based upon any scale of morality or ethics, but just the roll of the dice, the luck of the draw, fate. I find this question the most curious one of all.

Mother of Tears
2.0
Dimension Extreme

Dario Argento is among the finest horror film director of the second half of the 20th century, and even at 70 when this film was made, the Italian director still had plenty of blood to spill, plenty of nerves to fray. Most recently, Argento directed two successful *gialli*, *The Card Player* and *Do You Like Hitchcock?* And anticipation was running feverish when it was announced that Argento was ready to tackle the third installment of his Three Mothers trilogy (beginning with *Suspiria* and continuing with *Inferno*), his loosely connected world view of three witches, sisters, inflicting ruin on an unwary world. Of course *Suspiria* was Argento's most successful movie (coming early in his career), and artistically, along with *Deep Red*, remains his best. *Inferno*, wildly visual and violent, falls one rung lower artistically. But audiences waited 30 years for the trilogy to conclude, and as Argento's career enters its twilight, *Mother of Tears* might well be one of his final films (films such as *Giallo* and *Dario Argento's Dracula* followed in its

wake). So he needed to make this a fitting conclusion to his Three Sisters mythology.

To help insure the film's success he re-teamed with his family, casting both his life partner Daria Nicolodi and daughter Asia Argento (Nicolodi is Asia's mother) in key roles. Scoring the movie is former Goblin member Claudio Simonetti, who composed most of Argento's recent movies. Frederic Fasano is the cinematographer, and Walter Fasano is the editor. Fasanos worked with Argento on the wildly imaginative *Do You Like Hitchcock?* So Dario Argento's comfort zone, working with actors and technicians with whom he worked before, had to be conducive to making *Mother of Tears* successful.

Unfortunately *Mother of Tears* is ultimately a failure, but it is a film that has a great deal going for it anyway. It is not the classic the horror film community craved, and making fans wait 30 years only makes this disappointment more profound. At this point in his career perhaps Argento is better at creating the giallo film and not supernatural horror movies. As he proved so distinctly in his recent past with *Do You Like Hitchcock?*, Argento used music, cinematography, acting and editing to weave a suspense thriller filled with deepest dread and surprises, his pacing evolving into a crescendo of terror by the final minutes. In other words, Dario Argento was still operating near the peak of his artistic talents, even in his twilight years.

However, with *Mother of Tears*, using most of the same crew, the film feels half-baked and flat. The film's scope depicts

the "second falling of Rome" with armies of citizens infected by Argento's version of "The Rage," culminating in bloodshed and anarchy. The film cries out for a larger budget that can better visualize this sudden moral decay after the Third Mother returns. Such similar sequences were captured beautifully in lower-budgeted films such as Hammer's *Quatermass and the Pit*, but here Argento's visual apocalypse seems woefully lacking. And when his chic coven of witches appears at the airport, the sequence, while brash, seems more like a walk on the wild side of the fashion runway than the occult evil loosed upon humanity. And when an Asian witch upstages the reigning Third Mother, we know the film is in trouble. In several delicious sequences the witchy Asian, a gold tooth front and center, becomes the most terrifying vision of witchcraft in the entire film. Her death on a train at the hands of Asia Argento comes too fast and too soon. Moran Atias, who plays the Third Mother mostly in the nude, becomes the Matilda May of her generation (remember the naked alien from *Lifeforce*?). Atias, a scrawny young woman with bouncy breasts, seems oddly devoid of power. To make her seem more demonic, witchy cronies, male slaves and kinky human followers always appear in her presence. The Third Mother hardly has a word of dialogue, meaning the role lacks characterization that could make her appear to be the deliverer of world's end. Her major actions require draping herself in a talisman, a burlap sack dress, or stripping it off. Sometimes stripping, sometimes redressing in the same sequence. Atias wears demonic makeup and uses intense glares, but ultimately she becomes another naked model actress poseur. She pouts when she needs to command.

Argento's use of gore is both overdone, yet never gonzo enough. In Argento's classics the gore always pushes the envelope of taste, but it is executed in the most visually arresting manner. Take the beginning sequence from *Suspiria*, where a female victim is cut by shards of glass and left hanging by the neck only inches from the ground. Argento manifests an opera of visual horror that is both excessive and artistic, the imagery lingering long in the viewer's imagination. Here, the gore seems gratuitous and uninspired. We have similar sequences with throats be-

Moran Atias as the Third Mother, in one of her rare fully clothed moments

ing sliced and axes bashing in a human's skull. We have one woman who has a metal spear rammed up the entire length of her torso, finally penetrating from her bloodied mouth. We have servants of the Third Mother use an ancient tool to disfigure the face and mouth of a female victim as a blade slices open her guts, her intestines flopping to the floor. The woman, still conscious, is strangled when her own intestines are wrapped around her throat. All this is totally ridiculous. Argento was the modern master for orchestrating gore for horrifyingly effective results, but the splatter in *Mother of Tears* always looks like a visual effect and fails to involve us emotionally. It may be blasphemy to admit, but maestro Argento has lost the ability to terrify us and get under our skin.

Argento must be given props for his inspired use of CGI, the bane of most filmmakers. He creates a ghostly world when magic dust is thrown into the wind. Images of ghostly, former occupants of an Italian household create a true sense of the supernatural and remain one of the film's most effective sequences. In several scenes the ghostly presence of Asia's dead mother tries to help her child from the great beyond. In another sequence,

Asia Argento's apartment door comes to demonic life as those denizens of the other world bend the wooden door into the shape of demons that bring the door to terrifying life. A similar sequence was attempted in Robert Wise's *The Haunting* with similar effect, but with the magic of CGI, the effect is even more terrifying and mesmerizing.

The movie's worst flaw is the lack of a fully fleshed-out script, the story based upon Argento's original idea (both he and four other writers are given screenplay credit), so the movie becomes little more than a sketchy premise. By the movie's end, all it takes for Asia to defeat the Third Mother is to use a metal rod to rip the burlap dress off her quivering body and burn the talisman in an urn. At this point the entire house collapses and a huge phallic wooden stake crashes through the wall, pinning the naked witch beneath it. Classic Argento this is not!

But what does work in *Mother of Tears*? The now mature Asia Argento (still featuring the prettiest bags under her eyes), still oddly beautiful, becomes the perfect heroine to both flee the horrors and finally confront them … and finally to defeat them. Also, Argento's effective imagery of having a demonic monkey announce the appearance of the world of the occult is wonderfully executed. Sequences where the monkey sniffs out the hidden Asia are tense and frightening, becoming the scariest sequences in the entire movie. The catacomb tunnel sequence at the end featuring Asia searching for the Third Mother and her nasty entourage becomes effective.

But enough already!

Dario Argento can still deliver the goods though inconsistently, but *Mother of Tears* fails because the movie appears to have been executed without a fully realized script or the budget to deliver the visuals as Argento would wish them to appear. Think of *Suspiria* or *Deep Red* and their success is based upon imaginatively conceived visuals edited and scored to perfection. Those productions become visual dreams that lure the viewer into their off-putting vision. Here, with *Mother of Tears* Argento's visuals are literal, seldom poetic, and the result sputters when it needs to soar. Perhaps Argento was working too fast with too little money, perhaps age has sapped Argento's creative abilities, but the entire production has that unfinished feel. Even cult star Udo Kier appears far too briefly and dies in much too silly a manner.

After waiting 30 years to finish this trilogy, the disappointment is that much more heartbreaking.

Gog
(3-D version)
3.0
Kino Lorber

Ivan Tors is mainly remembered as a television producer, the man who brought *Science Fiction Theatre*, *Daktari* and *Flipper* to the small screen. But he was first a movie producer who made a string of hard-science sci-fi movies, *The Magnetic Monster* (1953), *Riders to the Stars* (1954) and *Gog* (1954), before making the move to TV. What hampered Tors was the fact that he loved to exploit the mysteries of actual science in his work and shunned the use of monsters and alien invaders. Tors thought the misuse of science by flawed humans was more realistic and believable and pointed children toward a future of scientific exploration. But to the kids back in theaters in 1953 and 1954, and even

the kids who watched locally produced "Early Show" movie programs when the films were sold to TV, Ivan Tors was generally considered to be a snooze, his films generally talky, overlong and dull. As a kid I hated *Gog*, then shown in worn black-and-white television prints. Often the prints shown were cut or had too many splices and we were hoping that any old variety of schlocky monster would enter the scenery soon.

Bravo to Kino Lorber for releasing a meticulous restoration of both a 2-D and 3-D version, now boasting over-saturated colors that bring the movie to life. Unfortunately *Gog* arrived in 1954, at the very tail end of the 3-D craze, and because of the added expense for two projectors/two prints needed for 3-D projection, the film only saw a very limited release as a 3-D movie. Instead, it was mostly shown in theaters in the 2-D version. But most

children only saw the film in black-and-white on TV, which was the most un-cinematic way of all. The truth is that *Gog*, while it's not *Creature from the Black Lagoon*, *House of Wax* or *It Came From Outer Space*, does contain some of the best 3-D photography and wow-factor pop-outs of the era. Lothrop B. Worth photographed the film under the direction of another one-eye-blind director, Herbert L. Strock. Strangely, the opening credits are 2-D to allow time for both projectors in theaters to be synched, but as soon as the movie proper begins, we see two gloved hands handling a syringe, whose needle pops out and is pointed directly at the audience. When it comes to 3-D effects, this one is a classic opening. Later during the movie, we are treated to sequences featuring flame-throwers directed outward toward the audience, two robots attacking human beings with their metal arms fluttering. While the film lacks lots of action and is very talky, visually the 3-D keeps the audience occupied and fascinated by the ambitious visuals.

Actually the movie starts quite dramatically with two back-to-back deaths. In this four level underground laboratory hidden beneath the desert, scientists are working on freezing human beings for long space voyages, working just as hard to thaw them out alive at the end of the journey. In the opening sequence one scientist is left alone in the freezing chamber when the controls suddenly start operating by themselves, the chamber door lock spinning shut trapping the doctor inside. Then automatically the freezing controls are activated and the temperature drops dangerously within a matter of seconds. The doctor is photographed in the rear plane and the frosted glass window and windshield wiper capture the middle plane, as the doctor quickly freezes and falls backwards to his death (supposedly shattering into a hundred pieces). Suddenly the temperature returns to normal and the locked doors are open. A female doctor goes inside the chamber and screams as she looks down at the remains of the deceased doctor, but the door suddenly closes and locks, as the temperature controls plummet, trapping the woman inside just like before. Unlike the prolonged death of the first victim, the female screams and is covered in a cloud of frosty fog as she falls to her frigid death within moments. The suspense generated by these sequences is never quite matched, as a conspiracy theory is revealed as outside investigator Richard Egan works with doctors and scientists (including Herbert Marshall, Constance Dowling, Philip Van Zandt and William Schallert) to solve the mystery. In a rather clever but less than dramatic scenario, it turns out that the computer that runs the entire underground laboratory, NOVAC, protected by robots Gog and Magog (triangular metal bots with four arms), has been tampered with when built and programmed in Eastern Europe. At that time a special receiver and transmitter was installed that allows a mysterious low-flying aircraft to control the underground military installation. While NOVAC is only a stationary giant computer, Gog and Magog become the enemy's "muscle" and are able to fight against their human

programmers and protect the Far Eastern threat.

In a rather unspectacular finale, humans armed with flame-throwers combat the charging robots (one at a time of course) and eventually fry their circuitry and render them as the patchwork tin cans they so resemble.

Gog is basically too scientific for its own good and it is only the bright color film stock and 3-D photography that elevates the film into becoming something special for the fans. Compared to the early TV prints, this restoration by Kino Lorber is a revelation and allows viewers to appreciate the film's stronger aspects. But even with these improvements *Gog* is at best an adequate way to spend 85 minutes on a Saturday afternoon. But gosh, does the 3-D photography and restored color help!

The Monster That Challenged the World
3.0
Kino Lorber

Jules V. Levy, Arthur Gardner and Arnold Laven met in the film unit of the U.S. Air Force during World War II, ultimately becoming Levy-Gardner-Laven Productions (also known as Gramercy Pictures) around 1951, hoping to produce successful independent motion pictures. Working with United Artists as their financial backer and distributor, the team soon found that the horror and science fiction market was the fastest way to financial success during the mid-1950s, when the genre's B-productions were in high demand. Levy and Gardner were the production end, while Laven directed (until he left for greener pastures, being replaced by director Paul Landres). Gramercy produced four horror-science fiction movies, three of which are among the best genre programmers made during the 1950s (*The Monster That Challenged the World*, *The Vampire* and *Return of Dracula*), while the forth, *The Flame Barrier*, is best forgotten.

The Monster That Challenged the World, released in 1957, was the first monster movie produced by Levy-Gardner-Laven, and it was an exceptional B-production (but as a child I remember asking my dad, what does "challenged" mean?). The production company never liked that title

Mimi Gibson plays Sandy, in this publicity shot with *The Monster That Challenged the World*.

and intended to call the movie *The Jagged Edge* (which seemed a terrible title, one that implied a psychological thriller rather than a monster-rama that appealed to the *Famous Monsters of Filmland* Monster Kid generation). But obviously the production team knew exactly what they were doing.

First of all, the entire cast was populated with highly effective professionals, always anchored by a veteran actor of high talent. Here veteran "cowboy" star Tim Holt starred (at age 37, with squat build and crew-cut, not the dashing romantic lead of many genre productions) and did a fine job; in *The Vampire* veteran John Beal starred and was spectacular in his Jekyll-Hyde performance; and in *Return of Dracula* Francis Lederer played the suave Continental Count Dracula, crafting a performance that may be inferior but still stands tall alongside the iconic performances by Christopher Lee and Bela Lugosi. For *The Monster That*

The Monster That Challenged The World

Challenged the World, Hans Conried, Audrey Dalton and Casey Adams (aka Max Showalter, best remembered co-starring in *The Indestructible Man* with Lon Chaney, Jr.) supply ample support.

For added impact on a budget, Gramercy always filmed on-location, which gave their films either a hometown aesthetic (such as the small-town America feel in both *The Vampire* and *Return of Dracula*) or the Salton Sea canal system military base locale of *The Monster That Challenged The World* (visually highlighting the 1950s usual competitive war of wills between scientists and the military). One thing was for certain, Gramercy gave each of its films a unique look and none of its productions resembled the similar ware produced by Universal-International or American-International or anyone else. If anything, the actual location photography created a gritty

and dank canvas onto which horror film mayhem encroached. Another strength of these three Gramercy productions was that the scripts (written by female Pat Fielder for all four science fiction-horror productions) contained pivotal action sequences paced regularly throughout each production, while her stories maintained suspense and an eager sense of anticipation. For instance, *The Monster That Challenged the World* begins with a military exercise where a trainee parachutes into the Salton Sea (actually, the sequence was filmed off Catalina Island) and is almost immediately picked up by a small boat containing two naval men. However, after arriving on the scene, the parachute of the jumper lies limp in the water, with one of the naval rescuers jumping into the water looking for his missing body (the other man remains onboard the boat). In a highly effective sequence, the man

aboard the boat is photographed in close up, his face registering the most hammy fright reaction imaginable, as a scary dark silhouette appears across his body. When the bodies in the water are recovered, they are both found shriveled and disfigured, having been drained of blood and water, as the horrified man aboard the boat dies from a stroke … caused by fear! In other words the film immediately establishes the fact that we are now in monster-land and that something truly horrifying scares the shit out of a well-trained military team. When the sea monster (based upon tiny mollusks) is finally revealed, the 10-foot tall beast, slobbering a white pasty slime from its mouth, impresses. Actual underwater scuba divers are edited alongside shots (photographed in giant water tanks) of the monster and humans in extreme close-up horror reactions, so this final effect, while not quite seamless to more receptive adults, actually works quite effectively for the juvenile audiences that mobbed theaters for weekend matinees. Even the sequence of a human coming within range of the deadly talons of the beastie and the monster's pincer's penetrating his neck becomes terrifying in a B-universe sort of way. Unlike most horror movies of the period, this giant mollusk impresses and comes off as one of the most effective monsters of the period.

The film's final sequence is quite terrifying. A little girl who likes to watch the rabbits that are maintained in the lab finds them in cold cages and turns up the temperature of the huge water-filled tank in which rests a mollusk egg (which must be maintained at a cool temperature or it will hatch a new monster beastie). Of course cute young Sandy (Mimi Gibson) knows nothing about the monster lurking unborn in the tank, so when the mollusk hatches and emerges from the tank, she screams and her mother (Audrey Dalton) runs to her, picks her up and races to a storage room, barricading the door, but the monster easily breaks through the door, its bug-eyes staring the humans down. But hero Tim Holt arrives and uses a fire extinguisher to keep the monster at bay. What is very interesting and cuts against the grain here is the intense fear registered on Holt's face, as he attempts to defeat the monster, threatening his new girlfriend. However, when servicemen armed with rifles appear and shoot the sea beast, all is well as the 10-foot tall monster drops to the ground dead.

Sequences such as the climax described above abound in *The Monster That Challenged the World*, making the film an exciting monster-fest from beginning to end. I maintain that the sequence in the dark room when the witchy housekeeper appears in *House on Haunted Hill* is one of the best shocks in horror history, and the sequence where the old caretaker checks out his canal area after hearing a squishing-splashing sound outside his observation booth and is suddenly attacked by the monster is almost equally effective. The film is filled with suspense and well directed, shots suddenly cut to feature disfigured victims, sudden death attacks and well conceived battles between monster and mankind. And here as rendered remastered in this Kino Lorber Blu-ray edition, the film has never looked better. All in all, for all fans of 1950s horror films, *The Monster That Challenged the World* is one of the best and should be in everyone's collection. Once again my hat goes off to Levy-Gardner-Laven for raising the bar.

The Premature Burial
2.5
Kino Lorber

After the tremendous success with the Edgar Allan Poe-based *House of Usher* and *Pit and the Pendulum*, American International, director Roger Corman and star Vincent Price had a good thing going. For a modest budget, AIP was able to create Hammer-esque art direction (courtesy of Daniel Haller) and created a true cinematic Gothic foreboding mood, with the help of expert cinematographer Floyd Crosby. The AIP Poe movies (mainly the ones directed by Roger Corman, that is) became the American Gothic of horror, challenging the dominance of British Hammer Film Productions.

So where was Vincent Price for this third entry? Why was his obviously tormented lead role given over to aging Ray Milland? The true story involved Roger Corman attempting to be too clever for his own good. Corman did not intend for this third Gothic Poe entry to be made and released by American International. Instead Corman intended to redress older sets used in earlier AIP productions but

release the film under the banner of his own film production company (one he operated with his brother Gene), Filmgroup. Since Vincent Price was under contract to AIP, Corman felt that Ray Milland would be a wonderful replacement and could play insanity just as well as Price. The only problem was that American International co-owner Samuel Z. Arkoff happened to appear on Corman's set unannounced one day and we can imagine what hit the fan. Arkoff, not wanting to submarine a potential moneymaking vehicle in his successful AIP Poe movie franchise, had Corman agree that he was making the movie for American International, even though Gene Corman's name still appeared as executive producer on the project. Arkoff received an unbilled producer's credit, and all was once again happy on the set, now that *The Premature Burial* was to be released under the AIP banner.

If this movie accomplished only one thing, it demonstrated the importance of having Vincent Price signed on as the face of the Poe franchise, because even though Ray Milland was an Academy Award-winning actor, his performance, while solidly intense, could not hold a candle to the performances that Vincent Price delivered in the first two Poe entries. Even though Milland could be melodramatic when required, he was always very professional and delivered successful but nondescript performances at this stage in his career. The more ham-fisted Vincent Price always over-played his role and did so quite delightfully, always imbuing his performances with passion. Just think of Vincent Price with the white hair delivering that effective soliloquy about being sensitive to visual and auditory stimulation in *House of Usher*, his eyes burning outwardly yet feeling so much pain internally, that

Guy (Ray Milland) toasts Emily (Hazel Court) and Miles (Richard Ney), showing off his fool-proof burial vault, from *The Premature Burial*.

the performance becomes one of his all time best. The tight photography of his face carefully conveys words that meld the audience's eyes and ears to the screen. Ray Milland has similar opportunities in *The Premature Burial* but the performance merely appears to be a journeyman one that seems polite and exudes little else in its craft. Milland, once he returns from the dead completely insane, his mental illness is conveyed more by dark eye makeup and bulging eyes, not the reality of a character who has lived long enough to experience the worst nightmare imaginable ... being buried alive. Vincent Price would have delivered a performance with quiet subtlety and over-played nuance ... for a Price performance could be both, subtle and yet overplayed to produce a performance that long lingers in the audiences' mind. Roger Corman could produce an effective AIP-style Poe movie without James Nicholson and Samuel Arkoff, but he could not do an effective one without the presence of Vincent Price. That's just how important Price became to the franchise.

The small ensemble cast includes Hazel Court, Heather Angel, Alan Napier, Dick Miller and Richard Ney. It seems that the majority of the cast is kept around merely to help drive Milland insane, even before he has a catatonic fit and appears dead while attempting to exhume his father's corpse, in an attempt to find out if his father were buried alive. While Milland is assumed dead (foolishly after talking about his catatonic condition and fear of being buried alive throughout the entire movie) and his body is prepared for burial (even as his body is being carted to the gravesite, his bulging eyes flicker open and dart here and there as seen through a solid plate glass casket window. Yet no one sees his open eyes or realizes that he is alive, although he is obviously the center of attention at his funeral.

Another curious (an actual centerpiece of the movie) sequence also confounds the audience. Milland has an outdoor burial vault constructed as a foolproof means of making sure he is never buried alive. It seems that Milland spends all his time there during the day painting and isolates himself from the rest of the world. New wife Hazel Court tells her husband that he might as well be dead if he remains in his burial vault all the time. So, being so much in love and eager to please, he blows up his vault with dynamite. What makes the vault so curious is that it is tricked out with devices that

will ensure that he cannot be buried alive. Inside his casket, stored in the upper lid, are tools that can be used to dig his way out of the buried ground. If he twitches a finger, the casket sides blow out. If he pulls a specific curtain, a section of the stonewall opens up, allowing access to outside the vault. If he pulls another curtain, a section of the ceiling opens and a rope ladder falls down. He even has several sticks of dynamite buried in the vault, allowing him to blast his way out. He can pull another chord and a bell rings. And this goes on and on. But after spending so much planning and construction time to protect his life, one little conversation with his wife makes him decide to abandon his foolproof sanctuary. And when he ultimately has that fatal-appearing catatonic fit, everyone assumes he is actually dead and they can't wait to get his body into the ground as fast as possible.

The Premature Burial is very inferior to the first two Vincent Price Poe vehicles, but when accepted on its own, it is not a bad movie, just a mediocre rehash. Roger Corman is the master of building outdoor sets (mainly the foggy cemetery) on a studio soundstage, with obvious solid walls disguised in the mist and fog, the set consisting of assorted gnarly trees and tombstones erected here and there. In many ways his outdoor sets remind us of the similarly-created outdoor sets from Universal movies such as *Frankenstein* and *Bride of Frankenstein*, where the imagination and vision of its director means more than realistic on-location settings. When watching *The Premature Burial* we know that the cemetery set is not an actual exterior location, but its stark visuals and creative design make it more than worthy. Since the movie was planned as a lower-budgeted alternative to the first two American International productions, *The Premature Burial* lacks the imagination and resources of the first two entries, but it still fits the formula and has that Gothic look that made all the Poe movies so very distinct. It is definitely worth a look.

The Whip and the Body
3.0
Kino Lorber

Most European horror movies suffered grievous harm when released on America shores during the 1950s, 1960s and 1970s. Many such movies were re-dubbed into English with mostly less than satisfactory results (subtitled versions back then were rare). Many releases were trimmed and reedited to fit the time slot for a matinee double feature that appealed to youthful horror film audiences. And to a lesser degree the movies were re-scored, with cast and credit names omitted or changed (Mario Bava becoming John M. Old, for example).

These were some of the reasons why I hated Mario Bava's *What!* when I first saw it at a drive-in theater in 1963. Ubaldo Terzana's dark and moody cinematography was effectively lost at the open-air theater and, being a child, the dreamlike and somnambulistic pacing was deadly and under-appreciated. The fact that the release print of *What!* was shortened and reedited did not help matters.

But now in its complete director's cut mastered from a clean, restored 35mm source presented in high definition, *The Whip and The Body* (a far better title than the senseless *What!*) can now be appreciated for the minor classic it is. Even though Mario Bava historian Troy Howarth tells me that the coloring for the Kino edition is not accurate and over-extenuates the blues, the pristine condition of the digital print and the deeply saturated colors held me transfixed, finally appreciating what I was formerly bored to tears watching decades earlier.

The Whip and The Body presents another decadent aristocratic family living in a dank and hollow-sounding castle, presided over by the elder and sickly patriarch Count (Gustavo De Nardo), whose second favorite son Christian (Tony Kendall) is set to inherit the Count's wealth and titles. Former favorite son Kurt (Christopher Lee, who has never looked more handsome) becomes the prodigal son returning from self-imposed exile, having seduced and abandoned the daughter of servant Giorgia (Harriet Medin), the daughter taking her own life with the same knife that is now enshrined in a glass case with a red rose. Giorgia vows revenge. Kurt returns to help celebrate brother Christian's recent marriage to the lovely Nevenka (Daliah Lavi), the woman Kurt claimed for himself. Of course the younger brother with the inferiority complex one-ups his brother by marrying the woman Kurt (not him) loved. However,

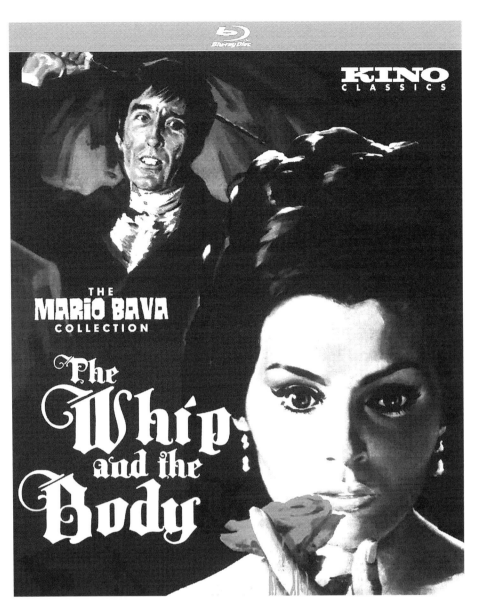

a cousin Katia (Ida Galli) becomes the sexual object of desire for Christian because he never truly loved Nevenka. Katia makes it clear to Christian that it is too late for them, now that he has married another woman. Kurt knows how to satisfy his former lover Nevenka, who still lusts after him. Kurt rightfully tells her that she loves violence and he takes her to the beach where he flogs her with his whip ripping the back of her blouse and causing welts to appear. Yet after the initial pain, Nevenka turns with carnal desire and the couple lustfully embraces. And finally servant Losat (Luciano Pigozzi), looking like a cross between Peter Lorre and Oscar Homolka, plays the red herring role by always appearing when least expected. Christian hates Kurt and Kurt hates his father the Count, who disinherited him when he abandoned the family

and brought disgrace upon them all when the servant's daughter stabbed herself to death.

Like Bava's classic *Black Sunday*, *The Whip and the Body* is a visually lush tale that reveals itself through inspired cinematography rather than dialogue or character development. Occurring in an oppressive castle, large and lumbering, that has seen better days, the film often seems to be a color version of *Black Sunday* but with ghostly apparitions rather than vampires. However, one sequence does play homage to the earlier Bava classic when son Kurt mysteriously enters the Count's chambers through the ornate fireplace, startling the sickly patriarch.

The bulk of the movie focuses on dream-like walks throughout the castle by all the major participants at night. Early on, in a marvelously staged nightmarish

FROM **BLUMHOUSE** THE PRODUCER OF **THE VISIT, INSIDIOUS & THE GIFT**

WRITTEN AND DIRECTED BY
JORDAN PEELE

GET OUT

rection makes everything work once audiences give the movie a chance and do not demand the rapid-pace rhythms of today's modern horror movies. Similar to a nightmare or becoming lost in one's visual imaginings, *The Whip and the Body* is very trance-like and deliberate in its ambitions, but such creepy-crawling pacing results in a big payoff. The movie lacks the mythic monsters of *Black Sunday* and *Black Sabbath*, but *The Whip and the Body* features performances that slowly get under the skin and allow us to understand warped, violent sexual attraction. This Kino Lorber edition delivers the goods.

Get Out
4.0
Universal

The only formulaic horror film trope occurs in *Get Out*'s pre-credits sequences, where a black man, obviously in the wrong neighborhood (echoed by his very own words on his cell phone) at the wrong time, walks down a tree-lined upper middle class very white suburban neighborhood, soon followed by an expensive white car that slows down to take a closer look at him. After enduring the car's slow crawl, the black man twists and quickly starts walking in the opposite direction, hoping to elude the car. But the car also turns around. But when he looks over his shoulder and finds the car stopped in the middle of the street and the driver's car door left wide open, the audience realizes it's only a matter of time before the driver will appear out of nowhere, render the black man helpless and drag his dead weight to the trunk of the car. Creating his version of a standard horror movie sequence to get his audience hooked, *Get Out* will advance in novel new ways from this point onward. Screenwriter and director Jordan Peele, in his debut film, knows how to make the commonplace terrifying, generating fear and dread just by the way in which he pans and edits his shots and cuts from one viewpoint to another. Here, he is already a visual master.

Chris Washington (Daniel Kaluuya) and Rose Armitage (Allison Williams) are headed toward the country to visit Rose's upscale but socially hip parents Missy (Catherine Keener) and Dean (Bradley Whitford), who do not know that their lily-white daughter is dating a black man.

sequence, Kurt drifts through the castle and stops at a window with wall length drapes. There the drapes seem to wrap around Kurt, who screams and fights the twisting cloth, soon pulling the very same dagger from his throat that Giorgia enshrined in glass, staring at the weapon before the bloody gash in his neck spells his slow demise. During the funeral in the castle chapel, all the members of the household appear to be glum as they attempt to hide their guilt, the actual murderer most definitely present.

Ah, but Christopher Lee appears periodically throughout the remainder of the movie, but only to his S&M lover, Nevenka, who often hears noises during the night and investigates, following the muddy boot prints that result in a shocking reveal whenever the mute Kurt appears. Of course no one believes her that the ghost of Kurt is stalking the castle, but in such sequences the sexually charged Daliah Lavi has never looked more ravishing, whether sitting at her piano or striking a midnight pose of both fear and anticipation. And these striking walks and visuals,

complimented by the concerto-like musical score by Carlo Rustichelli, the piano score alternating between spare, lush and romantic. The music is unlike any other horror movie score but, when paired with Mario Bava's ghostly walks through the bowels of the castle, produces a somber effect.

Soon others fall victim to the knife, leading Christian to go to the creepy family crypt and enter Kurt's tomb, hauling out his coffin and burning the already decaying corpse inside. This leads to the exciting climax where the actual murderer is revealed and the surviving family members can at last live in some semblance of peace.

Euro-horror is an acquired taste and the leisurely-paced visuals always pay off in a major way when handled effectively by a masterful director such as Bava. The difference between a Euro-horror epic that transfixes and mesmerizes vs. one that drags and bores is usually due to performance and direction. Here Christopher Lee and Daliah Lavi light up the screen and Mario Bava's sure-handed di-

Chris is very, very nervous but Rose assures her lover that her parents are non-racist liberals who will adore him. But right from the start, *Get Out* suggests *Rosemary's Baby*, *The Stepford Wives* and *The Devil Bat*, but handled in an even more effective, subtle manner. It appears the only two servants at the Armitage homestead are black, but oddly black. The house-servant is Georgina (Betty Gabriel), a very prim and proper black woman who appears to be devoid of any "blackness." When Chris speaks in a vernacular that Georgina should understand, she remains clueless, such as the conversation where Chris speaks of not "snitching" and Georgina stares, pauses and then states, "tattle-tail," a phrase she recognizes. The other black servant, the groundskeeper, does not speak much at all, but he is seen in various quick cuts that show him mowing the lawn or running at breakneck speed at Chris, aggressively charging the house guest, before cutting to the side at the last possible moment. Is this his way of working out?

It seems that the Armitages are part of a social "club" and they host a party at their home once a year, and it just happens to fall on the weekend that Rose and Chris visit. The crowd, mostly elderly, is regal and polite but also subtly racist. One man, a former golf pro, immediately name-calls Tiger Woods as a friend and gushes that Tiger was the best of all time. Another couple they meet features a middle-aged woman who smiles tenderly at Chris and states how handsome he is, then she literally grabs and squeezes his arm and runs her hand down his chest, then she looks at Rose and states, "Is it true … is it better?" as her smiling eyes dart to his genital area. Another couple states fair-skin has been the rage, but now the pendulum has swung back and "black is in fashion." Soon, to escape such small talk, Chris goes off by himself to take some photos (he is a professional photographer) and he sees the back of a young black man at the bar table. Smiling, Chris taps the man on the arm, saying it sure is nice finding "a brother" at last, and in an amazing shot, the black man slowly turns around to greet Chris, his eyes dazed as though he were zombified, but when he speaks, his performance is one of a white man imprisoned in a black man's body. His white wife (at least 30 years his se-

Chris (Daniel Kaluuya) is brought to tears, remembering the night he allowed his mother to bleed to death in a ditch, from *Get Out*.

nior) appears, merely to drag him away from Chris, making sure they don't become too acquainted. At the end of their conversation, Chris goes for a fist bump but the black man (dressed in the most "white" outfit possible) goes for a typical handshake when he uses his hand to grab Chris' entire fist. Soon Chris encounters Jim Hudson (Stephen Root), a blind gallery owner and a man that Chris (from his profession) knows by reputation. Hudson admires and wishes he had the vision that Chris possessed, realizing he has a particular eye for the photographic.

By this time Missy Armitage, a psychiatrist, discovers Chris' weakness: that he stayed home and watched television the night when his mother, never returning from work, was the victim of a hit and run driver. After her death the next morning, Chris learned that his mother survived the initial impact but died bleeding on the side of the road and might have been saved if he went out looking for her the night before. Of course Chris was a kid at the time, but his guilt is used by Missy to hypnotize him and take him to "the sunken place" where he can be rendered unconscious by clinking her spoon against her teacup at any time. And slowly the sinister plan is revealed. Dean Armitage reveals that his father lost out to Jessie Owens (the black superstar) in the 1936 Olympic trials, and even though he seems

very compassionate to all races, here is the direct cause of his racism. Daughter Rose, as Chris discovers secretly going through a box of photos in her closet, is also part of the conspiracy, as there are multiple photos showing all the black men she has dated. She is the lure to bring black men to the family home, to be hypnotized, and then prepared for a brain transplant in the family laboratory in the cellar. During the party, during a pretend Bingo game, art gallery owner Jim Hudson wins the auction (the purpose of the party) to have his brain put into Chris' body (and he thus gets the young man's eyes to boot). It turns out that Georgina is actually hosting Rose's grandmother's brain and the groundskeeper is hosting the grandfather's brain (see, a variation on the typical PRC Bela Lugosi programmer). And Andre Logan King (Lakeith Stanfield), potential sex slave to a woman 30 years older than he is, was the young black man kidnapped in the opening sequence of the movie. Dean Armitage is a neurosurgeon and Rose's brother Jeremy (Caleb Landry Jones) is his surgical helper and kidnapper. Shades of movies such as *The Corpse Vanishes* or *The Devil Bat*, where Bela Lugosi would play a well-loved doctor in a small town who was actually an evil experimenter working from his hidden basement lab. As the victims piled up, the trail eventually leads to Lugosi.

SEE THE TWO-HEADED KILLER CREATURE!

"THE MANSTER
Half Man—Half Monster"

for family members. Critics noted how wonderful Daniel Kaluuya is as Chris, and he is fantastic, but Allison Williams is just as outstanding, playing the love-struck young liberal who is actually a different character by the end of the film, her cold steel eyes transfixed to a shotgun she wields in order to prevent Chris from leaving. Her transformation is valid and real and her performance has depth and resonates. All the supporting players do great work as well.

One suggestion … see the film twice, or even three or four times. I liked the film the first time I saw it and generally got it; however, it was the second viewing where the underlying subtlety shone through and the movie went from being a very good film to a great one. In this day of paranormal found footage, conjured dolls and witches from beyond the supernatural realm of horror cinema, it is about time to once again have an actual adult A-production make a formidable contribution to the horror film genre.

And even though the repartee between Chris and his TSA buddy Rod Williams (LilRel Howery) is hilarious and provides inspired comic relief, no way should *Get Out* be considered a comedy (let alone a musical), as the Golden Globes characterized it. This is horror of the classic variety, too long missing from the scene.

The Manster
2.5
Scream Factory

Amazingly, *The Manster* is still fondly remembered on the bad cinema circuit, even though it premiered as the bottom half of the double-bill with *The Horror Chamber of Dr. Faustus* (aka *Eyes Without a Face*, the reedited and dubbed version of the French horror film classic). What makes this low-budget re-imaging of *The Wolf Man* such a quirky little B-horror programmer is the fact that this United Artists of Japan release was actually an American production filmed in Japan, in English. Most of the cast is comprised of unknowns (this was co-star Terri Zimmern's only movie credit), but star Peter Dyneley came from the world of the theater and he quickly gravitated to television for the remainder of his career. Sa-

Only when Chris photographs Logan at the "club" auction party does the man's eyes literally change, and the possessed soul inside returns to momentary power, as he charges toward Chris while screaming "Get out," which at the moment Chris interprets to mean that the formerly gentle and kind man is now an insane threat who is attacking him, when in fact the man, in his precious few seconds free to speak his mind, is trying to warn Chris to get the hell out of Dodge while he can. This is a mesmerizing sequence.

At the movie begins to wind down, Chris knows enough to leave the house immediately, and he asks Rose to get the car keys so they can escape, but when Rose delays, fumbling for minutes looking for the elusive keys in her bag, and when

family members start to slowly assemble, young Jeremy flipping a lacrosse stick at the front door, Chris knows he's in trouble. Rose finally finds the keys but states that she can't give them to him and soon Missy dings the tea cup with her spoon and Chris falls to the floor unconscious, soon awakening in a chair, his arms and legs strapped tight, a mounted deer head in front of him. The ending is wild and nicely handled, and I would not wish to spoil the unraveling course of events.

Jordan Peele creates one of the best horror films in a decade or even longer and his subtle style shines. This is a movie that demonstrates a new side of racism but its primary function is to illustrate people in power and to what extremes they will go to maintain such power, in this case creating a sense of immortality toshi (actually Tetsu) Nakamura appeared in several notable Japanese productions, including *Atragon*, *The Human Vapor*, *Mothra*, *The H Man* and *The Mysterians*, so he is actually the best-known actor in the production.

Filmed in moody black-and-white, the film features many interesting and well-designed sets (a massive mountain-top laboratory, with a tiny smoking volcano in the background; a steamy Japanese bath house, wonderful location photography at a shipyard; etc.) and very effective photography (David Mason) that utilizes lots of smoke and steam. The monstrous make-up by Fumiko Yamamoto is also quite good for such a low-budget production. What immediately strikes the viewer is that this movie does not resemble any of the other B-horror programmers of the era. It is a movie that stands apart from the rest. And while the film is not always entirely successful and is often hammy and overdone, it still elicits an interesting story and directors George Breakston and Kenneth G. Crane maintain an interesting pace.

Star Peter Dyneley, who plays *Larry* Stanford, is more than a tad similar in both acting style and physical appearance to Lon Chaney, Jr. Dyneley, basically a stage actor, likes to emote with a raised eyebrow and bulging eyes, all nicely overdone. And he conveys his fear and depression by hitting the liquor cabinet hard. In many ways *The Manster* becomes a atomic age reimaging of Universal's *The Wolf Man*, with an evil Japanese scientist and his experimental serum filling in for Bela the Gypsy. Dyneley does most of his acting juxtaposing extreme moods, moving from a regular Joe hard-boozing foreign correspondent to a ranting and raving tormented man, whose marriage is falling apart (because of his job and his drinking) while he slowly discovers that a parasitic monster is growing inside his body. Just as Larry Talbot transforms into a human wolf creature, Larry Stanford transforms into a Jekyll-Hyde monster where both Jekyll and Hyde are housed in one body that eventually splits into two entities.

The film's opening sequence is classic kitsch and goes for the full monty and succeeds by nature of its gonzo style. Japanese scientist Dr. Robert Suzuki presides over his spacious lab, where his failed experiment, his wife Emiko (Toyoko Takechi),

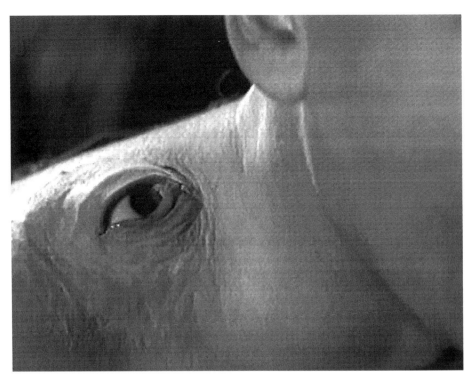

The bulging eye that grows out of Peter Dyneley's shoulder is the first hint that soon a second head will also emerge, from *The Manster*.

is locked in a prison with steel bars, her droopy melting eye, malformed mouth and thinning hair not as important as the fact that she has been rendered witless and uncommunicative. The doctor's brother Genji (Kenzo Kuroki), now transformed into an ape-man monster, comes back to the lab where Dr. Suzuki is forced to gas and kill him. This only occurs moments before we see Larry Stanford walking up the side of the mountain, wearing a full suit and dress shoes, ready to interview Suzuki for World Press. Suzuki, within moments, knows that this poor sap would be the perfect subject for his evolutionary transformation experiment (which did not work so well for his wife and brother) and fetches the drugged whiskey bottle in the back of his liquor cabinet to render the man unconscious, so he can use a syringe to inject his formula into his upper shoulder. The mad doctor plans to employ his assistant Tara (Terri Zimmern) to show Larry the town and keep a close watch as the transformation beings. As the couple slowly falls in love (contrary to the fact that Larry's wife Linda lives in New York and Larry just told her over the phone that he is homesick and plans to return for good, tired of the hard traveling life of a reporter), Larry's right hand and arm at first goes into spasms, then a new patch

of skin appears on his shoulder at the injection sight, his right hand soon turns hairy and beast-like (via a series of crude lap dissolves) and ultimately a human eye grows on his shoulder. This only leads to the sequence in a psychiatrist's office where a second monstrous head grows out of his shoulder, as Larry's own face gets plastered with dark grease paint to make him also look more monstrous. Finally, Larry returns to the scene of the crime, Dr. Suzuki's mountaintop lab, this time as the volcano starts to erupt. Tara gives Suzuki a hari-kari sword, which the doctor is prepared to use after shooting his wife to put her out of her misery, but Larry stabs the doctor with this very blade. Venturing up the mountain to the volcano, Larry pauses behind a tree where the final split occurs, the full-fur ape-man monster ripping itself apart from Larry's body, as now both creatures are totally free of one another. Larry attempts to wrestle with the fiend, who eventually picks up Tara and throws her into the volcano, but Larry, close behind, pushes the ape-man into the fiery hell. Soon Linda catches up to her husband and they embrace, the Japanese policeman reluctantly telling Linda that Larry will have to be arrested for murder as soon as he is well enough to comprehend the charges. Larry's boss delivers a sensitive speech about the good and evil housed in every human being and that he hopes the good wins out in the end. Rousing music swells as the end credits appear.

The more we watch Peter Dyneley register fear and pain in having his body transform without him knowing why, the more and more we see Lon Chaney, Jr. as his Larry undergoes the same sort of physical change. Of course Chaney, Jr. is much more effective an actor, but both men physically resemble one another and Dyneley uses many of the acting tricks that Chaney, Jr. employs. But when you add in the Japanese environment, mutant monster in the mountaintop lab, eyeballs erupting from Larry's shoulder and a melodrama involving Larry both wanting to fix things with his wife and yet still have his booze-fueled fling with the floozy Tara, we have a balls-out grade-Z gem. But too much is technically adept here for us to really call *The Manster* grade-Z and the movie is actually pretty much a hoot. Clocking in at a mere 72 minutes, *The Manster* is actually a forgotten bottom-of-the-double-feature programmer that is well worth revisiting, and on Blu-ray, it looks better than it deserves.

The Old Dark House
3.0
Cohen

Since Universal sold the rights to their 1932 James Whale classic to Columbia when William Castle made the remake in 1963, Universal allowed its negatives and prints to decay in vaults, until a young Curtis Harrington brought awareness to this cinematic tragedy and became the man who literally saved *The Old Dark House* (a documentary on Harrington's efforts appear as a supplemental feature on the disc).

So if Curtis Harrington saved the film, we have to thank Cohen Film Collection for releasing the digital 4k restoration (but, of course, only released in Blu-ray 1080p) of James Whale's follow-up to *Frankenstein*. In my younger days I never saw the appeal of *The Old Dark House*, and I knew why immediately after watching the Cohen restoration … I never actually *saw* the movie. Unlike the other 1930s Universal horror classics, which were never in bad shape and still looked even more stunning when re-mastered in Blu-

Morgan (Boris Karloff) reaches out for the frightened Gladys (Lilian Bond) in *The Old Dark House* (1932), directed by James Whale.

ray, *The Old Dark House* was in such poor condition that this restoration becomes a jaw-dropping revelation. This might simply be the best film restoration of the last decade … or even longer. The parties involved did a remarkable job of digitally restoring the black levels, the contrast, the shadow detail, and the image itself is devoid of speckles, blatant jump cuts, scratches and a hissy soundtrack. Visually and aurally, *The Old Dark House* can at last stand proudly alongside all the other Universal horror film classics.

For me, *The Old Dark House* could have been one of those early talkie movies that resembled a filmed stage play more so than an actual movie, and it might have been just that if director and visual stylist James Whale were not involved. Using the production design of Charles D. Hall (whose old dark house sets include stained high walls and steep staircases and rooms that appear to not have been inhabited for a multitude of years) and the photography of Arthur Edeson (such as the opening sequence featuring the violent mud-slide as a lone car tries to traverse the sloppy envi-

ronment), Whale creates a dazzling visual backdrop to the goings-on that even the theatrical quality of the film cannot undo. While the film is talky and misses having a musical score (even though the sound effects of the storm, the howling wind, the downpour of rain work almost as well as music), the visual quirkiness (the distorted faces in the mirror) always manages to keep things interesting.

Boris Karloff perhaps unfairly receives top-billing as Morgan, the brute of the family butler who becomes savage when he drinks too much, the booze making him sexually aggressive as he too soon tries to trap delicious blonde Margaret (Gloria Stuart) in a dark corner. For Karloff, Whale has given him another outstanding mute role and his mime abilities have to carry the performance, making him appear as the gorilla in a monkey suit, an attempt in domesticating the beast in all men (men fueled by lustful sex and alcohol). That first shot we get of Karloff, when he half opens the front door and Edeson's camera maintains a tight shot on Morgan's scarred face, is perhaps one of

A behind-the-scenes publicity photo of the entire cast and crew of *The Old Dark House* (with director James Whale in the middle of the back row, directly behind Melvyn Douglas)

Karloff's greatest entrances in cinema history. Then he mumbles incomprehensible language, prompting Horace Femm (Ernest Thesiger) to tell the houseguests that Morgan is "dumb" and that his sister Rebecca (Eva Moore) is "deaf." Karloff has a supporting role and, without the use of language, his performance, as effective as it may be, never generates very much importance except for those instances when he runs amok or tearfully carries the broken body of Saul Femm (Brember Wills) back up to his bedroom.

Horace and Rebecca Femm are truly odd siblings, old and set in their ways, Ernest Thesiger appearing older and frailer here in 1932 than he would appear in 1935's *Bride of Frankenstein*. The-

siger's Horace is a weak, frightened wisp of a man, tall, gaunt and colorless. He is too afraid to even venture up the stairs to the upper floor where his brother Saul is locked up, fearing that the arsonist will escape and burn the house down. It appears that Horace has not seen the light of day in a long, long time. Rebecca, on the other hand, hears more than she pretends to *not* hear, a religious figure who claims her 102 year old father Sir Roderick (played by female Elspeth Dudgeon in makeup with a hook nose to make her appear male) was wild and wicked and ordered her to go out and pray while he held depraved parties all the time in the house. Rebecca looks at beautiful Gloria Stuart—who changes from her wet clothes, either donning a

dressy negligee or the most flimsy and plunging dress imaginable—with scorn. Rebecca reaches out with her hand and touches Stuart's cleavage and declares her beauty will soon rot, as the young girl backs away half screaming. As mentioned earlier, as reflected in a warped mirror, we view first Rebecca whose features are ugly and twisted as she rants about depravity and sin, but then we view the distorted facial features of Stuart's in the mirror and this drives home the comment that her beauty and sexuality will soon rot and decay. And all this occurs in the dusty and neglected bedroom of a second sister who died at the age of 21, having lived a life of sin and debauchery making Rebecca seemingly very satisfied that her sinful

sister met an early demise. Only brother Saul later reveals that he has been locked away because he knows that "they" (Horace and Rebecca) killed her.

Sir William Porterhouse (Charles Laughton) arrives at the house, another victim of the violent weather, with an inability to drive a car through mud and rising lake water, with his young and perky mistress, a chorus girl who is paid for her companionship, but it's never of a sexual nature. Gladys (Lilian Bond) truly likes Bill but feels sorry for him, since he never fully recovered from losing his wife, who committed suicide feeling socially unworthy, never able to measure up to higher ups above her class. Her death only prompted Bill to amass money and, with it, rank and privilege, even though at heart he is basically jolly and charming lower class. Burnt out Penderel (Melvyn Douglas), a victim of the war and all the woes of the world, buries his sullenness under the guise of being a good friend, who sings songs aloud and drinks a tad too much, hiding the pain beneath. But when he sees Gladys, the chorus girl who smiles a lot and breaks out into silly little dances, this makes him happy and causes his heart to swell. And finally Philip (Raymond Massey), husband of Margaret, gets lost in the crowd literally, playing the decent but fairly quiet good guy. His only standout sequence is the opening one, showing

him argue comically with Margaret as he tries to drive the car around flooded-out roadways and avoiding high hills gushing forth mud.

The film is rather talky, even though the mere presence of the old dark house adds interest and dread to the proceedings. Key sequences occur when Morgan drinks too much and terrifies Margaret with his physical advances, which causes all the men (except Horace) to confront the butler and try to force him into a room that can be locked, so Margaret can be safe. This free-for-all as Morgan goes amok and literally knocks over furniture and pushes several men to the floor is rather dramatic and filmed quite effectively. A similar scene occurs in *Frankenstein*, with several men trying to subdue the frantic Monster by working together to hold the creature on the floor.

But the most effective sequence in the movie is the five-minute appearance of locked-away Saul, the youngest brother (and smallest) who lives to set fires and harm others. Brember Wills plays one of the screen's most subtle and interesting psychos, a man who appears for a brief instance to be the only normal member of the Femm family. His small curled hand almost clutches the banister of the long staircase, and all we see of him for the first several minutes is that slightly twisted hand and wrist. When Saul finally

charges down the staircase, he pleads with Penderel that he has been locked away because he knows the family secrets. He orders his "friend" not to touch him, but Saul reaches out and pleads for Penderel not to leave him alone. When Penderel momentarily leaves him to check a locked door, the camera focuses solely on Saul's face and we see how his lips curl and his eyes rise awkwardly, and in that brief and subtle change of facial movement, we know that Saul is insane—and evil. When Penderel returns, Saul picks up a knife from the wreckage of the debris when Morgan flipped the dining room table over, and Saul also stares at a burning candle and the knife, which he holds in his hand. Both men sit at a table while Saul rants on about how a flame is like the knife, and as he speaks, he sticks the knife into the table, gradually approaching Penderel. Finally Saul admits that Penderel is smart enough to know that he wants to kill him, and as Penderel lunges away from the table, he falls into a nearby chair and Saul throws the knife at him, but it sticks into the back of the chair. Penderel rushes to escape but falls, losing his balance, and without wavering Saul picks up a wooden chair and breaks it over Penderel's body, dazing the victim. Saul steals a burning log from the fireplace and rushes up the wooden steps to set a huge hanging drapery on fire, but Penderel regains his senses and fights Saul trying to stop him. But the insane little man leaps on Penderel, lunges toward his neck and attempts to bite his throat, and before long both men fall forward breaking the protective banister and plunge almost in unison backward to the first level, crushed and motionless. The stunt work is simply superb.

The Old Dark House sits nicely alongside other old-dark-house movies of the era, including *The Bat*, *The Bat Whispers* and *The Cat and the Canary*, but its tone is more quirky than horrific. While many fans consider *The Old Dark House* to be among James Whale's finest horror movies, I find the movie to be too talky, focusing entirely too much in the middle upon the budding romance of Penderel and Gladys and Bill's sad life. The most gripping sequence involves the introduction and gradually violent outburst of insane brother Saul, and somehow if the movie had focused on him, it would truly have been a horrific horror classic. As it is, becoming a concoction of James Whale's eccentric universe, the film is never entirely a character drama, warped comedy or intense horror picture. Perhaps with James Whale at the helm, we do not wish to have any of his productions become pigeonholed and formulaic, but with the strong silent performance of Karloff as Morgan (the proverbial bull in the china shop) and Brember Wills' stunning performance as Saul, we wish that these horror elements had been pushed more to the forefront with a little less melodrama. I do admit that the oddball brother-sister act of Ernest Thesiger and Eva Moore was also a strong positive of the production, and I wish they dominated the final two-thirds of the movie as they did the first third. I guess I am complaining the movie is a tad too episodic, with individual sequences crying out for further development, while other sequences are far less memorable. But for me, even if the film ultimately disappoints, those stand-out sequences are classic, and with James Whale's eccentricity enveloping the entire production, *The Old Dark House* still must be considered a slightly flawed Universal classic.

The Diabolical Dr. Z
3.0
Kino Lorber

Unlike many, I prefer Jess Franco's earlier black-and-white productions to his meandering, dreamlike color fantasies of the 1970s and beyond. *The Awful Dr. Orlof*, with its misty, haunting boat rides to the Gothic castle, where the mad surgeon constructs his laboratory, doing dirty work with the help of bug-eyed assistant Morpho, is my type of Franco thriller. Here, in 1966, Franco returns to the arena of surgical horror once again with moody and quirky black-and-white photography, with a futuristic lab constructed in the bowels of an abandoned mansion, with perhaps a hint of James Bond shenanigans added for oddball flavor. At this point in time Franco was making conventional (at least for him) movies that featured characters, tropes and situations from standard B-productions of the era, but as filtered through the eyes and vision of Franco, even the most conventional Franco movie is still very strange indeed.

Unfortunately, the Dr. Strangelove-like Dr. Zimmer (Antonio Jiménez Escrib-

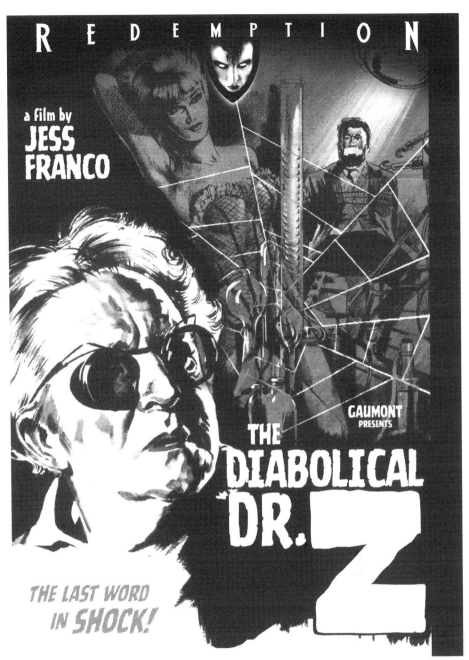

ana), who wears dark-tinted goggles and is confined to a wheelchair, is not along for long. While appearing at a neuroscience congress to support both the work of Dr. Orlof (a very curious in-joke, of course) and his own efforts (working on the theory that the good and evil within human beings is actually physical and can be altered by his invasive surgical techniques), the major members of the congress humiliate and denigrate Dr. Z's efforts, causing him to explode in rage and have a cardio episode and die, his last words a plea to his daughter Irma (Mabel Karr) to carry on his work. But Irma only seems intent on avenging her father's death in the most horrific and imaginative of ways.

First imagine the Zimmer mad lab, its centerpiece a metal-framed glass operating table, set at about a 45 degree angle, upright, where the patient (victim?) is held in place by a pair of mechanical metal arms with steel claws at the end. (Do you see the *Goldfinger* influence here?) Potential victims find that sharp metal probes (actually thick nails) with attached wires are connected to the beeping apparatus that shoots Z-rays into them, thus rendering the "patient" a slave to the will of Dr. Zimmer or his daughter. And did we mention that the very long and thick probes must be pushed deeply into the victim's temple and then several more are forced into the victim's back, in between specific

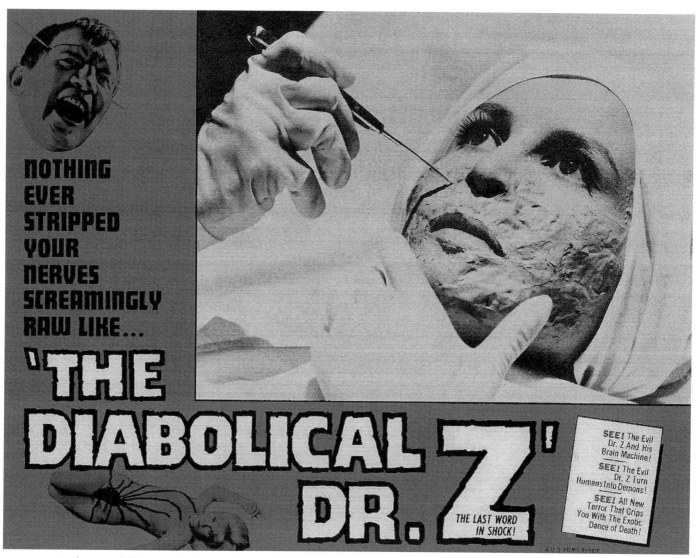

NOTHING EVER STRIPPED YOUR NERVES SCREAMINGLY RAW LIKE...

'THE DIABOLICAL DR. Z'

THE LAST WORD IN SHOCK!

SEE! The Evil Dr. Z And His Brain Machine!

SEE! The Evil Dr. Z Turn Humans Into Demons!

SEE! All New Terror That Grips You With The Exotic Dance of Death!

A U.S FILMS Release

In this U.S. lobby card, Irma Zimmer (Mabel Karr) operates on her own scarred face, to restore her beauty.

vertebrae? For some unexplained reason, a criminal/murderer Hans Bergen (Guy Mairesse) escapes from prison traveling a long distance through the woods to arrive at the gates of Dr. Z's home, where he collapses from exhaustion. He is immediately operated on in the manner described above and becomes a more handsome version of Morpho from *The Awful Dr. Orlof*.

Basically Irma wants to kill the three major doctors of power and influence who spoke out against Dr. Z at the congress: Dr. Vicas (Howard Vernon, who played Dr. Orlof from the earlier film), Dr. Morono (Marcelo Arroita) and Dr. Kallman (Cris Huerta). And Irma's instrument of murder is one hot tamale, Nadia (Estella Blain), who hosts a nightclub act as "Miss Death," where she dresses in skimpy outfits and appears on stage in a huge spider's web trying to seduce a male mannequin

who happens to have actual human eyes. In her most imaginative costume, she is nude beneath a fish net body suit that features a huge spider that covers her groin and has legs that extend upward to cover her nipples. Basically, all this is show biz and she is in love with our hero, another doctor, Philippe (Fernando Montes), and she is basically a decent girl just earning a living. But when Irma realizes that this hot dish would be the perfect "bait" for the men she hopes to murder, it is not long before Irma pretends she is a talent agent offering Nadia thousands of dollars to do her act in America, and she just has to go across the street to sign the contract in the nearby deserted theater; here Bergen is hiding out ready to kidnap her and transport her to the mad lab in the cellar of the Zimmer abandoned mansion, where she will become Irma's slave and instrument of murder.

Did we mention that Irma just happens to pick up a hitchhiker while driving in the country, and as the car passes a lake or river, the free-willed girl wants to stop and take a swim, Irma just happening to have an extra swimsuit in the back seat. Soon Irma runs her car over the poor lady, places her body in her car, puts her ring on the corpse's finger, soaks the car in gasoline, torches it and lets the car run into the water where it sinks below the water's surface. Ah, but just before doing that, Irma reaches inside to grab the car keys and burns the lower half of her face, which scars up immediately, but using a "surgical mirror," Irma operates on her own face, blood dripping from the surgical cuts, and fixes it. True, for the rest of the movie, her face is a little worse for wear, becoming oily with little bumps replacing the scar tissue. But to disguise the fact that Irma is now supposedly burned and dead

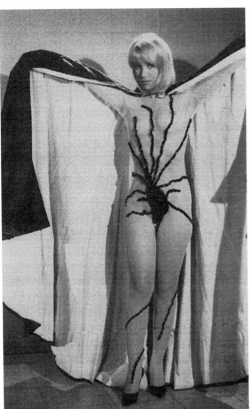

Nadia (Estella Blain), Miss Death, comes under the control of Irma Zimmer.

in the water, she now begins to wear glasses and dyes her hair brown. Even when she passes Philippe, who knows her well, he does not recognize her.

The three murders (actually more, as the Zimmer nurse Barbara [Lucia Prado] is subdued and placed in the household gas chamber, an item that is made to seem *de rigor*, as if every home has one) are inventively handled, as Dr. Vicas (a woefully wasted Howard Vernon, whose role is too brief to be memorable) is seduced on a train by Nadia, where she uses her elongated spider nails (which Irma has coated with poison) to scratch the throat of the doctor. While still barely conscious, Nadia tosses him out the window of the speeding train where he rolls down the hill, coordinated so that Irma and Bergen are waiting to stab the dying man to death. Dr. Moroni leaves his wife alone in bed, traveling to the nearby tavern to have a coffee, where Nadia is waiting and begins to stalk him and follow him home, but brute Bergen has already strangled Moroni's wife to death and waits in the shadows of his home. When Moroni finds his wife dead, he rushes outside to fetch a cab, one of course driven by Bergen (who

must move about very rapidly) who is secretly wearing a gas mask and sucking an oxygen tube as poison gas is pumped into the rear of the car. Hours later the police find Moroni's body on the side of the road, dead. Finally, Dr. Kallman, suspicious because of the first two murders, is almost lying in wait for Nadia to appear, and when he gets her in the sight of his gun, he phones his butler to call the police (but Kallman fails to notice that the butler is dead, replaced by Bergen), and when there's a knock on the door, Kallman assumes the police have arrived, so he foolishly places his gun on the table, opens the door and gets stabbed in the belly by Irma and dies.

This silly world of scientific horror is made real by the inspiring photography of Alejandro Ulloa, who loves to shoot scenes as high or low angles, usually after establishing s stationary shot, and then he pans his camera left or right to reveal more information in the frame. To be honest, the photography is the most creative aspect of the entire movie.

During the thrill-a-minute climax, hero Philippe has found Irma's isolated mansion and its haunted lab in the basement, but when Irma, Nadia (who is mostly locked away in a private cell after committing each crime, having to be surgically recharged to remain a slave to Irma, as the effect wears off soon enough) and Bergen return, there is a free-for-all fight, with Bergen and Philippe knocking over medieval armor and fighting with a metal spear (Philippe) and a large sword (Bergen), which ends with the metal spear stuck in Bergen's guts. The fight is well choreographed and photographed. Before his fitting end, Irma orders Bergen to get rid of Nadia, who is not needed any longer, but Philippe dives across the hallway to knock the knife out of his hand. Irma aims her pistol at Nadia, but out of the blue two police inspectors (one played by Jess Franco and the other played by music composer Daniel White) arrive on the scene and Franco fires the shot that drops Irma. Basically our two policemen are essentially superficial to the plot and their "wink-wink" performance is the main reason for their appearance, and the surprise gun shot at the end makes for dramatic resolution.

To be quite honest, I enjoyed *The Diabolical Dr. Z* very, very much. In 1966 it was a pleasure to see a black-and-white film so well photographed and edited, and with all the quirky aspects (simply the appearance of Nadia and the robot groping operating room) and the outlandish plot, which is handled with style and creative commitment, the film is outrageous fun. Think of *The Awful Dr. Orlof* crossed with a German krimi with a stronger dose of sexual appeal, and that pretty much sums up the movie. For me I can't wait to show the film to my friends.

Final Mutterings

I wish to thank all the people who encouraged me to produce this regular issue, after our 50th year anniversary issue arrived at the end of 2013. That issue took a lot out of me and at first it was difficult to build up the energy and enthusiasm to do another regular issue. People such as Richard Klemensen was there by the sidelines encouraging me, and I thank him (and others) for that. My wife Sue was also telling me, okay, we have several books waiting in the wings, but they can wait another few months for you to finish up your latest issue. I appreciate all her love and support as well.

Our busy schedule means I have to squeeze in the time to solicit, write, collect, organize, edit, and lay out the current issue. I would love to publish the magazine more frequently, but that means we need more articles written and submitted sooner than later. We encourage submissions from both seasoned veterans and first-time authors. However, it is always best to discuss your article ideas with me in advance. That is easily done by e-mailing me at:

midmargary@aol.com

Finally, thank you to everyone who submitted art, an article or purchased an issue of the magazine over the past decades. Also, thanks to anyone who wrote a letter of comment or helped me to distribute and sell copies of the magazine. I could not have done it without all the help and support the fan community (David Colton and the CHFB, among others) provided.

A portrait of Boris Karloff (left), alongside the Frankenstein Monster, both created by Mark Robinson

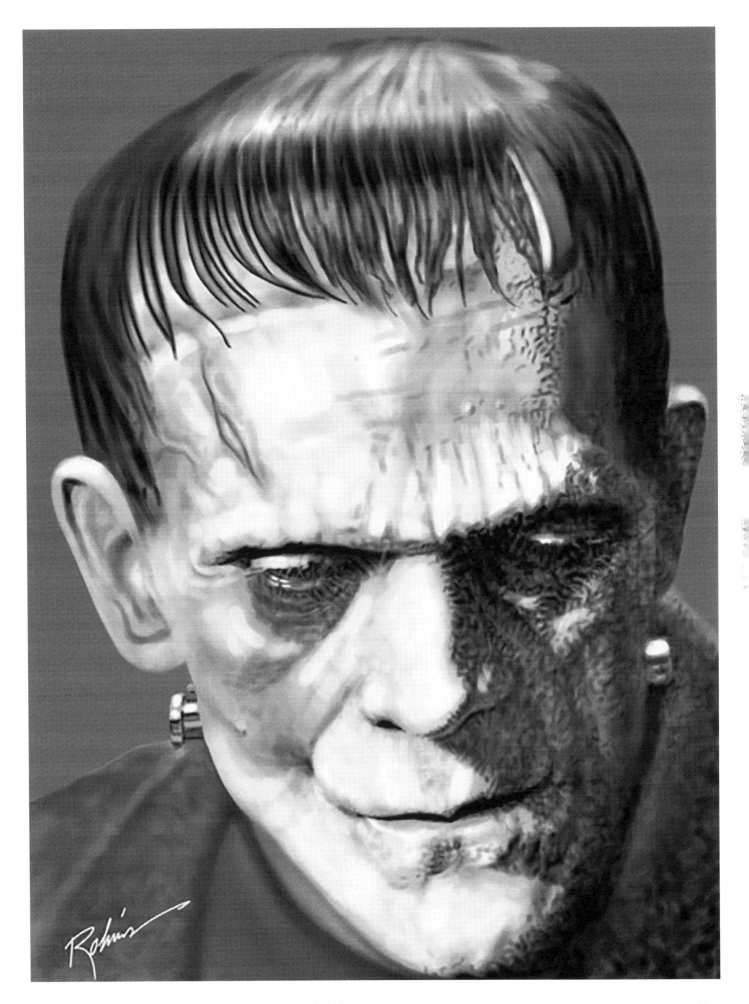

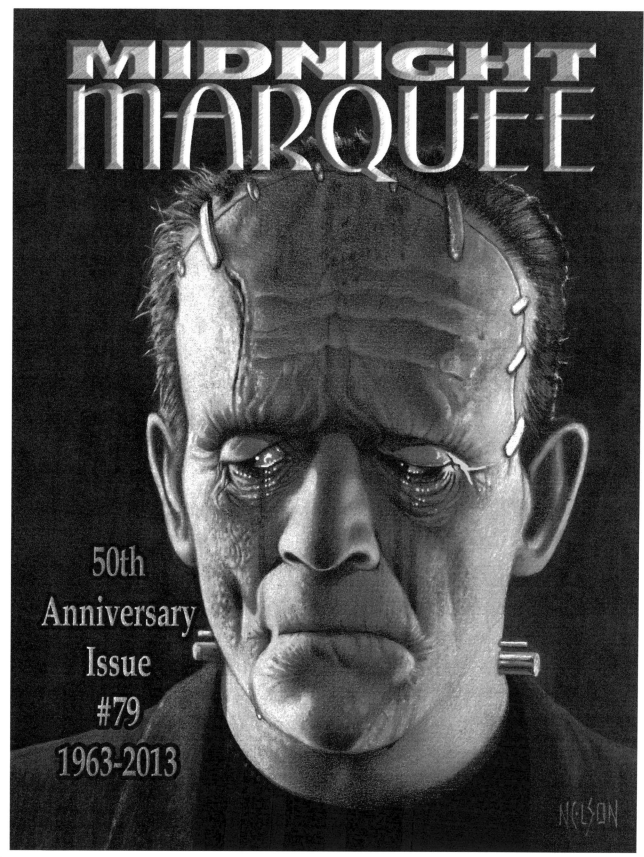

50th
Anniversary
Issue
#79
1963-2013

To order MidMar's 50th Anniversary Issue, or any of our books or mags, visit our website at www.midmar.com.

Made in the USA
San Bernardino, CA
27 August 2018